MW00768506

Take Back the Center

Take Back the Center

Progressive Taxation for a New Progressive Agenda

Peter S. Wenz

The MIT Press
Cambridge, Massachusetts
London, England

MIT Press books may be purchased at special quantity discounts for business or sales promotional use. For information, please email special_sales@ mitpress.mit.edu or write to Special Sales Department, The MIT Press, 55 Hayward Street, Cambridge, MA 02142.

This book was set in Sabon by the MIT Press. Printed on recycled paper and bound in the United States of America.

Library of Congress Cataloging-in-Publication Data

Wenz, Peter S.
Take back the center : progressive taxation for a new progressive agenda / Peter S. Wenz.
    p.   cm.
Includes bibliographical references and index.
ISBN 978-0-262-01788-6 (hardcover : alk. paper)
1. Progressive taxation—United States. 2. Income tax—United States. 3. United States—Social policy. I. Title.
HJ2327.U5W46   2012
336.24′150973—dc23
2012002291

10   9   8   7   6   5   4   3   2   1

This book is dedicated to our five grandchildren
Kiahna, Jasmine, Taylor, Michael, and Alyssa
With the hope that right-wing extremism doesn't degrade our
country and impair their lives.

Contents

Acknowledgments

I would like to thank Meredith Cargill, Berndt Estabook, Bob Kunath, Dick Palmer, Larry Shiner, Bill Underwood, and Mick Whittle for reading the manuscript in whole or in part and making valuable suggestions. I thank my wife, Grace Wenz, for reading on short notice many parts of the book and for giving sound advice. Also very helpful were my agent, Susan Schulman, of the Susan Schulman Literary Agency and my acquisitions editor at the MIT Press, Clay Morgan. Finally, I owe the greatest debt to Steve Allen, whose expertise in matters economic and financial saved me from many errors and gave me confidence that the arguments he accepted were sound.

1

Introduction

Much of the news lately is not just sad, it's infuriating. The United States has a crumbling physical infrastructure—roads, bridges, dams, levies, electrical grid, and more[1]—as well as an underused and poorly prepared human infrastructure—unemployment, underemployment, school dropouts, students less prepared than those in competitor countries, and higher education that many in the middle class cannot afford.[2] The middle class is generally hard pressed and thinning out as corporate profits soar, Wall Street bonuses often exceed the lifetime earnings of most workers, and the gap between the rich and poor increases. Most state budgets are in deficit, prompting many states to reduce spending on law enforcement, education,[3] and (if they have their way) health care for the poor.[4] The national debt is enormous and annual budget deficits discourage additional federal help for the states. Social Security and many state retirement plans are underfunded, which jeopardizes the welfare of future senior citizens.

This is all sad but what's really infuriating is that the obvious solution for many of these problems has little chance of legislative enactment: increase federal income taxes on the rich. The money collected from more steeply progressive taxes could be used to eliminate budget deficits and fund improvements in the country's human and physical infrastructure. K–12 education could become internationally competitive and a college education could again be made affordable to the middle class; jobs could be created in education and in construction related to infrastructure upgrades; Social Security and other retirement systems could be fully funded; and the middle class could be lifted up as the gap between the rich and poor is reduced. Yet, when the Bush-era tax cuts were renewed in December 2010, a Congress then dominated by Democrats wouldn't raise the top income tax rate from 36 percent to 39 percent, even though 39 percent is well below the rates wealthy Americans paid some decades ago.

Why is there such resistance to raising taxes on the wealthy? Since the 1970s American politics has been dominated increasingly by an unrealistic antigovernment-antitax right-wing ideology that has dislocated the perceived center of American politics. What were once considered extreme right-wing views are now treated as mainstream.

At one time the center of American politics was dominated by a more business-oriented Republican Party confronting a more labor-oriented Democratic Party. Together the two parties constituted a sane center because both made reasonable efforts to ground their views in available evidence. They had serious disagreements but most often stood together eventually (if not always promptly) to oppose extremists on both sides of the center, such as McCarthyites and segregationists on the right and ban-the-bomb peaceniks and drop-out hippies on the left.

The sane center of American politics from World War II through most of the 1970s inaugurated a new progressive era in American politics. Although it's not usually called a progressive era, "the greatest generation," with active Republican as well as Democratic support, accomplished a great deal that can be called progressive:

- the GI Bill extended higher education to millions of military veterans;
- state universities expanded enormously to bring affordable higher education to children of lower-middle-class families;
- the productivity of average workers doubled; the median wage doubled (after adjusting for inflation);
- the military was racially integrated;
- baseball was racially integrated;
- a host of immoral, racist policies aimed at African Americans in the South were abolished;
- the effective franchise was extended for the first time to millions of African Americans;
- the women's movement made a significant start toward gender equality;
- senior citizens were given public medical insurance;
- Social Security payments were increased and poverty among older Americans reduced;
- the interstate highway system was built, improving transportation for commerce and leisure;
- the Environmental Protection Agency was established; the exploration of space began; sensible deregulation catalyzed improvements in telecommunications and reductions in the price of air travel;
- cigarettes were recognized as hazardous to human health;
- and a crucial breakthrough needed for homosexual equality was accomplished because it was proved that same-sex preference is not statistically associated with any recognized personality disorders or mental diseases or defects.

There's more but that's enough!

These were accomplishments of the sane center composed of Republicans and Democrats who supported federal expenditures, which many of these accomplishments required, through progressive income taxes whose highest rate was 91 percent under President Eisenhower and remained between 60 percent and 70 percent until the Reagan administration.

Not everyone engaged in politics was part of this sane center during the post–World War II Progressive Era. The center was surrounded by radicals right and left whose agendas contributed little if anything to progressive developments. On the right were people, most of them Republicans, who believed that communists had infiltrated American government and threatened to undermine the United States in its Cold War contest with the Soviet Union. No reasonable understanding of available information supported most of Senator McCarthy's charges. Ultimately, a sane Republican president, Dwight Eisenhower, enabled by a bipartisan congressional coalition, brought an end to the witch hunts.

On the right also were people, most of them Democrats, opposed to racial equality and civil rights. They claimed variously (against the evidence) that blacks were morally and mentally inferior to whites, that separate educational and other public services for blacks and whites treated the races equally, that interracial marriage would weaken the genetic fitness of Americans, and that a major reason for black men to seek social and economic advancement was to make it easier for them to have sex with white women. In the end, the Civil Rights Act of 1964 crippled segregationist policies. It was championed by Democratic President Lyndon Johnson and was brought to a floor vote in the Senate through the work of Republican Senator Everett Dirksen.[5] A larger percentage of Republicans than Democrats voted for the bill.[6]

Radicals on the left were also addressed by the sane center without great partisanship. In the 1950s, for example, when some people on the left called for unilateral nuclear disarmament by Western powers, neither mainstream Republicans nor mainstream Democrats were moved. There was no credible evidence during the height of the Cold War that the Soviets and the Chinese would have behaved responsibly if they had become the world's only nuclear powers.

Another major leftist perspective from the 1950s through the 1970s was the beatnik-hippie mentality, which criticized American materialism and promised personal redemption through an alternate lifestyle. When combined with the drug culture, as it often was, the hippie saying was, "turn on, tune in, drop out." Reality-oriented politicians in the sane center saw this as adolescent economics. Many people in their teen years seek the freedom to do whatever they want with all the material possessions at their parents' disposal without any responsibility to earn the money needed to buy and maintain such possessions. The bulk of the youth drug culture was like this. Where did they imagine food, clothing, and housing would come from if most people dropped out? (Well, they were young.) No major political party considered this to be a serious alternative to a decent work ethic.

Of course, the center was itself not always sane, as when they supposed, against evidence available at the time, that if Vietnam were united under communist rule China would convert all southeast Asian countries to communism. Historical evidence, ignored by the center, indicated clearly that a united Vietnam, regardless of its form of government, was the most powerful force in the region to impede Chinese expansionism.

This tragic failure of reality orientation at the center of American politics was the exception rather than the rule from the mid-1940s to the late 1970s during the postwar Progressive Era. No group considered to be at the center during that period engaged in systematically unrealistic thinking that undermines most attempts at reasonable approaches to matters of law and public policy. But this is what we have today in the antigovernment-antitax movement. It has bewitched the country so thoroughly that the kind of solutions to national problems that were adopted by the bipartisan sane center during the postwar Progressive Era—high income taxes on the wealthy, federal support for higher education, federal overhaul of our transportation infrastructure—are now considered left wing instead of mainstream solutions to our problems.

$ $ $

It's time to take back the center for a new progressive agenda. The main elements of that agenda include the following:

• Because everyone who works full time should earn *a living wage*, the earned income credit (EIC), which currently gives low-wage workers federal tax credits to augment their incomes, should be expanded greatly so that no family of three with a full-time worker has income below $37,000 per year.

• Because, historically, higher rates of unionization correspond to better salaries for the middle class, the government should *promote unionization* through better policing of employers' illegal antiunion activities and through provision for union representation through employee signatures rather than through voting. (Voting gives employers opportunities for antiunion intimidation because voting typically requires onsite union organizing for the vote, which enables employers to identify union activists more easily.)

• Because our *transportation infrastructure* is in decay, many construction workers need jobs, and our dependence on foreign sources of oil impairs our national security and drains our economy, the government should invest massively in light rail within cities and intercity rail for passengers and freight. This project is for the twenty-first century what the interstate highway system was in the postwar Progressive Era.

• Because our *electricity grid* is outdated and poorly maintained, the government should design and fund a new, fully integrated electricity infrastructure.

• Because burning fossil fuels warms the planet and endangers our agriculture and our coastal cities, the government should increase its tax support for the development and deployment of *alternative sources of energy*, such as geothermal, solar, and wind power, just as it did in the postwar Progressive Era with nuclear power. It should also give more generous *tax credits* for purchase of *fuel-efficient and electric cars*, as well as for *home insulation* and *geothermal heating and cooling* systems.

• Because all Americans should have affordable *health care*, progress made through the 2010 Patient Protection and Affordable Care Act should be continued until all Americans have health insurance without intolerable financial burdens on families or businesses.

• Because education is increasingly important in our technological society, *preschool education* from the age of three should be provided free for every child.

• Because American high school students fare poorly in international tests, federal support for *K–12 education* should be increased so that teacher salaries are competitive with those in other sectors of the economy and teachers can be recruited in the United States, as they can in some other countries, from the top one-third of college graduates.

• Because many children of middle class and poorer families cannot afford a *university education*, federal support for higher education should be increased to expand opportunities and to ensure that graduates are not burdened with enormous debt.

• Because our national debt is already too high and, except for increased support for unionization, these initiatives and programs require significant government spending, the foundation of the new progressive agenda must be *more steeply progressive taxation*. Revenue from higher taxes on the rich should be used to increase income support to the *working* poor, invest in health care, pay for renewed infrastructures in energy and transportation, and fund improved education at all levels.

We need to take back the center for this progressive agenda so that public debate focuses on its implementation rather than on distractions created by right-wing antigovernment-antitax extremists.

There are many ways to take back the center. Protests, marches, petitions, campaign contributions, and work for progressive candidates can all help to focus public debate on progressive policies. But equally necessary are reality-oriented explanations showing that such policies, including the progressive taxes needed to fund them, serve justice, promote economic growth, and preserve democracy. That's the role of this book. Armed with its information and arguments, readers will be able to explain clearly why a new progressive agenda should be at the center of public debate and why objections from antigovernment-antitax conservatives should be dismissed as unrealistic.

$ $ $

How did such unrealistic thinking become central in American politics? The godfather of unrealistic antigovernment-antitax views is Ronald Reagan, who helped to move these ideas from the fringe to the perceived center of American discourse. He famously said in his first inaugural address, "government is not the solution to our problem; government is the problem." He complained, "Those who work are denied a fair return for their labor by a tax system which penalizes successful achievement and keeps us from maintaining full productivity." He decried excessive government spending that had resulted in "deficit upon deficit. . . ."[7] He added, "our present troubles parallel and are proportionate to the intervention and intrusion in our lives that result from unnecessary and excessive growth of Government."[8] He pledged "to get government back within its means, and to lighten our punitive tax burden."[9]

Reagan acknowledged that government does have a legitimate role to play in our lives, saying, "it's not my intention to do away with government. It is rather to make it work—work with us, not over us; to stand by our side, not ride on our back. Government can and must provide opportunity, not smother it; foster productivity, not stifle it."[10] But the message his supporters took away from his address was that less government and lower taxes are always preferable to more government and higher taxes, regardless of the situation, and this view pervades the perspective of most Republican stalwarts to this day.

Steven Moore, for example, a conservative who runs the Club for Growth, supported Pat Toomey in his 2004 primary race to replace Senator Arlen Specter as the Republican nominee in Pennsylvania's Senate race. Specter, Moore believed, was a "RINO" ("Republican in name only"), telling Philip Gourevitch of the *New Yorker,* "I think if you're a Republican in 2004 you've got to stand for a few things. . . . You've got to be . . . for cutting taxes and . . . for a smaller government. Otherwise, what are Republicans good for? That's why we keep saying Specter's a RINO—a Republican in name only—and let's replace him with a real Republican."[11]

Grover Norquist, president of the advocacy group Americans for Tax Reform, agreed that reducing taxes and diminishing the role of government in the economy was central to the Republican message, but didn't think it necessary to campaign against RINOs. He said, "What do these so-called moderates have in common? They're seventy years old. They're not running again. They're gonna be dead soon."[12] Like Moore, he envisioned a Republican Party united in its opposition to high taxes and big government.

So far, Norquist has proved more right than wrong. Although Specter was alive to run again in 2010, he left the Republican Party because he didn't think he could again defeat a conservative challenger in the Republican Party primary. (He became a Democrat and was defeated in the Democratic Party primary.) The antigovernment-antitax right wing of the Republican Party had gained on the sane center between 2004 and 2010 to the point of excluding people like Specter.

Already in 2004 Norquist claimed that "ninety per cent of Republicans in the House and the Senate will vote for every tax cut that's put on the table."[13] That was just after two rounds of significant tax cuts, one in 2001 and another in 2003 under a Republican president and with Republican majorities in both houses of Congress. After such tax cuts, how low did these Republicans think taxes could or should get? Norquist had previously said that he wanted government cut "down to the size where we can drown it in the bathtub."[14]

This is the heart of the dark nonsense that pervades (right-wing) Republican orthodoxy in our time. With the country's debt at more than $14 trillion, the Republican-dominated House of Representatives passed a budget plan in 2011 that was supposed to reduce future federal budget deficits by about $4 trillion over the next ten years. The plan would end Medicare as we know it because it would cover only one-third of seniors' health-care costs by 2030. Worse yet, the plan includes so many new tax cuts for wealthy people that the nonpartisan Congressional Budget Office estimates that it would actually increase deficits over the next ten years not reduce them.[15] However, merely failing to renew the Bush-era tax cuts would actually save $4 trillion,[16] but that would involve raising taxes, so Republicans won't consider it.

No matter what the issue, the answer is to have a smaller government and lower taxes. One size fits all. No serious questions need be asked about the public good if government gets smaller and taxes are lowered because an invisible hand will make everything work out for the best. There is no need for evidence in support of this general view or for detailed examinations of facts surrounding individual policy choices. This may not have been Reagan's belief, but it's certainly the prevailing view among Republicans today.

$ $ $

This view maintains its position at or near the center of American politics largely though right-wing deception, dishonesty, and distortion. The ends of lowering taxes and reducing government justify any means. And the mainstream media, rather than call these conservatives dishonest or crazy, accord them the respect that should be reserved for people who base their views on actual facts. Misplaced respect for right-wing radicals helps to move the center of American politics from sense to nonsense.

Consider, for example, candidate Obama's campaign encounter with Joe the Plumber (Samuel J. Wurzelbacher) a couple of weeks before the presidential election in 2008. Joe raised the issue of progressive taxation. Progressive taxes are those that impose a higher tax rate on higher incomes than on lower incomes. For example, a tax code that exempts the first $25,000 of income from taxation, applies a 10 percent tax rate to the next $25,000, increases the rate of taxation to 20 percent on the following $50,000, imposes a 36 percent tax rate on the next $150,000 and raises the tax rate to 39 percent on income over $250,000 would be progressive. Progressivity doesn't increase the percentage of taxation that high earners pay on their first increments of income. Like everyone else in the example, their first $25,000 would be exempt from income tax and their next $25,000 would be taxed at only 10 percent. Progressive taxation just imposes increasingly higher percentages of taxation on increments of income as income increases. Flat taxes, by contrast, require that the same percentage of income be paid in taxes no matter how high the income. For example, everyone might pay 20 percent on all income in a pure flat-tax system.

In his conversation with Obama, Joe the Plumber was objecting to Obama's plan to increase the progressivity of income taxes. Obama had proposed during his campaign that family income over $250,000 a year be taxed at 39 percent instead of 36 percent. Joe objected to the idea that if his business were to grow and make a profit of more than $250,000 a year, his income in excess of $250,000 would be taxed at a higher rate than at present. Joe seemed to prefer a flat tax. Obama justified increasing the progressivity of income tax by saying that his plan would reduce taxes for 95 percent of households, thereby giving them a better chance of moving up the income ladder. He concluded, "I think when you spread the wealth around, it's good for everybody."[17]

The right-wing blogosphere went wild. Here's a typical comment, which wouldn't be worth mentioning except that it's echoed by some conservative pundits who are mistakenly treated by mainstream media as responsible adults:

I think that all of you who say that the Republicans need to figure out what socialism is are a bunch of morons. You "liberals" so called can't recognize socialism when it is right in front of your face. Obama says that we should spread the wealth around. You should ask yourself what happened in the Soviet Union? The government took all of the wealth and spread it around "fairly."[18]

I'll assume, charitably, that this right-wing blogger didn't know that the tax code was much more progressive under Republican President Dwight Eisenhower, with a top tax rate of

91 percent. Eisenhower didn't see, nor did the American public in the 1950s see, any discrepancy between such steeply progressive taxes and the Cold War fight against the Soviet system.

Charitable attributions of ignorance can't apply, however, to Michelle Malkin, who is treated by the major media as a mainstream spokesperson for respectable, conservative views. She compared Obama's planned tax increase to the expropriation of farms in Zimbabwe.[19] She cited a story filed by Matt Ehlers in a North Carolina newspaper, the *Raleigh News and Observer*. Ehlers explains how Wally and Helen Herbst lost their prosperous farm in Zimbabwe. Zimbabwean president Robert Mugabe had become impatient with the continued prosperity of the 5 percent of Zimbabweans who were white compared to the 95 percent who were black. So, he allowed blacks simply to take farmland from whites, including the farm of Wally and Helen Herbst.

As a result of failure to protect property rights, matters have degenerated in Zimbabwe. It used to be the breadbasket of the region but now most of its people need international food assistance. Only 6 percent of the workforce is formally employed and a cholera epidemic started in 2008. Zimbabwe's inflation rate reached 231 million percent per year before the country abandoned its currency in favor of using the US dollar and some other foreign currencies.[20]

Could Malkin honestly believe that there is any similarity between Obama's tax proposal and the ruinous expropriation of farms in Zimbabwe? Of course not! She knows that we have had much higher tax rates than Obama was proposing without any expropriation and with improvements rather than declines in overall economic performance. Her column was purposely deceptive: a case of calculated disinformation.

But there's no outrage. We should all be outraged that she considers deception acceptable, that she thinks the end justifies the means, whether the end is furthering her career or advancing the goals of the antitax-antigovernment movement. She should be shunned and marginalized. There should be no place in journalism for such dishonesty. But there is. Malkin has since appeared on Sunday morning political round tables along with the likes of columnist David Brooks and economist Paul Krugman, as if her comments were as worthy of consideration as those based in reality.

Former vice presidential candidate Sarah Palin has been equally loopy about the health-care plan passed by Congress in 2010. The plan includes greater federal government involvement in health care and is therefore anathema to the antigovernment-antitax crowd. Palin said, "Nationalizing our health care system is a point of no return for government interference in the lives of its citizens."[21] But she didn't go on to critique the plan on matters worthy of debate, and there are many. Instead, she claimed that the legislation established what she called "death panels." She said, "The America I know and love is not one in which my parents or my baby with Down syndrome will have to stand in front of Obama's 'death panel' so his bureaucrats can decide, based on a subjective judgment of their 'level of productivity in society,' whether they are worthy of health care. Such a system is downright evil."[22]

It's difficult to assess the relative contributions of ignorance, self-deception, and plain old lying in Palin's claims. The new legislation does include money to fund end-of-life planning. For many years now, hospitals have employed clinical ethicists to help patients and their families decide how aggressively the patient wants to be treated. Does the patient want to be resuscitated in case her heart stops? Does she want to be intubated for long periods? And who would she like making decisions for her should she become unable to make decisions for herself? I sit on a committee that reviews the work of the clinical ethicists at Memorial Medical Center in Springfield, Illinois. The whole point is to empower patients and their families to receive the care that they want without being subjected to treatments that they don't want.

Another provision of the new legislation is to promote the use of treatments that clinical evidence shows to be most effective so that taxpayer money isn't wasted on treatments that don't work or that are more expensive than equally effective alternatives.[23] Nobody could look at these provisions and honestly detect "death panels." Yet the charge was widely reported and included in the health-care debate as if it had some basis in reality. As far as I know, the only prominent conservative commentator regularly willing publicly to dismiss Sarah Palin as a joke is David Brooks of the *New York Times*.

Of course, I don't favor censoring Palin's remarks. I just think the headline "Palin Finds 'Death Panels' in Health Care Plan" should be in the section of the paper with "Mozart Raised by Wolves" and "Lassie Caught in Love Triangle with Two-headed Man."

Here's another example of outrageous beliefs being taken seriously. Many people on the right claim that global warming is a hoax perpetrated by liberals who favor more government involvement in our lives. If global warming is real, these right wingers believe, government will have reason to intervene increasingly in private free markets to reduce emissions of greenhouse gases. These conspiracy theorists think that the whole point of claiming that the earth is warming is to justify this power grab by government.[24]

Of course, there isn't a shred of evidence supporting these claims. Can you really imagine that tens of thousands of people involved in the scientific reporting of evidence regarding climate change, all the people who have been measuring temperatures around the world over the last several decades, are part of some vast conspiracy? I guess the melting glaciers and ice caps would have to be in cahoots as well. This view is completely absurd.

Yet it affects electoral politics. Republican Senator Lindsey Graham, for example, was attacked by Tea Party activists at a Greenville, South Carolina, town hall meeting. The Tea Party, a recent manifestation of long-standing antigovernment sentiment, is composed of citizens who are upset primarily about the increasing role of government in people's lives. Their very vocal opposition in 2009 and 2010 almost derailed Obama's health-care legislation, which the Tea Party considered an inappropriate government takeover of health care. They are equally opposed to climate change initiatives that increase the government's role in energy-related decisions. Accordingly, they attacked Senator Graham for agreeing to work with Senator John Kerry on climate change and clean energy legislation. He was called a RINO, a traitor, a disgrace, a Democrat in drag, and a fake Republican.[25] It seems that in the view of these Tea Party activists, if Republicans oppose a bigger government, all true Republicans are obligated to ignore all evidence of global warming. Ideology is more important than reality.

During the presidential election of 2008, rather than oppose Obama merely on the issues, right wingers attempted the uncomfortable contortion of claiming simultaneously that Obama was a Muslim and that he was unduly influenced by his controversial Christian pastor, the Reverend Jeremiah Wright Jr. To his enduring credit as an American and as a human being, John McCain disallowed the racially divisive issue of the pastor's views to be used by his campaign. But the irrational assault on Obama was pursued by others, with the result that although only 13 percent of Americans thought Obama was a Muslim in 2008, 24 percent thought he was a Muslim in 2010.[26]

These outrageous examples should not be taken to suggest that Republicans should be excluded from debates at the center of American politics. There are plenty of sane Republicans now, just as there were during the post–World War II Progressive Era. John McCain and Lindsey Graham are sane on climate control, energy, and torture. We can all learn from them. Elder statesmen of the Republican Party, such as James Baker, Alan Simpson, and Colin Powell, can make invaluable contributions, as do such Republican pundits as David Brooks and George Will. These are among the people whose views should share the center as we debate the new progressive agenda. But we can no longer afford to treat right-wing extremists such as Grover Norquist, Paul Ryan, Sarah Palin, and Michelle Malkin as mainstream contributors to public debate. We can no longer allow their right-wing fantasies to share the center of American politics.

$ $ $

One key to reclaiming the center of American politics for reality-oriented views is to remind voters of government's value, because most of the idiocy and dishonesty stem from attempts to discredit people and policies that require maintaining or increasing government involvement in our lives. The other key is to justify in the popular mind taxing the rich more than the rest so that government services can be paid for without harming the middle class or increasing public debt.

Most Americans still want an activist government that solves national problems rather than a smaller government that can be drowned in the bathtub. A Pew Research Center poll released in February 2011 reveals that the majority of Americans prefer increased rather than reduced federal government spending on education, public schools, veterans benefits, college financial aid, Medicare, health care, aid to poor Americans, Social Security, combating crime, infrastructure, environmental protection, scientific research, energy, agriculture, terror defense, and military defense.[27]

A *New York Times*/CBS poll revealed in 2010 that even most Tea Party supporters, who claim to oppose big government, send their children to public schools. Follow-up interviews showed that these Tea Party enthusiasts aren't ready to give up Medicare or Social Security either, two of the government's largest programs.[28]

These findings convince me that in general people do appreciate the importance of government services. I believe that substantial majorities, when they think about it for a moment, recognize that most of us depend on public fire departments to protect us from fire and on the National Weather Service to warn us of dangerous weather. We all rely on government oversight to make air travel safe. Many people use life-saving or health-preserving medicines developed under the auspices of the National Institutes of Health and certified for use by the Food and Drug Administration. We all put our lives on the line regularly when we use highway bridges inspected by government entities. We depend on the Federal Deposit Insurance Corporation to guarantee our bank savings against bank failures. We rely on the Securities and Exchange Commission to reduce the level of insider trading and other forms of stock manipulation and cheating so that our stock portfolios and 401(k) retirement savings aren't devastated by unscrupulous stock manipulators. Most people use the services of the United States Postal Service, trusting that their letters and packages will arrive as promised, and this faith is (statistically) almost always justified.

The sticking point is not so much American appreciation of government services as the willingness to pay for them. The 2011 Pew Research Center poll cited previously found that most Americans think state budget problems should be addressed through a combination of increased state taxes and reduced state services. However, when polled on the state services that they would like to see reduced, respondents rejected reductions in state funding of colleges and universities, roads and transportation, health-care services, and K–12 education, which constitute the bulk of most state budgets. In other words, the majority generally rejected reduced government funding when particular programs were at issue. Nor did they approve increased taxes to pay for these programs when particular forms of taxation were considered. Majorities rejected increased sales taxes, increased business taxes, and increased personal income taxes.[29]

It seems that many Americans want the services of a large government without the large government. They want freedom from government (no new taxes) without giving up government aid, just as adolescents want freedom from parents (no parental restrictions) without giving up parental support. Like the hippies of old, they suffer from adolescent economics.

$ $ $

Such adolescent economics may be an understandable, although unhelpful, reaction to the growing gap between the rich and poor in our country and to the related impoverishment of the middle class (chapter 2). Feeling pressed, many people seek a scapegoat and unrealistically blame the government for their problems. But such government bashing does no good. Instead, foundational to a realistic solution is taxing wealthy people at much higher rates than at present. The majority of hard-pressed Americans could then avoid higher taxes and still have increased government services, thereby reducing gaps between the rich and poor through the funding of programs called for in the new progressive agenda.

This solution is opposed by free-market ideologies behind the antigovernment-antitax movement. According to these ideologies, rich people always deserve their wealth because they get wealthy by providing goods and services that people want, which spurs economic growth and helps everyone (chapter 3). Such ideological approbation of the underdeprived stands in the way of a new progressive agenda, and this book takes back the center for that agenda by undermining that approbation.

Much of the wealth accumulated by rich people, which increases the gap between the rich and the rest of us, has been gained through underhanded means, including defrauding the public (chapter 4), cheating the poor (chapter 5), and fleecing the taxpayer (chapter 6). What is more, when entrepreneurs are successful through improved productivity, much of the credit is due to social and technological change for which the entrepreneurs can take no more credit than any other member of society. To that extent, entrepreneurs shouldn't reap rewards any greater than other workers receive. Redistribution from the rich to the working poor through a more robust EIC is justified on this basis (chapter 7). In addition, if people didn't know their own status in society, they would want everyone to be treated fairly, and fairness would require not only higher taxes for the rich and a robust EIC for the working poor, but also massive investments in education from preschool through graduate school to give everyone equal opportunity. Higher taxes on the rich are needed for these massive investments in education (chapter 8).

A large government that redistributes wealth through taxation and aids the middle class through support of unionization (which was much more prevalent during the post–World War II Progressive Era) is needed also to save our democratic form of government from rule by the rich (chapter 9). Finally, the economy flourishes and grows fastest when tax money is used to create and maintain public goods in such areas as education, energy, transportation, and health care (Conclusion).

When readers can explain all these points to independent voters across a dinner table (my formula for ruining Thanksgiving dinner), the stage will be set for progressives to take back the center for a new progressive agenda. The fantasy of reducing government will be removed from the center of debate and replaced with discussion of balancing the federal budget through more steeply progressive taxation; providing more income support for the *working* poor through the EIC; improving the wages of lower- and middle-income workers through government support for unionization; funding education at all levels more generously to promote equality of opportunity; developing infrastructure in energy and transportation to regain energy independence and improve transportation efficiency; and completing the task of universal health care begun with passage in 2010 of the Patient Protection and Affordable Care Act.

2

The Rich Get Richer

Much of the anger that is common among Americans today and that animates antigovernment-antitax activists—anger at the bailouts of financial institutions in 2008, anger at the lavish bonuses that many high-flying workers at those institutions have received since then, and anger at the deteriorating financial situation of many middle-class families—stems from widespread frustration in the face of the growing gap between the rich and the rest in our society. Such anger is understandable because the gap has been increasing for almost forty years. But the antigovernment-antitax solution of less government and lower taxes on the rich is counterproductive. The problem of inequality today stems in large part from government retreating from public projects and lowering taxes on rich families.

In this chapter, stories of individuals with different levels of income and wealth illustrate the problem of economic inequality, which the new progressive agenda will address boldly when it takes center stage in political discussions. Concluding statistics show these stories to be representative of America today. Later chapters show that a new progressive agenda, not a smaller government, is the best way to help the poor and the middle class attain greater security and opportunity.

$$ \$ \quad \$ \quad \$ $$

The rich are now richer than they have been since the 1920s, and some of them are living in a favorite haunt of old money, Nantucket. This island off the coast of Massachusetts contains homes owned by the Vanderbilts, Mellons, duPonts, and other families prominent in the Gilded Age of the late nineteenth and early twentieth centuries. Many of their descendents still have summer homes here but they don't display their wealth ostentatiously. Nina Chandler Murray, a woman in her eighties from a family connected to the investment rating firm Standard & Poor's, explained to Geraldine Fabrikant of the *New York Times* how the descendents of old money differ from the current generation of hyper-rich:

Coming from a New England background, you had a honed discipline of what was expected. Showing off money was a sin. It was not that status was not important, but marriage was very closely controlled and predetermined, and everyone knew where everyone else fit.

What has happened in America is that achievement is so important that everyone wants everyone else to know what they have done. And in case you don't know, they want to tell you with a lethal combination of houses, cars and diamonds.[1]

Murray recalls this example. A woman at a dinner party told her, "My husband paid $250,000 to join the golf club, and he doesn't even play golf."

L. Dennis Kozlowski was among the new, hyper-rich of Nantucket before his 2005 conviction for criminal larceny in connection with Tyco International. He was known for having a $6,000 shower curtain in his Manhattan apartment, and for a multimillion-dollar party he gave for his wife's birthday in Sardinia. The party included a copy in ice sculpture of Michelangelo's *David* spewing vodka.[2] (I wonder where the spout was.)

Michael Kittridge, a fifties-something entrepreneur who sold his Yankee Candle company in 1998 for $500 million has a ten-thousand-square-foot house on Nantucket with a movie theater and a wine cellar with two thousand bottles of wine. He thinks people with money like to be with those who are similarly rich. "Successful people want to be with other successful people. . . . On Nantucket you don't feel bad because you want a nice bottle of wine. If you order a three-hundred-dollar bottle in a restaurant, the guy at the next table is ordering a four-hundred-dollar bottle."

The fact that the new hyper-rich have more money than the old rich can create awkward moments. Kittredge explains:

Money makes a lifestyle. It creates a division between the old money and the new. It is a little bit of class jealousy. We go to a cocktail party and a guy is telling my wife about his airplane. So finally the question comes up: "How do you get over to the island?" and she says, "We come by plane." And he says, "What kind of plane?" and she says, "A G-IV." And so the wind comes out of the guy's sails.

The old money guy has a twin-prop airplane and that is pretty incredible. For his time, that is pretty great. Now he is talking to a guy who is half his age who has a transcontinental jet. That is the end of the conversation.

Or you meet someone and they start telling you about their boat. He has a forty-five-foot boat and he is very happy with it. Then he'll say, "Do you have a boat?" And you say, "Yes." "Well, what kind of boat do you have?" And you say, "A Fead Ship." And he says, "How big is it?" That's how people rank them. So I have to say, "It's two hundred feet." It's the end of the conversation. Is there envy? Yes, could be. Was he a wealthy guy in his day? Absolutely, but relative to today—no.[3]

The hyper-rich cause housing difficulties for others on Nantucket. By 2004 the average house price on the island was $1.672 million, a result of new money bidding up prices. H. Wayne Huizenga, who founded Blockbusters and owns the Miami Dolphins, already had a house on Nantucket, but paid $2.5 million for another house just to have more room. Another hyper-rich resident, Richard Mellon Scaife, bought an extra house for his staff.

As the hyper-rich buy up real estate on an island of only fifty square miles, price increases make it difficult for people of modest means to live there. The former principal of Nantucket

High School, Paul Richards, left his job, and his wife, Martina, a nurse, left hers, because they couldn't afford to buy a house on Nantucket. Richards said, "It was frustrating to be driven away from two jobs that we very much enjoyed, but a starter home for our family would have cost over $600,000."[4]

The Nantucket Housing Office, a nonprofit organization, has proposed that a tax of eight dollars per square foot be placed on any construction exceeding three thousand square feet. They want to use the money raised in this way to help families earning $120,825 or less afford housing on the island. Where the hyper-rich take root, even families earning over $120,000 a year may need housing assistance!

Greater differences between the rich and the rest are evident in intercontinental air travel. My wife, Grace, and I, both retired, are able to travel by air once or twice a year, often overseas, but always in the cheapest seats we can find. Typically, we arrive at the gate early, finding only a few fellow passengers reading newspapers, drinking coffee, keeping their eyes on their carry-on luggage, and trying to control their bored children. We hope that this is a good sign, that the flight won't be full, because we know how uncomfortable an eight- or nine-hour flight to Europe can be when the seat rows are so close that your knees get crushed when the person in front of you reclines; when elbows of strangers come dangerously close to Jell-O deserts; and the wait at the restroom after the movie seems endless. Still, I'm old-fashioned enough to feel like it's a miracle and a privilege that I can fly across the ocean in a day to attend the theater in London or see the Parthenon in Athens. As the time for boarding arrives, hoards of people descend on the gate. Oh well, it's a miracle and a privilege.

The hyper-rich do not share this experience. Joe Sharkey reports in the *New York Times* on the flying experience of "the tremendously rich." I don't mean the people who enter commercial flights before the rest of us because they sit in first class. As I pass by first class Brahmins on my way toward the coach-class area I wonder how much these people paid for their tickets and, if it's anywhere near as much as I imagine, how extra leg and elbow room can be worth that much. I guess they're rich enough not to care. But they're not the hyper-rich or "the tremendously rich." The tremendously rich escape our notice altogether because they're not on our plane at all. Like the hyper-rich traveling to Nantucket, they have their own planes. But they don't just have transcontinental jets. Many of them have *commercial-size* transcontinental jets.

One of these people is prominent liability lawyer Willie Gary who owned a Boeing 737 when he discussed the matter with Joe Sharkey in 2006. Coming from a family of migrant workers in Florida, Gary became "weary of wasting valuable time away from his family in commercial airports and [was] eager to have the space to conduct business in the air." So he bought a 737 to complement what is now his "second plane," a Gulfstream G2 that seats 16. Gary finds the 737 very convenient, because "on the 737, we can take depositions. . . . We have meetings and settlement conferences. It gives me the luxury of getting in and getting out and moving on. I've touched down in as many as five states in a day." However, he's not wedded to the plane, adding, "I'm a goal setter, and I'm always looking for something new."[5]

That "something new" may be the Boeing 787, called the Dreamliner, which is expected to carry between 210 and 330 passengers, depending on how the seats are configured, when used commercially. But the very rich can have it configured differently. Lufthansa Technik showed its VIP version at the National Business Aviation Association trade show in Orlando, Florida, in 2006. It will have only thirty-five seats "most of which can also be used as single lie-flat seats, queen-size beds or double beds. . . ." The Dreamliner lists for upward of $150 million.

Even the Dreamliner, however, is small compared to a jumbo jet, a Boeing 747, which normally carries about four hundred passengers. It can be modified to carry fewer passengers in better style, passengers who want to fly, for example, with their Rolls Royce and race horses. These planes list for $180 million with a bare interior. Expect to spend another $50 million or more to make the inside really livable. Thirty-nine such VIP-configured 747s currently ease the pain of travel for the overprivileged.

More is to come. The Airbus A380 will be the largest plane in the sky, allowing even more room for luxuries, including perhaps the greatest luxury of all, class distinction among passengers. The plane has an upper and lower deck, like the ocean liners of old. Although no place on the plane corresponds to the steerage level my grandparents inhabited on their way from Europe to Ellis Island, some extremely wealthy people may enjoy excluding ordinary VIPs from the plane's most cherished quarters.

New York Times correspondent Jennifer Steinhauer claims that services distinguish the wealthy from the rest of us even more than goods:

These [rich] Americans employ about nine thousand personal chefs, up from about four hundred just ten years ago, according to the American Personal Chef Association. They are taking ever-more exotic vacations, often in private planes. They visit plastic surgeons and dermatologists for costly and frequent cosmetic procedures. And they are sending their children to $400-an-hour math tutors, summer camps at French chateaus, and crash courses on managing money.[6]

Like the two-tiered A380, the greatest reward is status, Steinhauer claims. Rich people can get what others can't. This explains why people pay $800 for a haircut and pay $350 for a meal at a Japanese restaurant that seats only twenty-six people, ensuring exclusivity and making reservations hard to get.

The underdeprived receive other services as well. Ellen Perry, for example, counsels rich families on how the younger generation should be trained to handle great wealth so that it doesn't harm them. The families she counsels have an average wealth of $100 million. Polly Onet plans parties for wealthy families, including a children's party with a "Charlie and the Chocolate Factory Theme" in which everything was edible, even the flowers. The party cost $120,000. Dr. Jana Klauer is a nutritionist who scopes out restaurants where her clients are expecting to dine. After examining the menu, she chooses what her clients will order to ensure that they are eating healthy meals.[7]

$ $ $

Not everyone is so prosperous. I drive through a leafy suburb of a major city, past modest, extremely well-kept houses with green lawns, a beautiful public high school with all the latest amenities, and small parks adjacent to up-market public grade schools. The streets are wide and cars glide by at an even pace, except when they meet at four-way stops and politely defer to one another. I turn into a driveway that is actually the entrance to a long parking lot that sits alongside a two-story brick apartment building. Camouflaged by trees and reduced to minimal street presence by construction that is perpendicular to the road, we enter what is for this town the low-rent district (or patch), an area where less affluent middle-class people can rent apartments in a town where they could never afford to buy a house.

This is 2006 and I'm visiting my eldest daughter Ami, a white-collar worker with a college degree and the single parent of two children, ages two and five. My five-year-old granddaughter Taylor jumps into my arms as her younger brother Michael seems unsure whether we are people he knows. We haven't seen them for a few months. He warms up to my wife

Grace first because they had spent a couple of hours a day together at the Chautauqua Institution during one week of the previous summer while my daughter took a special studies class. Taylor soon finds Grandma Grace and leads her to the small bedroom that the two children share. The other small bedroom in this two-bedroom apartment is Ami's. The place is covered throughout in off-white carpet, except in the linoleum-tiled kitchen, which has a small table that seats four. There's no dining room, just a living room that accommodates a large sofa against one wall and a television in an entertainment center on the opposite wall. The impressive cleanliness of the small apartment, Ami assures me, is in honor of our visit.

While Grace entertains the children in their bedroom, Ami and I sit down at the kitchen table to look at her monthly budget. Her 2006 budget is interesting because it's based on an annual income of $48,000, which was close to the median household income that year. As you look at the budget, remember two things: first, half of all single-earner households have less income. Second, median household income fell almost 10 percent between 2007 and June of 2011, so the situation for nearly half of American households is even worse now.[8]

$800	rent
$630	daycare (for her two-year-old)
$100	hot lunches, after-school enrichment, and intersession fees (for her five-year-old in kindergarten)
$80	Internet and cable (she uses the Internet for work)
$50	electricity (water and gas are included in the rent)
$100	cell phone (a bad deal but it lasted two or three years)
$120	college loan repayment
$150	other debt payments
$150	gasoline (she has a long commute)

$40   car insurance

$2,220   total

After deductions for taxes, health insurance, and such, my daughter took home $1,300 every other Friday in 2006. So, ten months of the year her income was $2,600. This left her just $380 a month for everything that isn't represented yet in her budget. I point out to her that she hasn't put anything in her budget for clothing, car repair (or car payments when the car is replaced), lessons for her children (they're very talented), Christmas presents, entertainment, birthday parties, toiletries and, oh yes, food. She says that for all of this she has more than just $380 a month. She gets a tax return that is usually over $1,000, and twice a year she gets three paychecks instead of two, because she's paid every other Friday, and therefore twenty-six times a year. This suggests to me that three months of the year, the two with extra paychecks and the one when she gets her tax return, her budget works. But the other nine months she's left with big holes in her budget.

Ami realized this. Reacting to her unsustainable financial condition, she took a job for several months in 2006 delivering about 230 papers a day for an additional $720 a month before taxes. Between getting her children to and from daycare and school, commuting to her day job, performing her day job, and doing the paper route, she didn't sleep much and, in the opinion of this concerned parent, was jeopardizing her health. I'm not sure how she's getting by right now, but she stopped her paper route at the end of 2006 and has had some modest raises. The $630 day-care expense disappeared in fall 2009 when Michael entered kindergarten, replaced by the lesser expenses associated with school attendance.

$ $ $

As mentioned previously, Ami is a middle-income white-collar worker with a college degree. Budgets are even tighter for many blue-collar workers with only high school diplomas or less. Medical sociologist Susan Sered and health systems analyst and activist Rushika Fernandopulle discuss the situation of blue-collar workers Dave and Judy who live in Decatur, Illinois, just thirty-five miles from where I live. At the time of their interviews several years ago, Dave and Judy had been married just five years, even though Dave was fifty-five years old and Judy only a few years younger. It was a second marriage for both of them. Judy had concentrated on raising her children until she was in her mid-thirties when she went to work at an Eagle supermarket. She worked hard and liked her work but lost her job and its health benefits two years into her marriage to Dave when the store closed as a result of competition from a new Walmart.

Dave started working when he was only sixteen. He realized that menial factory jobs wouldn't get him far, so he pursued technical education:

I got an apprenticeship in construction, in '76, I guess it was. It took me almost a year to go through the whole process, and I finally got hired in '77. And, boy, that was great. It started out at six dollars and fifty cents an hour, which wasn't a lot, but I had been making five dollars. So that was a lot for me. And then every six months or a year, I got another raise. And it just kept going up, and it was wonderful. And everything was good. You could buy a new car once in a while; you could have a home.[9]

Dave was a member of the pipefitters' union and enjoyed a steady stream of work for many years at local manufacturers such as Caterpillar and Firestone. When unions were strong, factory work, although often grueling, included health insurance and paid enough to allow workers to buy cars and homes and live a middle-class life. Health insurance was particularly important to Dave when he had open heart surgery to unblock four arteries. He continues to have high blood pressure and high cholesterol, for which he is supposed to take medications, including Lipitor. But that has become a problem.

In recent decades, corporate mergers, acquisitions, and downsizing have reduced the availability of high-paying jobs with health insurance. "In the 1980s alone, west-central Illinois lost 64,033 jobs in manufacturing through layoffs and mergers of corporate mainstays such as Case, John Deere, and Caterpillar."[10] Matters have gotten worse since the 1980s with increased outsourcing of manufacturing overseas, where workers may earn only one-tenth of the American wage. Over a number of years Caterpillar laid off a lot of workers but fewer than fifty people at a time so they could avoid the kind of disclosure required when more than fifty people are let go at once. The biggest hit to Decatur's economy, however, was the complete closure of the Firestone plant in 2001. As one former factory worker put it, "You know, they move the plants down to Mexico to those—what do they call them?—*maquiladoras*—like sweatshops, with no unions and no benefits. And they pay them peanuts to work like slaves. I don't blame those people for taking our jobs. They need to eat, too. I feel sorry for them."[11]

But there's reason to feel sorry for Dave as well. He works only intermittently now and has little prospect of steady employment in the future. He doesn't think the major employer that remains in the area, Archer Daniels Midland, would hire him full time or that he could keep up with younger workers if they did. A job retraining administrator in Decatur explains:

Factory workers like Dave worked extremely hard. They worked terrible hours. They worked on shifts. They would work at night. It's filthy inside the plants, dangerous, very hot and very noisy, up to a hundred twenty degrees, with no air conditioning. The work was dangerous. They would risk life and limb. They worked really hard for their money, and they felt they deserved what they earned. Having lived through all that, they now want a job with low stress and a job that's less physical. Sometimes it's necessary because they have arthritis or other kinds of degenerative problems as a result of the very hard work, the heavy lifting, and repetitive lifting they've done inside the plants.[12]

Dave and Judy had medical insurance through his union, but the deductible was so high—$500 per person per year—that the insurance did them little good, Judy says, "By the end of last year, we just met our deductible. And then the year starts over again. So we never get anything paid [for by the insurance]."[13] Then the insurance added another deductible for medications as they eliminated coverage for dental and eye care altogether. In addition, the insurance would pay 80 percent of the costs of a hospital stay until the patient's portion equaled $5,000; then it would pay 100 percent. But Dave and Judy couldn't come up with the 20 percent to pay their portion. Finally, Dave and Judy will have to forgo insurance completely because Dave isn't employed regularly enough to qualify for union benefits. Dave explains:

Well, right now, with things the way they are, they have also changed our insurance so that you have to work ten out of twelve weeks in a quarter to qualify for the insurance. So, now, I've been laid off a month. I no longer will qualify after this quarter. So I'd have to self-pay. Well, our self-pay is like—what are the rates, twelve or fourteen hundred dollars? It's way up there per quarter. I can't pay that.[14]

Dave risks a serious cardiac event for lack of medication.

Judy suffers, too, for lack of coverage. One month after she lost her job because of the closure of the Eagle supermarket, Judy's daughter was hit and killed by a train. Lacking a job and insurance that would provide grief counseling, Judy hasn't been able to get over her terrible loss. All she has is a prescription for antidepressants. She exudes sadness, which diminishes her chances for finding work in Decatur's anemic economy, as does the fact that she's been out of work for three years.

Her continued sadness is augmented by their housing situation. When Dave and Judy met, shortly after each had gotten a divorce, neither was in good financial shape, which is common after divorce. Still, they managed to buy a modest home near some railroad tracks. After the death of her daughter, Judy experiences renewed pain every time she hears a train go by. The couple would like to move, but they can't sell their house for a price that would enable them to buy another house in a more favorable location.

Their money pressures are sometimes extreme. When Dave was out of work, Judy says, they went three weeks with no money at all, which included three days without eating, before Dave's unemployment check arrived. They've sold many personal possessions and would sell more to keep food on the table and save their home, but buyers are hard to find. They don't want to give up their home because it's the sole remnant of their middle-class life and they fear homelessness.

$ $ $

Writer Barbara Ehrenreich chronicles the difficulties of many people, the working poor, who don't make enough money to rent a decent apartment, much less own a home. In her popular book *Nickel and Dimed: On (Not) Getting By in America*, Ehrenreich shares her experiences in the world of the working poor in the late 1990s. She took various poorly paid jobs in different parts of the country. This was considered a time of general prosperity, yet the minimum wage of $5.15 an hour didn't come close to a living wage.

Working in a restaurant in Florida, Ehrenreich lived in a small apartment for $500 a month. But she could afford to rent the apartment in the first place only because she had $1,000 to put down on a deposit and the first month's rent. People who earn between $6 and $10 an hour can seldom amass $1,000. One of Ehrenreich's colleagues is Gail, who's "sharing a room in a well-known flophouse for $250 a week. Her roommate, a male friend, has begun hitting on her, driving her nuts, but the rent would be impossible alone."[15] Gail says she's

thinking of escaping from her roommate by moving into the Days Inn herself. I am astounded: how she can even think of paying $40 to $60 a day? But if I was afraid of sounding like a social worker, I have come out just sounding like a fool. She squints at me in disbelief: "And where am I supposed to get a month's rent and a month's deposit for an apartment?" . . . In poverty, as in certain propositions in physics, starting conditions are everything. . . . If you can't put up the two months' rent you need to secure an apartment, you end up paying through the nose for a room by the week. If you have only a room, with a hot plate at best, you can't save by cooking up huge lentil stews that can be frozen for the week ahead. You eat fast food or the hot dogs and Styrofoam cups of soup that can be microwaved in a convenience store.[16]

One of Ehrenreich's colleagues at the restaurant in Florida had even worse housing problems; she was homeless. She wore tasteful outfits to work, which made her seem prosperous, but the outfits came from a thrift store and the woman actually lived in a van parked behind a shopping center. She showered in a colleague's room at the Days Inn.

Homeless people elsewhere are often poorly received by more prosperous residents of the areas where they congregate. The city of Las Vegas, Nevada, passed an ordinance in 2006 that prohibits feeding homeless people in public parks. It's a misdemeanor punishable by a fine of up to $1,000 or a jail term of up to six months to provide "food or meals to the indigent for free or for a nominal fee." The ordinance explains: "an indigent person is a person whom a reasonable ordinary person would believe to be entitled to apply for or receive public assistance."[17]

Gail Sacco, a retired restaurant owner, regularly feeds homeless people at Huntridge Circle Park, a three-acre expanse of green lawns and trees in a residential area near downtown. The nearest shelter for the homeless, where homeless people can get free food under government auspices, is about three miles away. Walking that distance when the temperature is over 100 degrees can be downright dangerous.

However, there are about twelve thousand homeless people in Las Vegas, and apparently their congregating in parks can upset or scare local residents as well as harm the park's landscaping. The city had recently spent $1.7 million on landscaping and other improvements at Huntridge Circle Park. But the city already has an ordinance against more than twenty-five people gathering in parks without a permit, so the ban on feeding people in parks doesn't seem aimed at discouraging the formation of large groups in the parks because the other ordinance already takes care of that.

Gary Reese, the mayor pro tem and a member of the city council who represents the area around Huntridge Circle Park claims that people who want to feed the homeless can take them to McDonald's or Kentucky Fried Chicken. He doesn't consider the fact that you can feed many more people for the same money making meals at home than patronizing fast-food restaurants. Allen Lichtenstein of the American Civil Liberties Union in Nevada said the ordinance is unconstitutional and absurd. If you're picnicking with friends at a local park it would be legal to share your food with friends who have enough money to buy their own food but not with people who are too poor to buy food for themselves.

Fort Myers, Florida, and Santa Monica, California, also restricted feeding the homeless in public parks but relaxed these restrictions in response to legal challenges. Orlando, Florida, by contrast, passed an ordinance making it illegal to feed more than twenty-five people in downtown parks or in other public facilities without a permit. Clearly, if you're desperately poor and homeless, hunger can be an issue. As we've seen, it has even been an issue for home-owning Dave and Judy in Decatur, Illinois.

Dave and Judy are not alone either when it comes to lacking medications necessary to treat serious illness or injury. Barbara Ehrenreich cites an example she learned about while working as a waitress in Florida. The boyfriend of one of Ehrenreich's colleagues at the restaurant lost his job for failure to return to work soon enough after he got a cut on his foot. The cut healed very slowly because the man couldn't afford the prescribed antibiotic.

The inability to afford prescribed medications increased with the recession that began in 2008. Kevin Sack reports in the *New York Times* on conditions in Rocky Mount, North Carolina, an economically depressed area in the eastern part of the state where the unemployment rate was 14 percent in 2009. One resident, James Crawford, went home from the hospital after his third heart attack with six prescriptions. They included "a pair for high blood pressure, one each for angina, cholesterol, and acid reflux, and a renal vitamin for his kidney disease."[18] Mr. Crawford, sixty-one, who lives on $1,800 a month that he receives from Social Security and veteran's benefits, bought only the heart, blood pressure, and acid reflux pills. He won't even consider buying Plavix, which helps to prevent future heart attacks by reducing the chance that new blockages will form in his arteries, because the copayment is $160. He received that prescription in February after his second heart attack. Now that he's had a third attack, he still feels he can't afford to fill the prescription.

Children can be at risk as well. Lisa Hylton lives with her husband, a pipefitter, in the nearby town of Sharpsburg, North Carolina. His work is intermittent and they can't afford insurance during the stretches when he's idle. So, they don't fill all of the twice-monthly prescriptions for inhalers to treat their son Hunter's asthma.

These are not isolated cases, according to Sack. Pharmacists at the town's Almand's Oakwood neighborhood store stopped the automatic refilling of prescriptions because they found that about half the time customers didn't show up to buy the refills and pills had to be restocked. Dr. John Avent, who treats patients at a low-income clinic nearby, estimates that 80 percent of his patients were not taking medications as prescribed. Like Dave in Decatur, James Crawford with heart disease, and Hunter Hylton with asthma, these patients are risking their health because their financial situation is so poor.

$ $ $

Statistical evidence shows overwhelmingly that the kind of divide between rich and poor illustrated in the contrasting stories of the hyper-rich building enormous homes on Nantucket and the working poor sharing motel rooms so they can wait on tables in Florida grows almost every year. In my county, Sangamon County, Illinois, which reflects national trends, median family income declined 8.4 percent between 1999 and 2005. Adjusted for inflation, it was $50,320 in 1999, but only $46,115 in 2005. In nearby Decatur, where Dave and Judy live, median family income declined twice as much between 1999 and 2005. One of the reasons, of course, is the loss of well-paying factory jobs that have been replaced by much-lower-paying service work. Clinton Lay's story is typical of what has happened in Decatur:

For almost 10 years, Clinton Lay—a Springfield native with a high-school equivalency diploma—could afford new cars, vacations and cross-country outings with his family, all because of his $70,000-a-year job at Decatur's Bridgestone/Firestone plant. . . .

The 12-hour shifts at the factory were monotonous and exhausting, but Lay planned to stay until retirement. . . .

But Lay and more than 1,500 other people lost their jobs when the plant closed in fall 2001.

Lay has been retrained through a program at Springfield's Capital Area Career Center and now works as a home health-care nurse. But in the job turmoil, his car and his wife's were repossessed. They can't afford to buy a home. They live paycheck-to-paycheck, Lay said.

Although he enjoys nursing much more than factory work, he earns slightly more than half of what he made at Firestone.[19]

Before their slide between 1999 and 2005, people of moderate means had already experienced declining incomes relative to rich people. During the 1990s the earning power of the average worker increased 5 percent (adjusted for inflation), whereas the average increase for CEOs (chief executive officers) of major corporations increased 571 percent, from $1,952,806 in 1990 to $13,100,000 in 2000. Now consider this. The average worker made $17,957 a year in 1990, compared to $24,667 in 2000 (without adjusting for 17 percent inflation during the decade). If those workers had received the same percentage increase in earnings during the 1990s as the CEOs of major corporations, they would have been averaging an income of $102,502.40, or more than $49 an hour by 2000.[20] I doubt many stores, restaurants, bars, cinemas, or contractors would consider it realistic to pay their average employee over $100,000 a year.

The decline of income among median workers compared to the rich goes back even farther. In 1988, Lawrence Summers, former US treasury secretary and more recently economic advisor to President Obama, wrote, "The U.S. today is in the midst of a quiet depression in living standards. The median income of the typical American family is right now the same as it was in 1969."[21] An analysis of Congressional Budget Office data shows that after-tax income for the top 1 percent of households increased 115 percent between 1977 and 1999, whereas *after-tax income for the middle 60 percent of households actually declined during that period.*[22]

The top one-tenth of 1 percent did even better than the top 1 percent. Their average income of $4.3 million in 2007 was 390 percent higher (adjusted for inflation) than that group's income in 1980.[23] By the year 2007 this group's income exceeded 8 percent of all the income earned in the United States, a percentage greater than any since the 1920s.[24] And the top one-hundredth of 1 percent did better still. These are the fourteen thousand households with income of at least $5.9 million in 2005. From 1950 to 1970 for every additional dollar earned by the bottom 90 percent, those in the top 0.01 percent earned an additional $162. From 1990 to 2007, for every extra dollar earned by those in the bottom 90 percent, each taxpayer at the top brought in an extra $4,740.[25]

The growing gap between the rich and the middle is no surprise to those who watch trends in CEO compensation compared to average wages in the companies that the CEOs run. In the 1960s corporate CEOs made twenty-five times as much as hourly production workers. At the beginning of the 1990s they made ninety-three times as much as production workers and by 1999 they made 413 times as much.[26] Here's an example of the change as expressed by former US labor secretary Robert Reich: "The CEO of General Motors took home about $4 million in 1968 (translated into today's dollars), which was around 66 times the pay and benefits of the typical GM worker at the time. In 2005, Wal-Mart's CEO Lee Scott, Jr., took home $17.5 million, some 900 times the pay and benefits of the typical Wal-Mart worker."[27]

Wealth is distributed even more unevenly than income, and the trend of increasing difference between the rich and the rest is the same. The Economic Policy Institute writes in its report *State of Working America 2006–07* that between 1962 and 2004 "the wealth share held by the bottom 80 percent shrunk by 3.8 percentage points, and that 3.8 percent share of wealth shifted to the top 5 percent of households."[28] Writers for the League of Women Voters Jeff Kolnick and Doug Anderson add,

The wealth held by the wealthiest 1 percent was 125 times the median wealth in 1962, but 190 times the median in 2004. For the super-rich who make *Forbes Magazine's* annual list of the 400 wealthiest Americans, the expansion of wealth has been particularly dramatic. In the 11 years between 1995 and 2006, this group saw its total wealth more than double from $470 billion to $1.25 trillion. At the same time, the personal savings rate of Americans overall—one indicator of wealth among the 80 percent who work for wages—has declined precipitously since 1982, dropping into negative territory in 2006.[29]

Much has been made in recent years of the investment in 401(k) retirement funds by average Americans, leaving the impression that investment in the stock market is widespread among people in the middle of the income spectrum. However, as long ago as 1999 the *Wall Street Journal* pointed out the error of this view: "For all the talk of mutual funds and 401(k)s for the masses, the stock market has remained the privilege of a relatively elite group. Nearly 90% of all shares were held by the wealthiest 10% of households. The bottom line: that top 10% held 73.2% of the country's net worth in 1997, up from 68.2% in 1983."[30] By 2010, the top 1 percent owned 33 percent of all privately held wealth in the United States.[31] Political and economic commentator Kevin Phillips adds,

Given the stagnation of median family net worth, talk about the United States becoming a Republic of Shareholders hardly applied to a family whose miniscule stock "portfolio" or pension fund interest had grown by $2,600 or even $6,100 while its debt load for college, health insurance, day care, and credit cards had jumped by $12,000. Still less did it apply to . . . [many] Americans who didn't own any stocks, even indirectly through pension funds or mutual funds.[32]

To make matters worse, about 46 million Americans lacked health insurance in 2010. This means that many people like James Crawford and Hunter Hylton were risking their health and their lives by failing to take medications needed to properly manage heart disease, asthma, and other serious conditions. When medical crises arose as a result of inadequate medical care, these people went to emergency rooms for costly life-saving interventions that put them further into debt. All too often, however, it was too late. Using figures from the The Institute of Medicine, correspondent T. R. Reid estimates that by 2009, over twenty thousand people were dying each year in the United States for lack of access to health care.[33]

The Patient Protection and Affordable Care Act, passed by Congress and signed into law by President Obama in 2010, addressed this situation. When fully implemented in 2014, the number of uninsured in the United States will be reduced dramatically and people will not be turned away by insurance companies because they have preexisting conditions.[34] This is all part of the new progressive agenda, but it's only a start. More will be needed to provide *all* Americans with affordable and effective health care coverage.

$ $ $

The new progressive agenda addresses the problems of increasing inequality, grinding poverty, financial insecurity, and medical inattention through more progressivity in the tax code, an increased EIC, stepped-up government funding to create jobs and renew our infrastructures in transportation and energy, better funding for education at all levels, and universal health care. Capturing the center for this agenda requires exposing its opponents to the withering criticism of reasonable scrutiny, which is the goal of this book.

Among the most influential opponents of the new progressive agenda are free-market conservatives who call for lower taxes and reduced government involvement in the economy. We examine this conservative vision in chapter 3 before showing in later chapters that the free-market conservative view is completely unrealistic.

3
Progressive Taxation and Free-Market Prosperity

Many opponents of the new progressive agenda are free-market conservatives who object to increasing taxes on rich people because, these conservatives think, people typically become rich in a free-market economy by improving productivity and creating jobs, both of which enrich society in general. High taxes on the wealthy, they say, unfairly punish people for success and discourage future innovation, thereby impoverishing society.

But higher taxes on rich people are foundational to the new progressive agenda. Its many components cost a lot of money and, as we've seen, poor and middle-income households are already under such financial stress that their taxes can't be raised much. So, taking back the center for the new progressive agenda requires explaining the errors of this free-market thinking. That is the subject of this and following chapters. We'll find that up to a point (which we are far from reaching) high taxes on the wealthy are economically beneficial.

First, however, let's look at the world through free-market conservative eyes so that we understand clearly the conservative view that we oppose. As luck would have it, I received an e-mail in March 2009 from my friend Arlie Beane that expresses beautifully a free-market conservative case against raising taxes on rich people. It's called "A Letter from the Boss."

To All My Valued Employees,

There have been some rumblings around the office about the future of this company, and more specifically, your job. . . . The good news is this: The economy doesn't pose a threat to your job. What does threaten your job, however, is the changing political landscape in this country. . . .

First, while it is easy to spew rhetoric that casts employers against employees, you have to understand that for every business owner there is a back story. . . . Sure, you see me park my Mercedes outside. You've seen my big home at last year's Christmas party. . . . However, what you don't see is the BACK STORY.

I started this company 28 years ago. At that time, I lived in a 300 square foot studio apartment for 3 years. My entire apartment was converted into an office so I could put forth 100% effort into building a company which . . . would eventually employ you.

My diet consisted of Ramen Pride noodles because every dollar I spent went back into this company. I drove a rusty Toyota Corolla with a defective transmission. I didn't have time to date. . . .

Meanwhile, my friends got jobs. They worked 40 hours a week and made a modest $50k a year and spent every dime they earned. They drove flashy cars and lived in expensive homes and wore fancy designer clothes. . . . I, however, did not. I put my money and my life into a business with a vision that eventually, someday, I, too, will be able to afford these luxuries. . . .

So, while you physically arrive at the office at 9am, mentally check in at about noon, and then leave at 5pm, I don't. There is no "off" button for me. . . . There is no rest. There is no weekend. There is no happy hour. Every day this business is attached to my hip like a 1-year-old special-needs child. . . .

Now, the economy is falling apart and I, the guy that made all the right decisions and saved his money, have to bail out all the people who didn't. . . .

Yes, business ownership has its benefits but the price I've paid is steep and not without wounds.

Unfortunately, the cost of running this business, and employing you, is starting to eclipse the threshold of marginal benefit and let me tell you why:

I am being taxed to death and the government thinks I don't pay enough. I have state taxes. Federal taxes. Property taxes. Sales and use taxes. Payroll taxes. Workers' compensation taxes. Unemployment taxes. Taxes on taxes. I have to hire a tax man to manage all these taxes and then guess what? I have to pay taxes for employing him. . . .

On October 15th I wrote a check to the US Treasury for $288,000 for quarterly taxes. . . .

The fact is, if I deducted (Read: stole) 50% of your paycheck you'd quit and you wouldn't work here. I mean, why should you? That's nuts. Who wants to get rewarded for only 50% of their hard work? Well, I agree, which is why your job is in jeopardy. . . .

Had the government suddenly mandated to me that I didn't need to pay taxes, guess what? Instead of depositing that $288,000 into the Washington black-hole, I would have spent it, hired more employees, and generated substantial economic growth. My employees would have enjoyed the wealth of that tax cut in the form of promotions and better salaries. But you can forget that now. . . .

If any new taxes are levied on me, or my company, my reaction will be swift and simple. I'll fire you and your coworkers. . . . Then, I will close this company down, move to another country, and retire. You see, I'm done. I'm done with a country that penalizes the productive and gives to the unproductive. My motivation to work and to provide jobs will be destroyed. . . .

So, if you lose your job, it won't be at the hands of the economy; it will be at the hands of a political hurricane that swept through this country. . . .

Well, there it is. I don't know if this memo was really sent by any boss to his employees during the 2009 bailout period, but the e-mail containing it had a large, bold print heading: "Wonderful letter: Hits the nail on the head." The memo represents a free-market conservative critique of high taxes on the wealthy. Low taxes and a correspondingly small government encourage free-market activity that increases job opportunities and generates social wealth for everyone. This belief is behind Speaker of the House John Boehner's claim that higher taxes to deal with the nation's debts will reduce prosperity by eliminating jobs. In spite of the debt, Boehner wants the government to "stop job-killing tax increases."[1]

$ $ $

You don't need to be a free-market conservative to recognize that free-market activity has benefited humanity tremendously.

The extraordinary productivity increases that began with the industrial revolution demonstrate the power of the free market, without recourse to big government programs, to generate social wealth that helps everyone, including the poor. Economic historian Natalie McPherson summarizes the improvement in human life attributable to industrialization:

In 1770, the average European farmed from sunrise to sunset six days a week. This individual ate mostly bread and owned one outfit of clothing. If this person was British he was slightly richer: He probably owned a pair of shoes. Travel to the next village was an occasion to remember for a lifetime. People went to bed when the sun went down because oil lamps were expensive and homemade candles and fat lamps were not bright enough to allow much activity at night. . . .

In industrialized countries today we work forty-hour weeks. Our modern closets are full of clothes and shoes. We jet to vacations in sunny spots far away. Our homes are full of electric lights, washing machines, refrigerators, soft beds, and chairs. We have personal computers, television sets, and automobiles. The change in the lifestyle of the average person in the United States in the past 250 years is greater than the change in lifestyle in the preceding 2,000 years.

This is true because the amount of economic output produced per worker has increased astronomically in Europe and the United States, providing us with a wealth of goods and services.[2]

Christopher DeMuth, president of the American Enterprise Institute, a free-market-oriented think tank, attributes the benefits of industrialization to incentives inherent in the free market. Attempting to maximize profit in a free market, entrepreneurs compete with one another for customers by creating new products and services, improving products and services, and lowering prices. They lower prices in part by reducing labor costs through the development and use of more efficient tools, machines, and methods. The result is that American free enterprise spreads the wealth without government programs or tax policies designed specifically for that purpose. At present, DeMuth maintains, owing to labor's increased productivity the economy produces enough food, shelter, clothing, and other necessities to meet everyone's material needs. "The problem of poverty, defined as material scarcity, has been solved."[3]

Second, DeMuth continues, improvements in human health have been dramatic as a result of an improved infrastructure of sanitation and clean water, the conquest of some dreaded diseases, and the availability in abundance of nutritious food. He cites the view of Nobel Prize–winning economist Robert Fogel who says that the average lifespan has just about doubled in the last three hundred years owing to our increasing control of the biological environment. The effects can be seen in just a generation in Seoul, South Korea, by comparing the physical appearance of younger and older Koreans.

"Third," DeMuth maintains, "the critical *source* of social wealth has shifted over the last few hundred years from land (at the end of the 18th century) to physical capital (at the end of the 19th) to, today, human capital—education and cognitive ability."[4] This change doesn't mean that complete equality among Americans is on the horizon because individuals differ significantly in intellectual potential and educational opportunities, the new source of wealth. However, the trend is in the direction of greater equality when you consider how unequally land ownership was distributed at the end of the eighteenth century and physical capital (factories, railroads, etc.) was distributed at the end of the nineteenth. In addition, most people are smart enough to occupy responsible, well-paid positions in our society, even if they're not potential Nobel Prize winners. So the shift to intellectual ability as the main source of wealth tends to have a leveling effect.

The widespread possession of helpful and entertaining material goods also illustrates the tendency toward greater equality. *New York Times* correspondent Jennifer Steinhauer points out that when the movie *Wall Street* came out in 1987, Michael Douglas's character, a Wall Street tycoon, possessed a cell phone as a sign of privilege and power. By 2004, half of all Americans had cell phones, largely because their cost had plummeted during the previous decade. Steinhauer continues: "The pattern is a familiar one in consumer electronics. What begins as a high-end product—a laptop computer, a DVD player—gradually goes mass market as prices fall and production rises, largely because of the cheap labor costs in developing countries that are making more and more of the goods."[5] During the same decade the price of clothing was steady and prices in general at department stores actually declined about 10 percent, also largely the result of lower-wage foreign workers making products for global trade.

Cruise vacations clearly illustrate the democratization of what was once a consumer item reserved for the rich. Up-market cruises now make up only about 10 percent of the business; 90 percent is for people of moderate income. The average price per week per person, about $1,500, has remained the same for fifteen years, according to Oivind Mathisen, editor of the newsletter *Cruise Industry News*. Yet the ships still contain up-market features such as spas, boutiques, and sophisticated restaurants, as well as new amenities, such as ice skating rinks and rock walls.[6]

Many other areas of leisure activity show the same trend toward the equalization of consumption patterns. DeMuth points out that

expenditures on recreation . . . have become strikingly more equal as people of lower income have increased the amount of time and money they devote to entertainment, reading, sports, and related enjoyments.

Television, videocassettes, CD's, and home computers have brought musical, theatrical, and other entertainments (both high and low) to everyone, and have enormously narrowed the differences in cultural opportunities between wealthy urban centers and everywhere else. Formerly upper-crust sports like golf, tennis, skiing, and boating have become mass pursuits . . . and health clubs and full-line book stores have become as plentiful as gas stations.[7]

Writing in 1997, DeMuth emphasizes the role played by the free market in the increased opportunities for middle-income people:

Anyone who has been a business traveler since the late 1970s, for example, has seen firsthand how deregulation has democratized air travel. Low fares and mass marketing have brought such luxuries as foreign travel, weekend getaways to remote locales, and reunions of far-flung families—just twenty years ago, pursuits of the wealthy—to people of relatively modest means.[8]

This democratization of air travel is the result of deregulation, which unleashed the forces of the free market. New air carriers were allowed to compete for customers with established airlines. The free market is equally responsible for the development of the cruise industry, for the falling prices of cell phones and other consumer electronics, and for the steady or falling prices, through global trade, of clothing and other items sold at department stores.

In sum, the free market is already providing all the progress anyone could expect, so a new progressive agenda is unnecessary.

$ $ $

Worse than unnecessary, free-market conservatives claim, raising taxes on the wealthy to fund a new progressive agenda—government programs designed to provide better education for the poor and middle class, develop public transportation, and so forth—are likely to reduce economic growth and thereby disrupt the general tendency toward greater prosperity and equality. Such programs, they think, absorb funds that entrepreneurs need in order to develop new products, improve old products, expand markets, and enlarge employment opportunities. In addition, as the letter from the Boss indicates, the high taxes needed to fund new government programs harm the economy by reducing incentives for entrepreneurs and other highly skilled individuals to work their hardest to deploy wealth-generating innovations.

Philosopher John Hospers articulates many of these free-market conservative views. He writes that the reason we are so wealthy today is that thousands of people took the risk of using the ideas of the great inventors to produce goods in new ways:

Between the invention of the steam engine, and the existence of railroads spanning a continent, there is an enormous gap. Between the invention of a process for the manufacture of steel, and the actual use of that process in factories around the world, there is a gap. The gap is filled by many hundreds or thousands of men who . . . can take the ideas of others and put them to commercial use through the facilities of mass-production. . . . [9]

But to start a factory and to install large and complex machines takes much planning and a great deal of capital. It may be years before the man who initiates these moves is out of debt, and still more years before he turns a penny of profit. . . . The entrepreneur who undertakes these jobs is the *risk-taker* of a society, laying all his capital on the line and borrowing more in the hopes that the enterprise will succeed. Moreover, once factories are built they cannot easily be moved; so before he will take such risks, of course, he wants to be quite sure that he will not be taxed to death once he breaks even. . . . [10]

If the risks are to be worth taking, the entrepreneur must live in a country that is politically stable; his property rights must be secure, so that he can start a major enterprise without fear of losing all he has through nationalization or excessive taxation. Only then can he go ahead with confidence. . . . Then he can mass-produce his products so that thousands or millions of them can come into existence where few or none existed before—lowering the prices through mass-production, so that great masses of people can afford to buy them. [11]

In sum, high taxes on rich people and corporations reduce the incentive for entrepreneurs, such as the Boss, to take the risks necessary for economic development that creates jobs and benefits society in general. Therefore, when the government raises taxes it actually impoverishes the poor, whose best chance for economic advancement is through the free-enterprise economic development that taxes impede.

$ $ $

Free-market conservatives claim evidence for their view from comparisons of taxes in the United States with those in other wealthy industrial countries. Prominent economist Paul Krugman pointed out in 2003 that total taxation in the United States—including federal, state, county, and municipal taxes—tends to be about 26 percent of gross domestic product (GDP)—the total value of output in the country. In Canada, by contrast, total taxes are about 38 percent of GDP; in France 46 percent, and in Sweden 52 percent.[12] Krugman thinks that Americans could pay much higher taxes, because people in other countries do.

But free-market conservatives look at these numbers differently. They think that the American economy is the most dynamic in the already-wealthy, industrialized world and attribute its vitality at least in part to its lower taxes. They point out that our per capita GDP is about 30 percent higher than in some of these other countries. Perhaps our lower taxes result in business investments that boost productivity, just as free-market conservatives would expect.

Krugman doesn't think so. He looks behind the GDP figures and finds no support for the free-market conservative view. He acknowledges that per capita GDP in France, for example, is about 30 percent lower than it is in the United States but attributes most of the difference to how many people are working and how many hours they work. Per capita, fewer French are in the workforce, and this accounts for most of the difference in per capita GDP. The employment rate of prime-age adults (ages twenty-five through fifty-four) in the two countries is about the same, but employment rates among younger and older people in France are lower than in the United States. In the fifteen- through twenty-four-year-old group, 25 percent of the French are employed compared to 54 percent of Americans. Correspondingly, the French stay in school longer. In the fifteen- through nineteen-year-old group, 92 percent of the French, but only 84 percent of Americans attend school. In the twenty- through twenty-four-year-old group, the figures are 45 percent for France and 35 percent for the United States. Krugman sees this as a greater problem for the United States than for France. France is developing the more educated work force.

Even when the lower workforce participation among the French is taken into account, Krugman writes, "French GDP per *worker* is . . . 10 percent lower than in the United States."[13] But that's only because the average French worker gets more time off. In general, Europeans work 350 hours less per year than Americans, which is the equivalent of nine weeks less work per year.[14] However, when they are at work, they are just about as productive as Americans. In fact, Krugman reports, "worker productivity per hour appears to be slightly higher in France than in the United States."[15] There's no support here for the view that high taxes discourage productivity-enhancing investments that enrich society. All we have here is the preference in Europe for more leisure and less total output.

What is more, there's no reason to believe that their lower per capita GDP deprives the European middle class of decent lives. Whereas many Americans go bankrupt each year because they have unpaid medical bills,[16] Europeans all have some form of universal health insurance that precludes this middle-class nightmare. Whereas many Americans go deeply into debt to afford housing in areas where there are good schools so that their children will have a leg up in pursuit of the American Dream,[17] high taxes in Europe allow for schools that do better at promoting social mobility. In fact, in Scandinavia, where taxes are generally highest, social mobility is higher than in the United States.[18] In sum, international comparisons supply no evidence that our lower taxes compared to western European countries improve our productivity or help the middle class.

Free-market conservatives sometimes claim that the history of tax policies at different times within our country shows that low taxes stimulate economic growth better than high taxes. They note, for example, that according to Congressional Budget Office estimates, the average federal tax rate of the top 1 percent of taxpayers fell between 1979 and 1983 from 37 to 27.7 percent, and they attribute the unusually large economic growth of 4.2 percent per year between 1982 and 1989 to this reduction of the tax burden.

Krugman replies convincingly, however, that this conservative argument mishandles the relevant statistics. Economic growth is always greater than usual when the economy is coming out of a recession. The reliable yardstick that economists use to measure economic growth is growth throughout the entire economic cycle, from one peak to the next. Measured this way, from the peak of 1979 to the peak of 1989, the American economy grew at 3 percent a year, just as it had done between the previous business cycle peaks in 1973 and 1979 when taxes were much higher. Contrary to what Hospers and other tax foes would expect, the data don't suggest that lower taxes on rich people stimulated the economy.[19]

In case that test wasn't enough, President Clinton subjected the economy to the opposite test. "He raised the marginal rate on high-income taxpayers," Krugman writes. "In 1989, the top 1 percent of families paid, on average, only 28.9 percent of their income in federal taxes; by 1995, that share was up to 36.1 percent." What happened?

Conservatives confidently awaited a disaster—but it failed to materialize. In fact, the economy grew at a reasonable pace through Clinton's first term, while the deficit and the unemployment rate went steadily down. And then the news got even better: unemployment fell to its lowest level in decades without causing inflation, while productivity growth accelerated to rates not seen since the 1960s. And the budget deficit turned into an impressive surplus.[20]

Krugman attributes some of these positive developments to "the maturing of information technology: business finally figured out how to make effective use of computers, and the resulting surge in productivity drove the economy forward."[21] But the fact that businesses invested massively in new technology when tax rates went up is exactly the opposite of what conservatives expected. And the investments were generally productive; computers are now integral to our lives.

Economic performance during America's postwar economic boom between 1947 and 1973 tells the same story. Former labor secretary Robert Reich tells us that during this period "real median family income doubled, as did the value of what the typical American worker produced."[22] Obviously, there was sufficient investment in capital formation and technological development to increase productivity. Yet the top tax rate during the Eisenhower years was 91 percent and during the Kennedy years it was 78 percent. Clearly, low taxes are not needed for the kind of productive investment that results in economic prosperity. So the association of low taxes with economic growth, which free-market conservatives rely on when they advocate the lowest possible tax rates, is not supported by our economy's actual performance.

In sum, none of the free-market conservative arguments for low taxes are well supported by economic data that compares some periods in American history with other periods or that compares the United States with other countries. Intuitively, of course, we believe that a 100 percent tax rate would discourage entrepreneurial activity and harm the economy. Nothing in the data or in this book disputes that assumption. The Boss is right; some after-tax income is needed for motivation. But there's nothing in the data to suggest that top tax rates of, say, 65 percent on earned income, investment income, and large estates would harm the country's economy. And such a rate, justified as we'll see on other grounds as well, is all that's needed to fund a new progressive agenda that reduces inequality and helps the poor and the middle class.

$ $ $

The argument that we've just considered—that high taxes on the wealthy will stifle innovation and impair productivity, jobs, and wealth—is not the only free-market conservative objection to raising taxes on rich people. A second objection to such tax increases needed to fund a new progressive agenda is that progressive taxation punishes successful people for their success. Even if this punishment doesn't discourage successful people from working hard, remaining productive, and helping the economy to grow, it still seems unfair. Ideally, the free market allows businesses to thrive only if they offer a product that customers willingly buy at a price that yields profits. Willing customers must think that the product adds value to their lives or they wouldn't buy it, and they must prefer this merchant over others or they would take their business elsewhere. No one is holding a gun to their heads. So, it's a win-win situation. The business makes a really big profit (a win for them) only by providing better products, services, or prices to customers than competitors are providing (a win for consumers). When businesses serve society in this way, it seems unfair to tax them extra (progressive taxation) for being successful.

The perception of unfairness in this situation isn't confined to free-market conservatives. It's a commonsense moral belief, widespread in our society, that benefactors should be rewarded, not punished. Politician and journalist Clare Boothe Luce was being ironic when she said, "No good deed goes unpunished."[23]

Everyone knows that good deeds should be rewarded, so the world is awry and unjust if they're punished instead.

Free-market conservatism is central here only because it makes the factual claim that wealthy entrepreneurs are, indeed, great benefactors of society. Given that belief, many people in our society would think that it's unfair to punish them with higher (progressive) taxes. A flat tax, which taxes everyone at the same rate, is fairer, they think.

But are wealthy entrepreneurs really benefactors? Is the free-market conservative belief correct? Starting in chapter 4 we'll look at many reasons to dispute it. First, however, we'll look at the world through the glasses of free-market advocates who believe that wealthy entrepreneurs enrich us all and consequently deserve all the rewards of their success. Therefore, progressive taxes on high incomes unjustly deprive rich people of some of the rewards that are legitimately theirs.

Consider the success of Sam Walton, founder of Walmart, now the largest retailer in the world. In October 1985 *Forbes* magazine named Walton "the richest man in America."[24] How did he get so rich? Although we'll find much to criticize about Walmart in later chapters, consider first Sam's account of his own success, an account that makes his work appear highly beneficial to society.

According to Sam, "the secret of successful retailing is to give your customers what they want. . . . You want a wide assortment of good quality merchandise; the lowest possible prices; guaranteed satisfaction with what you buy; friendly, knowledgeable service; convenient hours; free parking; a pleasant shopping experience."[25] Sam believes that he succeeded by pleasing customers, thereby improving society through private enterprise, not government programs.

As World War II ended Sam bought the franchise of a Ben Franklin variety store in Newport, Arkansas, a town of seven thousand people near the Mississippi River. Inexperienced in business, he didn't realize at first that the previous owner was eager to sell because he was losing money. The store grossed about $72,000 a year whereas the competition across the street was grossing more than double that amount.[26] Sam had to figure out how to turn this loser into a winner. He started by attending helpful seminars run by the Ben Franklin franchise program and initially ran the store according to their guidelines, which included buying at least 80 percent of the store's merchandise from the parent company Butler Brothers.

Sam quickly learned, however, that he could increase sales and serve customers better if he went outside the guidelines and searched for wholesale bargains on his own. He tried to get suppliers to sell items, such as ribbons and bows, directly to him instead of selling them to Butler Brothers who jacked up the price 25 percent before reselling. In short, Sam wanted to eliminate the middle man to get a lower price for his customers. However, most suppliers refused because they depended on their relationship with Butler Brothers. So, Sam started making trips in the evening across the Mississippi River to Tennessee, hauling a homemade trailer which he would stuff with whatever bargains he could get from wholesalers, often ladies undergarments and men's shirts. He could price these items low and still make a profit. Sales were brisk.[27]

Sam then started to work with Harry Weiner of Weiner Buying Services in New York City. Weiner would find out what items manufacturers were selling at bargain prices so he could direct store owners like Sam to those manufacturers when they placed an order. Weiner took 5 percent for this service, which was better than the 25 percent that Ben Franklin took. Sam tells a story about one of these deals that set the stage for Walmart's eventual success:

If you're interested in "how Wal-Mart did it," this is one story you've got to sit up and pay close attention to. Harry was selling ladies' panties—two-barred, tricot satin panties with an elastic waist—for $2.00 a dozen. We'd been buying similar panties from Ben Franklin for $2.50 a dozen and selling them at three pair for $1.00. Well, at Harry's price of $2.00, we could put them out at four for $1.00 and make a great promotion for our store.

Here's the simple lesson we learned—which others were learning at the same time . . . : say I bought an item for 80 cents. I found that by pricing it at $1.00 I could sell three times more of it than by pricing it at $1.20. I might make only half the profit per item, but because I was selling three times as many, the overall profit was much greater. . . . In retailer language, you can lower your markup but earn more because of the increased volume.[28]

It's a win-win situation for the store and its customers. The store increases its profit and customers get the same items at lower prices. Sam's business volume increased from $72,000 the year before he bought the store to $105,000 in his first year as owner and then to $140,000 a year and $175,000 a year in the next two years.[29]

After selling his store in Newport for a good profit, Sam bought a store in Bentonville, Arkansas, another small town, where he lived the rest of his life. He had an eye for new items that customers at his new Walton's Five and Dime would like. For example, he went to New York City and bought a whole bunch of what were then called *zori sandals,* which we know as *flip-flops.* One of his clerks thought these sandals would give people blisters on their toes, but Sam priced them at 19 cents a pair and sold pile after pile of them until everyone in town, it seemed, had a pair.[30] Again, this kind of retail innovation results in a win-win situation. The store makes a good profit and customers get what they want at a low price.

By 1960 Sam could see that large discount stores were the wave of the future, so he started a chain of such stores alongside his chain of five and dimes. The volume of business at the discount stores, the Walmart chain that started in 1962, soon overshadowed the five-and-dime business. The new stores, like the old ones, were in small towns because the already established, large retailers were putting their discount stores in large metropolitan areas.[31]

Relationships with suppliers remained key to Sam's success. The established stores were supplied by vendors who took a 15 percent commission, which required that the store add 15 percent to the price it charged customers. Sam, by contrast, established his own supply network, often buying directly from manufacturers to cut out the middleman and give his customers the lowest possible prices. Relationships with suppliers were sometimes contentious because Sam wanted the lowest price so he could pass along the savings to his customers. Claude Harris, a major buyer for Walmart who also trained other buyers, explains: "I always told the buyers: 'You're not negotiating for Wal-Mart, you're negotiating for your customer. And your customer deserves the best price you can get. Don't ever feel sorry for a vendor. He knows what he can sell for, and we want his bottom price.'"[32]

Walmart wouldn't pay for the cost of kickbacks or for the supplier's transportation or promotional program. Walmart would use its own trucks to pick up merchandise and its own marketing to sell it. If a supplier said that the lowest price was $1.00, Claude Harris would say that he'll see if he can get it for 90 cents from a competitor. Harris concludes, "If you buy that thing for $1.25, you've just bought somebody else's inefficiency."[33]

Eventually, Walmart developed good relationships with its major suppliers, such as Proctor & Gamble. In order to get the highest quality at the lowest price, Walmart would sit down with suppliers to plan together. "By doing that," Sam writes,

we give the manufacturer the advantage of knowing what our needs are going to be a year out . . . , or even two years out. Then, as long as they are honest with us and try to lower their costs as much as they can and keep turning out a product that the customers want, we can stay with them. We both win, and most important, the customer wins too. The added efficiency of the whole process enables the manufacturer to reduce its costs, which allows us to lower our prices.[34]

Now we have a win-win-win situation. The manufacturer, retailer, and customer all win.

The company's employees win as well, according to Sam. He admits that he was initially stingy with employees and regrets that the *associates*, the Walmart term for *employees*, weren't included along with managers in the profit-sharing program that began in 1970 when the company went public. A profit-sharing plan was started for associates later. Sam writes,

The more you share with your associates—whether it's in salaries or incentives or bonuses or stock discounts—the more profit will accrue to the company. Why? Because the way management treats the associates is exactly how the associates will then treat the customers. And if the associates treat the customers well, the customers will return again and again, and *that* is where the real profit in this business lies. . . . Satisfied, loyal, repeat customers are at the heart of Wal-Mart's spectacular profit margins. [35]

It's a win-win-win-win situation, with corporation, customers, suppliers, and employees all winning. BUT WAIT! THERE'S MORE! GET ONE MORE WIN AT NO EXTRA COST! When the corporation does well, its shareholders also win. Walmart went public in 1970 to finance expansion. Largely as a result of expansion, its profits went from $1.2 million in 1970 to $41 million in 1980.[36] Its shareholders benefited greatly. The stock sold initially at $16.50 a share. Someone who bought one hundred shares at that time for $1,650 and held on to the stock would by 1992 have Walmart shares worth about $3 million.[37]

Now this is how the free market is supposed to work. Walmart has grown enormously since Sam's death in 1992 and today, according to an estimate by former labor secretary Robert Reich, saves American consumers between $100 and $200 billion dollars a year.[38] This benefit is not only enormous but widely distributed among Americans, especially those of modest means who are the mainstay of Walmart's customer base.

Looking at business success in this light, many free-market conservatives object to progressive taxation because it punishes people who are among society's greatest benefactors. Why should Walmart or its shareholders or its executives pay a larger percentage of their income in taxes than other people pay when the money is earned in the process of benefiting society, including its poorer members?

$ $ $

Perhaps the fairest system would be to fund the federal government by charging each individual the same amount of tax each year. Unfortunately, this is impractical. If we confined the tax-paying group to individuals over the age of eighteen and healthy enough to work, many people wouldn't earn as much money as their tax bill if everyone's tax bill were the same. Using round figures that are realistic enough to make the point, if the government spends $3 trillion in a year and this had to be paid in equal portions by the country's approximately two hundred million adults able to work, the tax bill would be $15,000 per person ($30,000 for a couple, $45,000 after the oldest child turns eighteen, and so forth). Many individuals don't make as much as the government would be asking them to pay in taxes, including those working full time near or at the minimum wage. Such people would literally have nothing to live on. And how many eighteen-year-olds would be able to afford a college education if they had to pay $15,000 in federal taxes every year in addition to their tuition, fees, and living expenses?[39]

I don't know of anyone who objects to this reasoning; it rules out every *person* paying the same *amount* in taxes. But perhaps every person could pay the same *percentage* of *income* in taxes. This resembles the flat tax idea that Steve Forbes proposed during his 1996 run for the Republican nomination for the presidency of the United States. Using 1996 dollars, his plan allowed a couple filing jointly to subtract from their gross income $26,200, plus an additional $5,800 per dependent. This amount of income wouldn't be taxed by the federal government at all, thereby avoiding the possibility that a tax bill will leave people destitute—unable to afford food, housing, clothing, and so forth. All earned income above this subsistence amount would be taxed at 17 percent. Other proposals say the tax should be 19 percent. In Forbes's plan, there would be no taxes on investment income (interest, dividends, and capital gains), on payments people make to the Social Security system, or on inheritance. There would be no itemized deductions.[40]

Allan Sloan, reviewing the proposal in *Newsweek*, claimed that Forbes's proposal didn't raise enough revenue. Perhaps we can correct for that, because our interest is in the fairness of the concept of a flat tax, by applying the flat tax to investment and inheritance income as well as to earned income. This would not only raise a lot of revenue but also make the overall tax burden flatter. The sense that fairness requires everyone to pay the same percentage of income in federal taxes would be satisfied better when all income is subject to the same flat tax.

In the opinion of flat tax proponents, the observation that David Cay Johnston made in the *New York Times*, intended as a rebuke, is no rebuke at all:

Under the Bush tax cuts [enacted in 2001 and 2003], the four hundred taxpayers with the highest incomes—a minimum of $87 million in 2000, the last year for which the government will release such data [at the time of Johnston's writing]—now pay income, Medicare, and

Social Security taxes amounting to virtually the same percentage as people making $50,000 to $75,000.[41]

Flat tax proponents think that this is fine. They think it's only fair that people of different income groups pay relatively equal percentages of their income in federal taxes (when all forms of federal taxation are included), so they applaud this effect of the Bush tax cuts. Why should successful people who provide great benefit to society, people like Sam Walton, be punished for their success with higher tax rates?

One answer is that riches are often gained by harming others. We shall see in the next three chapters that many people become rich through underhanded means and government handouts while harming the public. Raising awareness that wealth often results from harming others fosters taking back the center for progressive taxation because it shows that to a large extent rich people don't really deserve all their income. So, it's no injustice to raise their taxes and use some of their income to fund a new progressive agenda.

4
How Some People Make Millions in America

We saw in the last chapter that a major free-market conservative objection to progressive taxation that could provide funds for a new progressive agenda is the claim that such taxation is unfair. It's unfair, they say, because people become wealthy only by helping others, and benefactors shouldn't be punished with unusually high taxes.

This chapter disposes of this free-market conservative objection to progressive taxation by showing that people do not make their fortunes in the United States only by helping others. Some people do make their fortunes this way but others do more harm than good to the public in the process of becoming wealthy. Although most free-market conservatives join the general condemnation of dishonest and harmful business practices, they seldom acknowledge what this chapter demonstrates through stories backed up by statistics: unscrupulous business practices pervade so many key industries as to undercut the claim that progressive taxation is unfair because riches are evidence of benefit to society.

Consider the enviable wealth of Bruce C. Rohde, CEO of ConAgra from 1997 to 2005. The corporation started as a food processor in 1919. Under the guidance of former CEO Charles M. Harper, the company went on a buying spree beginning in the 1970s that gave it an interest in food from "dirt to dinner." Eventually, it owned more than 280 businesses, including such brands as Chef Boyardee canned foods, Hunt's ketchup, and Healthy Choice dinners. Investor returns from 1980 to 1993 were an impressive 22 percent a year, amounting to over 1,000 percent over the entire period. Mr. Harper was paid well for his performance, which always hit targets set by the board. His inflation-adjusted pay was $1.3 million in 1976 and rose to about $6 million a year by the early 1990s.[1]

By the mid-1990s, however, ConAgra's market share and sales stopped growing. According to Eric Dash of the *New York Times*, ConAgra's decentralized organization, which allowed great autonomy for its ninety subsidiaries, made it hard for ConAgra to compete for the business of supplying the large supermarket buyers such as Walmart. So in 1996 the company decided to reorganize.[2]

Bruce Rohde had already been an outside legal consultant for ConAgra, working with Mr. Harper on more than two hundred transactions. In 1996 he was brought into the company to help with reorganization. The following year he became CEO. In spite of its recent failure to grow, the company's stock was still near its all-time high, "and Mr. Rohde was paid handsomely. His first year's total compensation was $7.9 million, including an initial $4.3 million restricted stock grant, vested over 10 years, and a $500,000 long-term performance payout."[3] His mandate was clear: he was supposed to centralize operations and integrate ConAgra's many different businesses.

However, the company didn't flourish under Mr. Rohde's leadership. "From mid-1999 to mid-2001 . . . the company incurred $1.1 billion in restructuring charges. It terminated more than 8,450 employees and closed 31 plants."[4] Independent analysts thought that ConAgra wasn't investing enough in its brands for their profits to remain high.

But these setbacks didn't deter ConAgra's board of directors from continuing their generosity toward Mr. Rohde. Although they withheld his bonus and long-term equity awards in early 2001, citing weak results from his efforts, he still received in salary and stock options pay of more than $8.7 million during two years of difficulty. But in July 2001, independent compensation consultant Frederic W. Cook convinced the board that Mr. Rohde's compensation wasn't competitive. So the board awarded their CEO an additional 300,000 stock options. Mr. Cook defended his recommendation, saying, "There's nothing wrong conceptually with giving someone options after a bad year" because "an option is an incentive for the future. It is not a reward for the past." Still, Cook recognized that people would say "they rewarded him for failure" and admitted that "financially it's hard to argue with that."[5] But apparently that wasn't enough board penance for their initial failure to award Mr. Rohde a bonus early in 2001. In September of that year they granted him another 750,000 stock options, claiming that his total compensation through options had been "below competitive levels for a number of years."

If this was the board's reaction to two bad years, it's no surprise that Rohde did very well indeed during two years that seemed to be better, 2003 and 2004. For appearing to meet earnings targets, the board granted Rohde $16.4 million in bonus money during those two years as well as the part of his long-term incentive plan that he had already earned. It turned out, however, that as a result of accounting errors, earnings for those two years had been overstated by about $200 million, which was somewhere between 10 and 15 percent of total earning over the period. John M. McMillin, who was then an analyst at Prudential Equity Group, asked if the restatement of earnings for those years would be followed by a restatement of bonuses. A spokesman for ConAgra said that the restatement of earnings didn't affect the way Rohde's bonuses had been calculated. Rohde could keep all of his bonuses.

Correspondent Dash summarizes the situation this way: under Mr. Rohde's leadership,

ConAgra routinely missed earnings targets and underperformed its peers. Its share price fell 28 percent. The company cut more than 9,000 jobs. Accounting problems surfaced in every one of Mr. Rohde's eight years. . . . [Yet] Mr. Rohde's salary alone rose at 8 percent a year, and he collected more than $22 million in cash compensation. . . .

Even when ConAgra restated its financial results, which lowered earnings in 2003 and 2004, Mr. Rohde's $16.4 million in bonuses for those two years stayed the same.[6]

In 2005 ConAgra again declined to award Rohde a bonus and the fifty-seven-year-old resigned as CEO in September after being paid over $45 million during his eight years at the helm. The happy end to this sad story is that ConAgra was generous with Rohde's severance package. Dash reports,

Since stepping down in September, [Rohde] started collecting $2.4 million in severance pay, twice his most recent salary, as well as full health benefits, which he will have through 2009. ConAgra shareholders are footing the bill for a secretary and an office near his home. And that $984,000 annual pension? It reflects 20 years of service, even though he was a ConAgra executive for not quite nine.[7]

Cases like this, and there are many more like it, challenge the claim made by John Hospers and other free-market enthusiasts that progressive taxation is unfair to rich people because they have earned their riches by meeting the needs and wants of others.

Here's another example. Ivan G. Seidenberg, CEO of Verizon, was given $19.4 million in total compensation at the end of 2005, a 48 percent increase over the previous year even though Verizon's stock price fell 26 percent, its credit rating was reduced, its profits went down 5.5 percent, and fifty thousand of its managers had their pensions frozen.[8] A study in

2005 found eleven companies whose chief executives were each given more than $15 million over a two-year period in spite of the fact that shareholder returns had been negative for the previous five years. The companies include AT&T, Bellsouth, Hewlett-Packard, Home Depot, Lucent Technologies, Merck, Pfizer, Safeway, Time Warner, and Walmart.[9]

The more general picture can be gleaned from the statistics that we saw in chapter 2, which showed that the ratio of CEO pay to that of ordinary workers has increased dramatically over the decades. From 25 to 1 in the 1960s it increased to 93 to 1 by 1990 and 413 to 1 by 1999.[10] How could this reflect value as measured by productivity, as free-market proponents think it should? How could CEO productivity in general go up 1700 percent relative to worker productivity? Of course, it can't. To understand the spectacular rise in CEO compensation that is unjustified by market fundamentals we have to look at corporate boards of directors, compensation committees, compensation consultants, and peer-group comparisons. We find conflicts of interest and old boy connections that most free-market advocates condemn.

CEO compensation is voted by the corporation's board of directors. They are supposed to be looking out for the welfare of the company's shareholders, so they should base compensation on productivity. But many boards don't do a very good job. One reason may be that many board members are or were CEOs who empathize with a CEO's desire for greater compensation. In addition, current CEOs can benefit indirectly when any CEO's pay increases because the increase establishes a general climate in which an increase in their own pay becomes more likely.

Another factor making board members friendly to high CEO compensation is that board membership has its compensations in money (although not a great deal of money relative to the total income of most board members of major corporations), contacts, and prestige. Some board members may be flattered by being asked to serve and most probably want to avoid the embarrassment of being asked to resign. So how does one attain and retain a position on a board of directors? Pleasing shareholders is not central because shareholders seldom play a large role in the selection of the board. Board members are most often nominated by the CEO or other board members, and shareholders usually ratify those selections. So the way to become and remain a board member is to be the kind of person who fits in with other board members and keeps the CEO happy with his or her total compensation package. These factors explain why no members were voted off the boards at Citigroup or Bank of America at their annual shareholders' meetings in 2009 even though both companies were implicated in and hurt by the financial crisis of 2008–2009. The shareholders weren't happy but the process of board-member retention doesn't give them effective control.[11]

Boards of directors don't just decide by the seat-of-the-pants what the CEO is worth. They receive recommendations from a compensation committee, which is a subgroup of the board that does extra work and receives extra pay for making recommendations concerning compensation for top management. The composition of Verizon's compensation committee may help to explain why, even though shareholder value had declined 26 percent during the previous five years, its CEO Ivan Seidenberg nevertheless received a 48 percent pay raise. First, all four members of the compensation committee were CEOs or former CEOs, making them sympathetic to Seidenberg's financial desires. Perhaps more important, three of the four members of the committee, who each received about $200,000 a year for their services to Verizon, were members with Seidenberg on other boards of directors. Finally, Seidenberg sat on the compensation committee of one of them, John L. Stafford, when he was CEO at Wyeth. (I just love the Spanish word for this cronyism, *amiguismo*; it just oozes chummy bonding.)

The compensation committee wouldn't be doing its job if it didn't employ a professional consultant or advisor whose fees can be as much as $950 an hour. (Don't look for a decimal.) Here we come to plain old-fashioned conflict of interest. In Verizon's case, Hewitt and Associates provided the compensation advice. Although described as an "outside consultant," Hewitt has other lucrative business dealings with Verizon, writes Gretchen Morgenson in the *New York Times*:

Verizon is one of Hewitt's biggest customers in the far more profitable businesses of running the company's employee benefit plans, providing actuarial services to its pension plans and advising it on human resources management. According to a former executive of the firm who declined to be identified out of concern about affecting his business, Hewitt has received more than half a billion dollars in revenue from Verizon and its predecessor companies since 1997.

In other words, the very firm that helps Verizon's directors decide what to pay its executives has a long and lucrative relationship with the company, maintained at the behest of the executives whose pay it recommends.[12]

This cozy relationship with Verizon management is par for the course at Hewitt. Other companies that use Hewitt's compensation-consultation service also use the firm for actuarial, investment, administrative, or other services. They include Boeing, Maytag, Genuine Parts, Procter & Gamble, Toro, Morgan Stanley, and Nortel Networks.[13] A spokeswoman for Hewitt, Suzanne Zagata-Meraz, sees no problem in this, saying, "Hewitt Associates has strict policies in place to ensure the independence and objectivity of all our consultants, including executive compensation consultants."[14]

One sign that a consultant is biased toward high rewards for management is the selection of criteria for success. In Mr.

Seidenberg's case, for example, the Hewitt consultant decided that Seidenberg deserved a raise if Verizon performed better than 20 percent of companies in a sample of comparable firms. So three-quarters of comparable companies could do better than Verizon and Seidenberg's work would be considered successful enough for a raise. Brian Foley, a compensation consultant with no ties to Verizon said, "That hurdle is so low it's almost embedded in the ground."[15]

The consultant not only helps determine the criteria of success in relation to a peer group of companies but also helps to pick which firms are included in the peer group in the first place. An example of faulty peer-group comparison surfaced with questions concerning the total compensation, about $140 million, received by Richard A. Grasso when he was chairman of the New York Stock Exchange. The peer group was dominated by highly profitable investment banks and financial institutions that were much larger than the exchange. The median annual revenue of companies in this group was $26 billion, which was more than twenty-five times the annual revenue of the exchange. Their median assets were 125 times more than that of the exchange, and the median number of employees in the peer group was fifty thousand, about thirty times as many as at the exchange. One way to justify a hefty salary increase for top management is to compare their current salaries with managers heading much larger or more complex organizations.[16]

Another example of the questionable use of peer-group comparisons occurred in 2005 when the compensation committee for drug maker Eli Lilly compared its CEO's pay to the CEO pay at Johnson & Johnson (J & J). Here are some comparisons of the two companies. Eli Lilly made two acquisitions between 2002 and 2006; J & J made twenty-five. Eli Lilly operated in twenty-eight countries; J & J operated in fifty-seven. Eli Lilly spent $3 billion on research and development; J & J spent twice that amount. And Eli Lilly's revenue in 2005 was $15 billion, whereas J & J's was $51 billion.[17] It's no surprise that if these differences are ignored, senior management at Ely Lilly seems undercompensated and deserving of hefty increases.

Peer-group comparisons operate to increase executive pay also by enlisting the board of director's competitive instincts. Boards don't like to think that their CEO is below average in compensation; they tend to want their CEO to be paid more than most others in their peer group. But unlike in Lake Wobegon, everyone can't be above average and the attempt to make them so tends to inflate compensation packages.[18]

No doubt the compensation of many CEOs is justified by their performance but the blanket statement that this is generally the case seems unfounded when you consider the enormous inflation of executive compensation compared to total economic growth and compared to the pay of most other employees. In 2006, then treasury secretary John Snow told the *Wall Street Journal* that he trusted the marketplace to reward executives appropriately. "In an aggregate sense, [executive compensation] reflects the marginal productivity of C.E.O.s."[19] Snow seems out of touch.

Nobel Prize–winning economist Paul Krugman points out that international comparisons show American CEO compensation to be outside world norms. He notes that energy company British Petroleum, for example, is twice the size of its competitor Chevron, yet the CEO of the American company Chevron receives twice the compensation of his counterpart heading a British firm.[20] Another Nobel Prize–winning economist, Joseph Stiglitz, makes the same point in starker terms by comparing CEO pay to worker pay in different countries. In Japan, he notes, executive pay is about ten times that of average workers' pay and in Great Britain about twenty-five times that of average workers' pay, whereas in the United States by 2000 it was five hundred times as much. Stiglitz goes on to write that

during the nineties overall pay of American CEOs began to bear no relationship to the usual economic forces. In the nineties, compensation soared to unheard-of levels, defying all laws of economics. Competitive markets dictate that compensation is determined by demand and supply. If compensation were really determined by competitive forces, compensation would only have increased if there was a large shift in demand or supply. But the number of CEOs on the market didn't suddenly shrink and the productivity or performance of America's CEOs did not rise so much that they suddenly deserved 1,000 percent raises. During the nineties, American executive compensation rose by 442 percent in eight years. . . . [This] was completely out of line relative to the salaries of middle management, relative to the salaries of workers, relative to anything imaginable.[21]

Warren Buffett decries the fact that executive pay often defies any market logic because he recognizes that unreasonably high CEO compensation diminishes shareholder returns, as shareholders ultimately pay the bill. In his 2006 annual message to the shareholders of his investment company, Berkshire Hathaway, he wrote, "Too often, executive compensation in the U.S. is ridiculously out of line with performance. The upshot is that a mediocre-or-worse C.E.O.—aided by his handpicked V.P. of human relations and a consultant from the ever-accommodating firm of Ratchet, Ratchet & Bingo—all too often receives gobs of money from an ill-designed compensation arrangement."[22]

Although CEO compensation took some hit during The Great Recession of 2008–2009, the high flyers were flying higher than ever by 2010.[23] Heading the list was Viacom's Philippe P. Dauman, who received $84.5 million in 2010 after a 149 percent increase in compensation.[24] The median increase in CEO pay between 2009 and 2010 was 23 percent[25] even though total inflation during the year was only 1.6 percent.[26] Even companies that were bailed out by the federal government, such as Capital One and Goldman Sachs, gave their CEOs hefty raises.[27] The Dodd-Frank Wall Street Reform and Consumer Protection Act of 2010 contains a "say in pay" provision that helps shareholders express their views about executive compensation. But award committees are not bound by shareholder views, so any effect on CEO pay is uncertain.[28]

$ $ $

Executive compensation isn't the only area where results in the American market as it actually exists diverge from the results in an ideal market where rewards reflect service to others. High corporate profits are often earned by harming rather than helping consumers and the general public.

It's now well known, for example, that tobacco companies tried to fool the public for more than a generation after scientists had proved that smoking cigarettes is harmful to people's health. The industry established and funded the Council for Tobacco Research and the Tobacco Industry Research Committee, ostensibly scientific groups dedicated to investigating the effects of tobacco on human health. In reality, tobacco company lawyers and public relations staffs were in charge of releasing their research findings, and they tended to suppress, ignore, or distort any findings that indicated the health hazards of smoking. The council tried to create a climate of uncertainty that would give smokers an excuse to continue smoking in spite of a scientific consensus and government warning of smoking's harmful effects. Some council scientists claimed that a causal link between smoking and disease is unproved until biological pathways or mechanisms of the link could be found, prompting one of the council's critics, Dr. Peter Wilenski, to quip, "If the tobacco lobby were marketing sex, they would say that its connection with pregnancy was a random statistical correlation."[29]

Profits from this relatively successful deception were in the many, many billions, whereas some of the losses to consumers were priceless. By the 1980s some four hundred thousand Americans were dying each year from tobacco-related illnesses.[30] The tobacco companies continued to resist regulation of their deadly product even after its harmful effects were finally acknowledged in the 1990s. It was only in 2009 that tobacco, one of the most deadly substances consumed in the United States, finally came under the regulatory control of the Food and Drug Administration.

The tobacco industry is not alone in trying to hoodwink the public on vital matters of human welfare. For many years the auto, steel, petroleum, and coal industries combined efforts to fool people into thinking that the influence of greenhouse gases on global climate was merely an unsubstantiated theory, not a well-established scientific fact. Andrew Revkin writes in the *New York Times*, "For more than a decade the Global Climate Coalition, a group representing industries with profits tied to fossil fuels, led an aggressive lobbying and public relations campaign against the idea that emissions of heat-trapping gases could lead to global warming." Its budget in 1997 alone was $1.68 million.[31] Exxon Mobil also funded other groups with the same mission, including the Heartland Institute, to which it gave more than $600,000 between 1998 and 2002.[32] These organizations, like the Council for Tobacco Research, were intended to sow just enough doubt in the public mind to forestall serious efforts to address a serious problem, efforts that would have reduced industry profits. These campaigns of disinformation helped delay for more than a decade serious actions to curb greenhouse gas emissions.

Documents released in 2009 reveal that even the scientists employed by the Global Climate Coalition rejected the major arguments used by global warming skeptics, including the claim that flawed records of temperature were giving the false appearance of climate change. Leonard S. Bernstein, a chemical engineer and climate expert at Mobil Corporation, led the coalition's advisory committee when it produced a primer on climate change in 1995 that concluded, "The contrarian theories . . . do not offer convincing arguments against the conventional model of greenhouse gas emission-induced climate change."[33] The coalition's operating committee approved this primer in early 1996, but only after omitting the criticisms of contrarian arguments. William O'Keefe, who was then a leader of the Global Climate Coalition, says that he had no idea that a section questioning the arguments of climate skeptics had been written and then dropped from the primer before it reached his desk. He didn't say, "I am shocked, shocked!" but he did say, "One thing I'm absolutely certain of is that no member of the board of the Global Climate Coalition said, 'We have to suppress this.'"[34] (It's amazing how consistently the people paid big bucks to lead organizations—without their unique leadership skills the organization would flounder—turn out to have known nothing about its activities—"I wasn't there; no one told me; I was out of the loop; it's news to me"—as soon as the organization is caught in any kind of malfeasance.) The coalition dissolved in 2002 when some of its chief sponsors decided it's better to (at least appear to) fight global warming than to fight the scientific consensus on the subject.

The food industry has engaged in the same kind of obfuscation as the tobacco and energy industries. They have raised pseudo-scientific objections to legitimate scientific studies, counting on the general public to be incapable of telling the difference. According to former labor secretary Robert Reich,

The food industry has financed a squad of experts to debunk research showing that childhood obesity leads to health problems in adulthood and that sugar and fatty foods have a direct relationship to weight gain. It is not necessary that the research they sponsor prove otherwise; only that it raise enough questions that a legislator or regulator who wishes to side with the food industry can credibly claim to be unconvinced by the preponderance of research on the other side.[35]

The result is that food-industry profits increase as children's health declines.

These cases illustrate that not just single companies every once in a while, but whole industries over decades—large and important industries such as the steel, automotive, petroleum, coal, food, and tobacco industries—can maximize profits by harming the public through what amounts to fraud. These industries are rich enough to mount successful disinformation campaigns that forestall actions needed to promote the public good. The association between profits and serving the public, which exists in idealized markets, is often absent from real-life corporate activity.

The pharmaceutical industry, to a large extent aided by the medical community, also maximizes profit at public expense. Dr. Marcia Angell, Harvard professor and former editor of the *New England Journal of Medicine,* writes,

In 2001, the American drug companies in the Fortune 500 list . . . ranked far above all other American industries in average net return, whether as a percentage of sales (18.5 percent) of assets (16.3 percent), or of shareholders' equity (33.2 percent). These are astonishing margins. For comparison, the median net return for all other industries in the Fortune 500 was only 3.3 percent of sales. Commercial banking . . . was a distant second at 13.5 percent of sales.

In 2002, as the economic downturn continued, big pharma showed only a slight drop in profits—from 18.5 to 17.0 percent of sales. The most startling fact about 2002 is that the combined profits for the ten drug companies in the Fortune 500 ($35 billion) were more than the profits for all other 490 businesses put together ($33.7 billion). In 2003 profits of the Fortune 500 drug companies dropped to 14.3 percent of sales, still well above the median for all industries of 4.6 percent for that year.[36]

If profits reflect benefit to customers, the pharmaceutical companies must be extraordinarily beneficial indeed. Like "The Old Dope Peddler" in the satirical song by Tom Lehrer, they must be doing well by doing good. However, this is not what Dr. Angell found.

Conflicts of interest abound between drug companies, on the one hand, and physicians and institutions doing drug-related research, on the other. Dr. Charles B. Nemeroff of Emory University, for example, headed a five-year study funded by the National Institutes of Health (NIH) of some drugs made by GlaxoSmithKline. The doctor failed to disclose to the university that he had, contrary to university policy, received more than $10,000 a year from the company whose drugs he was investigating. In fact, he had received about $500,000 from the company for giving talks promoting the drugs. When in 2004 the university became aware of this conflict of interest and confronted Dr. Nemeroff about it, he assured them it wouldn't happen again and duly reported for that year receiving only $9,999 from GlaxoSmithKline. In reality, he had received another $171,031 from the company. Emory University may not have zealously monitored Dr. Nemeroff because the NIH grant of $3.95 million for Nemeroff's research included $1.35 million that the university received for overhead.[37]

This kind of conflict of interest is the norm, not the exception in relationships among researchers, research institutions, and pharmaceutical companies, according to Dr. Angell. One result is that negative results in drug studies are not reported. Just as the Global Climate Coalition failed to report its scientists' acceptance of key claims about global warming, negative test results related to new drugs are not reported or are underreported. Angell writes:

In view of . . . the conflicts of interest that permeate the enterprise, it is not surprising that industry-sponsored trials published in medical journals consistently favor sponsors' drugs—largely because negative results are not published, positive results are repeatedly published in slightly different forms, and a positive spin is put on even negative results. A review of seventy-four clinical trials of an antidepressant, for example, found that thirty-seven of thirty-eight positive studies were published. But of the thirty-six negative studies, thirty-three were either not published or published in a form that conveyed a positive outcome. It is not unusual for a published paper to shift the focus from the drug's intended effect to a secondary effect that seems more favorable.[38]

This is how GlaxoSmithKline's antidepressant, Paxil, was approved without any warning that it may be ineffective as well as harmful to children and adolescents.

New drugs typically receive Food and Drug Administration (FDA) approval if their sponsors can show one or a few positive clinical trials, regardless of whether other trials show the drug to be ineffective. In addition, new drugs are typically tested for safety and effectiveness against a placebo, a similar-looking pill with no known pharmaceutical properties. A review of studies done between 1987 and 1999 that formed the basis for FDA approval of the six most popular antidepressants—Prozac, Paxil, Zoloft, Celexa, Serzone, and Effexor—found that placebos were as effective as the drugs in 80 percent of cases, and that the association of the drugs with benefit was so weak as to undercut the claim that any of the drugs would be clinically helpful. But because only the positive results were published, clinicians had no knowledge of this and prescribed these drugs widely, to the enormous profit of the drug companies and their mostly wealthy shareholders.

GlaxoSmithKline was sued for its misrepresentation of Paxil and agreed in 2004 to pay $2.5 million for consumer fraud, but that was a small price to pay when it was grossing about $2.7 billion a year from the drug. An internal GlaxoSmithKline document uncovered during the law suit revealed a systematic attempt to suppress unfavorable research results. The document included this statement: "It would be commercially unacceptable to include a statement that efficacy had not been demonstrated, as this would undermine the profile of paroxetine [Paxil]."[39]

Conflict of interest also affects clinical guidelines concerning matters such as the safe level of "bad" cholesterol. The National Cholesterol Education Program released new guidelines that lowered the amount of such cholesterol that was considered safe. But in 2004 it was revealed that eight of the nine members of the panel who issued this recommendation were in the pay of pharmaceutical companies that make cholesterol-lowering drugs.

Pharmaceutical companies also engage in "disease mongering," as when they "promote diseases to fit their drugs." They invent serious sounding clinical names for common problems, thus turning heartburn into "gastro-esophageal reflux disease" and shyness into "social anxiety disorder."[40] This convinces normal, healthy people that they need medications. Angell writes:

It seems that the strategy of the drug marketers—and it has been remarkably successful—is to convince Americans that there are only two kinds of people: those with medical conditions that require drug treatment and those who don't know it yet. While the strategy originated in the industry, it could not be implemented without the complicity of the medical profession.[41]

When the industry has a drug for a disorder and advertises the disorder's prevalence, it's amazing how many more cases of the disorder doctors find. For example, there was a forty-fold increase—that's an increase of nearly 4000 percent—in the diagnosis of bipolar disease in children between 1994 and 2003, leading to the treatment of thousands of children with multiple drugs that the FDA had not originally approved for this purpose. Angell concludes: "It is simply no longer possible to believe much of the clinical research that is published, or to rely on the judgment of trusted physicians or authoritative medical guidelines. I take no pleasure in this conclusion, which I reached slowly and reluctantly over my two decades as an editor of *The New England Journal of Medicine.*"[42]

Another problem with health care in America today is that medical practices, which provide large incomes to wealthy physicians, may cost more than they're worth; they may increase the cost of medical care—now at 17 percent of the GDP—more than they improve health outcomes for patients. For instance, research at Dartmouth Medical School showed that the use of medical and surgical interventions varies widely from place to place in America. Some areas consume much more medical intervention than others, Dr. Donald Berwick reports in *Newsweek.* "For many procedures, the variation is stunning. Compared with the lowest-use areas, people in the highest-use areas get 10 times as many prostate operations, six times as many back surgeries, seven times as many coronary angioplasties and 10 times as many hospital stays if they have heart failure." The main difference between high-use and low-use areas seems to be the number of specialists and the number of hospital beds, according to Dr. Berwick. "The use of specialists visits varies by 660 percent, and what best predicts the rate is the number of specialists per capita. The more doctors, the more doctor visits. The more hospital beds, the more days spent in the hospital." Is this good? Are people benefiting from the extra medical attention that generates profits to hospitals and physicians? Not so much, Berwick reports: "In fact, for many measures, quality and outcomes were best in the low-use areas and worst in the high-use areas. The less, the better."[43]

Again, profit in the real marketplace in the United States does not correlate well with benefit to others. And we're not talking about a few "bad apples," such as the Ponzi schemer Bernard Madoff or the people at Enron who got rich (before their fall) through practices that harmed others. We're talking about practices that are common, systematic, and pervasive in large sectors of the economy—autos, steel, energy, food, pharmaceuticals, and medicine.

We can add auditing to that list. Much corporate misbehavior is abetted by conflicts of interest among auditors who are supposed to keep corporate bookkeeping honest so that the investing public can know the true value of companies before they invest. However, much like the compensation consultants who recommend high pay for senior executives who give them money for other services, auditing firms often provide consulting services to the companies they audit. An audit that overlooks some painful information can win money for the auditing firm in its capacity as consultant. This was the case with Arthur Andersen's audits of Enron and WorldCom. But those weren't the only cases. Over the years, Arthur Andersen was involved in corporate scandals at Sunbeam, Waste Management, Global Crossing, Dynergy, Halliburton, Colonial Realty, and Qwest (now called CenturyLink). In short, the profits of auditing firms and of the companies they audit cannot always be taken at face value.[44]

Many unsophisticated investors are at risk also because stock analysts, too, often have conflicts of interest. They work for investment banks that broker stock and bond offerings. These banks get a commission from the corporation whose stocks and bonds they are brokering. The stock analyst can also earn commissions from customers who buy stocks and bonds but those commissions have become small as a result of competition from discount brokerages. Low commissions from those who buy stocks and bonds gives investment banks and their stock analysts increasing willingness to please the companies that issue stocks and bonds because that is now where they get most of their money. Therefore they tend to hype stocks and bonds out of all proportion to a sober estimate of their current worth or their potential for profit and growth. According to most free-market conservatives, such practices harm investors and the market.

But this is just one of several problems with the financial sector of the economy, which accounts for 7 percent of wages and income in the United States.[45] The real estate market is now well known for practices that yielded enormous profits and high salaries before the mortgage crisis began in 2007. One way financiers made a lot of money was by removing the ordinary relationship between borrowers and lenders of money for real estate. In the old days lending institutions would hold the mortgage, which gave them an incentive to make sure the money would be paid back by the borrower. Then new financial instruments were invented, called *mortgage-backed securities*. A bunch of mortgages were packaged together to form a kind of property of its own, the value of which was based on the value of the expected return on the packaged mortgages as borrowers paid off their loans. The issuer of a mortgage no longer lost money if the borrower defaulted on the loan because the initial lender had already sold the debt to others as part of a mortgage-backed security. The lender made money not from the repayment of the loan, but from fees, commissions, and profits related to transactions that generated the mortgage, packaged it with others, and sold the package on the financial market. These practices, begun in the 1970s, made more money available for mortgage loans.

The additional money available for mortgage loans, combined with federal government policies that kept interest rates low, increased demand on the housing market and drove up real estate prices. Still, as long as the mortgage-backed

securities contained only traditional mortgages—mortgages issued to credit-worthy borrowers—there was no problem. Problems arose and increased very quickly in 2005 when subprime
mortgages—mortgages issued to people who did not meet standard criteria of credit worthiness—were added to the packages.
Many people formerly excluded for reasons of financial risk
from home purchase could now buy a house, and the additional demand further increased the value of real estate, which,
according to economist Paul Krugman, became significantly
overvalued by summer 2006.[46] This meant that a lot of people
would lose money, especially those who had relied on prices
going up, when the housing bubble finally burst.

Here's an example given by Steve Eisman, a financial analyst. The former babysitter of his twins, a woman from Jamaica,
told him that she and her sister now owned five townhouses in
Queens, New York. They bought one, and when its value rose
they were told that they could refinance and take out $250,000
to buy a second one. When prices continued to rise, she and
her sister repeated the process until they owned five. But then
prices began to fall and they couldn't make the payments.[47]
They lost everything; the people who bought the mortgage-
backed securities lost a lot of their money, too. But the people
who wrote the loans and packaged them into mortgage-backed
securities kept all of the money they earned on these transactions. The old dope peddler had been replaced by the old debt
peddler.

Part of the problem that led to the meltdown of the financial
sector of our economy, explains Nobel Prize–winning economist Robert Solow, is that banks and other lending institutions
increased their rate of leverage. They used to leverage their
funds at 10 to 1, meaning that they retained one dollar for
every ten that they lent to others. In that case, they had enough
funds on hand if 5 or 6 percent of the money they lent went

into default. But then many large financial institutions, such as Bear Stearns and Lehman Brothers, decided to make more money by lending more money. They could do this by leveraging at 30 to 1 instead of 10 to 1, which tripled their potential lending. This extra infusion of money into the mortgage market also helped to push up real estate prices, but now the institution itself would be in trouble financially if 5 or 6 percent of its debtors defaulted, because they had retained capital to cover losses of less than 4 percent, not 10 percent as in days of old.

To make matters worse, Robert Solow explains,

many highly-leveraged financial institutions—banks, hedge funds, and insurance companies among them— . . . borrowed from other financial institutions to make complicated bets on risky assets, and they have lent to other leveraged financial institutions so that those institutions could make complicated, risky asset bets. These are the "toxic assets" that weigh down the balance sheets of banks. *No one knows for sure what anyone else is worth: they own assets of uncertain value, including the debts of other institutions that own assets of uncertain value.*[48]

The situation got so bad that almost all mainstream economists agreed in fall 2008 that the federal government had to step in to rescue the financial industry because its collapse could have plunged the country into a depression like that of the 1930s. Of course, experts differed among themselves significantly on what kind of bailout would be most helpful. The amazing thing is that some of the Wall Street firms that had just received bailout money gave hefty bonuses to some of their employees. Ben White wrote in the *New York Times*, "Despite crippling losses, multibillion-dollar bailouts and the passing of some of the most prominent names in the business, employees at financial companies in New York . . . collected $18.4 billion in bonuses for the year."[49] This made it the sixth highest bonus year on record, but constituted a 44 percent drop from the previous year. The firms giving bonuses said they had to give bonuses to retain valued employees. And get this! "A poll of 900 financial industry employees . . . by eFinancialCareers .com, a job search Web site, found that while nearly eight out of 10 got bonuses, 46 percent thought they deserved more."[50] They thought they deserved more bonuses in an industry that for the year in question had lost so many billions of dollars that it required hundreds of billions of dollars from taxpayers to bail it out. I guess no matter how enormous and undeserved a privilege may be, its beneficiaries consider its continuation to be their right.

$ $ $

My point in this chapter is not that no one deserves to be rich on the basis of work in the free market. Thomas Edison became rich inventing and selling to the public electric lights, phonographs, and many other helpful items. Henry Ford became rich reducing the cost of automobiles so that ordinary Americans could afford them. More recently, Jeff Bezos, founder of Amazon.com, has become wealthy by providing people with improved opportunities to buy books and many other items. And these are just three examples among a host of others. People do often get rich in the United States by serving customers well.

My point in this chapter is, nevertheless, that the correlation is weak in our society between free-market-generated riches and their traditional justification in meeting the needs and wants of others. In the real free market, it's a mixed bag. Practices that are widely condemned by advocates of an honest free market, such as fraud and conflicts of interest, result in billions of dollars of earnings, are common among major corporations and pervade leading industries. One way to take back the center for a new progressive agenda is to use these facts to rebut conservative claims that the foundation of the progressive agenda, raising taxes on rich people, is unfair. We can answer, "Not so much." Still, the practices exposed in this chapter do not constitute a reason *for* progressive taxation; they just undermine one objection to progressive taxation—the unfairness objection. Chapters that follow give positive reasons for the progressive taxation needed to pay for programs in a new progressive agenda.

5
Workers Are Cheated

We've seen that a lot of people become rich in the United States through fraud, disinformation, and conflict of interest, without doing much good for others. We now look at ordinary workers and find that in many cases the poverty of the working poor is another factor that augments the wealth and income of the rich. This chapter argues that unfair treatment of the working poor is a positive reason for the kind of progressive taxation needed to fund a new progressive agenda. Again, more general knowledge of these facts will help progressives take back the center.

Here's an example of unfairness that, like many others, involves Walmart, the nation's largest private-sector employer with a workforce of about 1.3 million. It sells more in a year than Target, Sears, Kmart, JCPenney, Kohl's, Safeway, Albertsons, and Kroger combined. Walmart sales represent 2.6 percent of America's GDP. Its influence on working life is commensurate with its size, so let's look at how they treat their employees.[1]

One of those employees was Mike Michell, whose job was to catch shoplifters and fellow Walmart employees who were stealing from the company. He was twenty-eight years old and good at his job. He caught 180 shoplifters during a two-year

period at the stores where he worked in East Texas. He installed secret cameras at the loading dock to catch any employees who took a five-finger discount on merchandise arriving
at the store, and he watched out for cashiers who stole money
from cash registers. He told Steven Greenhouse of the *New
York Times*,

I didn't look at associates [the Walmart term for employees] as employees. I looked at them as potential thieves. Any time anyone was
injured and filled out a workers' comp claim form, we were told they
were trying to get something for nothing, so let's get rid of them. If
anyone filed a workers' comp claim that cost Walmart a lot of money,
we tried to terminate them. The rationale was, they're faking it.[2]

Built like a middle linebacker, he was proud to think of himself as playing defense for the company in its fight against theft
and fraud.

But then one day the Walmart system turned on him. A manager had told him that a woman who had just left the store was
using false checks, so Mike went out to the parking lot to apprehend her. She quickly jumped into a car, and while Mike was
trying to read the license plate the car's driver gunned the engine and came right at Mike. Mike jumped onto the hood of the
car, holding on to the windshield wipers, but soon realized that
he could be killed if he fell off after the car had reached a high
speed. So he let go and fell to the ground. He recalls: "After I
hit the ground, the car's front tire came so close to my head I
could see pebbles in the tread. I wound up with a torn rotator
cuff and two ruptured disks in my spinal cord. I also wound up
with part of my kneecap broken on my left knee. They removed
a section of my kneecap."[3]

Mike went back to work the very next day to show that
he was still a good employee and even caught a shoplifter, but
his doctor told him that he should only do light duty. He soon
found that the doctor was right. He was in too much pain to

work his ordinary forty-hour week. When he told his supervisor that he needed help with his work, he was told that if he took a disability leave he would be demoted to a $6-an-hour store greeter when he returned to work.

Because the pain was so bad, Mike told the store manager that he would nevertheless take disability leave the following month so that he could have an operation. During that month he saw the manager of his store when they were both forty miles from the store in another town. Mike believes that the manager was spying on him to discredit his claim of disability and use that as a reason to fire him. A manager might go to this trouble because at Walmart the medical costs of a disability claim come from the profits of the store where the claimant worked, thereby reducing the store's profits and jeopardizing or reducing the bonus the manager would receive at the end of the year.

When, still in pain after his operation, Mike returned to his old job, they finally found a reason to fire him. He was called to the front of the store to apprehend a shoplifter before he got away. The shoplifter was a large seventeen-year-old male who, Mike could see, was wielding a knife. Mike quickly got the knife out of the young man's hand and walked him toward the back of the store where there's a holding area. But, as Mike recalls, "As I tried to search the guy, he kept pulling away. I said, 'If you don't stop, I'm going to put you on the floor.' I believed he was trying to go for another weapon so I pulled his leg out from under him. I didn't slam him down. I just took him to the ground. I had not done anything that had not been done before."[4]

When the police came, they confirmed Mike's suspicions; the young man had a second knife. But the next day the store manager claimed that Mike had beaten up the young man for no good reason and Mike was fired for using excessive force and for assaulting a customer.

Having helped the store fire employees just because they had filed workers' comp claims, Mike knew what was going on but there was really nothing he could do about it. He still needed another operation, according to his doctor, one to fuse ruptured discs to reduce the pain he was still experiencing. It would cost $20,000. Walmart wouldn't pay for the operation because, they claimed, Mike's discs were impaired to begin with; the disc fusion was needed to treat a preexisting condition having nothing to do with Mike's workplace injuries. Mike couldn't afford the operation without financial help, so he sued the company. In pain, out of work, and out of money, Mike moved in with his parents, but still couldn't afford to pursue the lawsuit, giving up after two years of fruitless effort. Eventually, because he's now really poor, Mike will be able to get the operation he needs through Medicaid, which gives public health insurance to the very poor. Taxpayers will have to foot Walmart's bill.[5]

If this situation were unique, it wouldn't be worth mentioning. Unfortunately, it's typical of Walmart behavior toward employees and illustrates the plight of many low-wage workers—the working poor—in jobs at many firms. At Walmart, some of the callous treatment of employees is documented by former managers who implemented draconian policies. Melissa Jerkins was a store manager for Walmart in Decatur, Indiana, when she was only thirty-one years old. Because it was a relatively small store (for Walmart), it wasn't open twenty-four hours a day, but there was a twelve-person night crew to clean up the store and stock shelves. It was too costly to have a night manager to look after just twelve employees, so they needed another method of preventing employee theft. The method was to lock employees in the store, usually from 10 p.m. to 7 a.m.[6] Even though one person is believed to have died in 1988 as a result of being locked in a Walmart store all night, the practice continued at least until 2004.[7]

Higher management at Walmart set limits for employee payroll as a percentage of total store sales. One year, Melissa recalled, it was down to 5.9 percent. To meet this goal she needed to fire or push out more experienced, higher-paid employees making $9.50 an hour (that one does have a decimal) so she could replace them with new employees making only $6 an hour. She also reduced the hours of full-time employees from forty hours a week to thirty-five hours a week or even twenty-eight hours a week. Some of these employees would plead with her for more hours, Melissa said. "They couldn't afford their bills, they couldn't afford food for their family, they couldn't afford diapers for their children, but we were told to cut them back. You hated to do it, but by the same token, you can't have a heart."[8]

At that time new employees were eligible for benefits after working six weeks in a row full time, so Melissa, like many managers, often scheduled employees for part-time work after they had worked five weeks in a row. She also followed the company practice of challenging all employee claims for unemployment insurance, no matter how clearly justified the claim. She would tell state officials that the employee was fired for misconduct and therefore shouldn't be eligible for state benefits, which would increase the amount of money the store would have to contribute to the unemployment compensation system.[9]

Walmart's pay for its ordinary workers is quite low. Investigative reporter Greg Palast had volunteers around the country apply for cashier jobs in 1999 and found that the average wage offered was $6.10 an hour.[10] Around the same time, best-selling author Barbara Ehrenreich took a job at Walmart for $7 an hour, which she still found inadequate.[11] A single person with a child can't live even on $8 an hour, she points out, because after taxes the take-home pay is only about $1,200 a month. If rent is only $500 a month and day care is another $500 a month, there's only $200 a month left for food, clothing, transportation, entertainment, health care, health insurance, and everything else. Federally subsidized day care exists, but only about 14 percent of eligible families actually get the subsidy.[12]

In 2004, only about half of Walmart employees were covered by the company's health insurance plan because full-time workers weren't eligible for the plan until they had worked six months, part-timers had to wait two years, and the cheapest plan cost $228 a month, which was out of the reach of many employees anyway. As a result, in Georgia alone in 2002, among the dependents of Walmart's approximately forty-two thousand employees, 10,261 children were enrolled in the state's health-care program for kids, which is meant for children whose parents were too poor to afford health insurance.[13]

Walmart's admission that it doesn't give a living wage comes in the form of advice during employee orientation on how to apply for state and federal assistance for the poor.[14] A committee of the House of Representatives in Washington, DC, Ehrenreich tells us, "estimated that a 200-employee Walmart store may cost federal taxpayers $420,750 annually—about $2,103 per employee—in subsidies for free and reduced-price school lunches, Section 8 housing assistance, federal tax credits and deductions for low-income families, state health insurance programs, and energy assistance, among others."[15]

Walmart keeps wages low in part by discouraging unionization. Sometimes their methods are legal, as when the orientation for new employees explains that a union is unnecessary at Walmart because the company treats its associates as family. New employees are told, according to Ehrenreich, who attended one of these orientation sessions, that unions "no longer have much to offer workers," which is why people are leaving them "by the droves. . . ." But . . . "unions have been targeting Walmart for years." Why? For the dues money of course. Think of what you would lose with a union: first, your dues money, which could be $20 a month "and sometimes much more." Second, you would lose "your voice" because the union would insist on doing your talking for you. Finally, you might lose even your wages and benefits because they would all be "at risk on the bargaining table."[16]

Walmart also is credibly accused of illegal methods of discouraging unionization. Mike Michell, for example, said that his Walmart job included discouraging unionization as well as catching thieves. He was told to spy on some meat department workers because they were talking about joining a union. He secretly installed a hidden camera in the store's walk-in freezer. This was against federal law, which doesn't allow spying on workers simply because they want to form a union.[17]

Greg Palast adds this story:

In 1982, well on his way to becoming America's richest man, Sam [Walton, the founder of Wal-Mart] dropped by an Arkansas distribution center and told the loaders, as one regular guy to another, that if they voted to join a union in a forthcoming representation ballot, he would fire them all and shut down the entire center.

The words, corroborated by eight witnesses, may have been in violation of U.S. labor law, but they were darned effective. The workers voted down the union, keeping Sam's record perfect. Out of 2,450 stores in America today, exactly none is unionized.[18]

The antiunion tradition continues at Walmart. In 1994 Linda Regalado was fired after she failed to heed a warning from management that they would terminate her employment if she continued to talk to coworkers about unionization.[19]

Low wages at Walmart affect the wages received by workers elsewhere. David Neumark, an economics professor at the University of California at Irvine, found that after eight years of Walmart's presence in a county, average worker earnings in the county, from retail and nonretail employment, had fallen by an average of 2.5 to 4.8 percent. The basic reason is that Walmart drives some high-wage employers out of business and forces others to lower wages in order to be price competitive with Walmart.

A four-and-a-half-month strike in 2003–2004 in Southern California that involved fifty-nine thousand workers at Safeway, Albertsons, and Ralphs (owned by Kroger) was a dramatic example of this phenomenon. Fearing the entry of Walmart into their market, management at these grocery chains pointed out to labor that their unionized cashiers could earn as much as $17.90 an hour, whereas Walmart paid its cashiers only $8.50. The union eventually caved in and accepted a $.90 an hour cut in beginning pay and a cut in top wages from $17.90 to $15.10. They accepted a lowering of company health coverage contributions from $6,900 a year per full-time worker to just $2,000 a year.[20]

Walmart became the largest retailer in the world in part by getting suppliers, whether of electronics, clothing, or food, to reduce their prices. Suppliers in turn must reduce the pay they offer their employees in order to comply with Walmart's insistence on lower prices. Craig Cole, the CEO of a supermarket chain in the Pacific Northwest, Brown & Cole Stores, puts it this way: "Wal-Mart has developed a business model based on being an employer of the working poor. [This] business model is undermining communities by pushing out locally owned retailers while driving employee wages down. . . . Socially, we're engaged in a race to the bottom."[21]

As we saw in chapter 3, former labor secretary Robert Reich sees the glass as half full. He points to studies showing that Walmart saves American consumers between $100 billion and $200 billion a year, and doubts that consumers would accept higher prices if Walmart decided to raise its prices in order to offer better compensation to its workers. Instead, he thinks, many customers would simply shop elsewhere, where prices (and employee compensation) are at rock bottom.[22] The major alternative, that of Walmart absorbing the cost of higher wages by lowering profits, Reich says, would be unacceptable to shareholders.

Steven Greenhouse calculates, however, that Walmart could raise its average wage $1.70 an hour to the average wage in the big-box retail industry, spend $3 per worker hour on a decent health-care plan instead of the $1 it spends at present, and have to raise its prices by only 1 percent if it were willing to lower its annual profits from $11.3 billion to $8.1 billion. Frankly, I doubt that customers would notice a 1 percent rise in prices as much as shareholders would notice a 30 percent decline in profits.

Libertarian John Hospers claims, as we saw in chapter 3, that rich people become rich by creating wealth from which the whole society benefits, so there's no real conflict between rich people getting richer and poor people thriving. However, the possibility of improving the lives of more than a million Walmart employees if Walmart profits were trimmed by 30 percent shows that the people who are getting richer in this country, including those who are heavily invested in stocks, are getting richer in part by impoverishing the working poor. It's not a win-win situation.

The same logic of lowering costs to consumers while maintaining high profits accounts for the widespread practice of time-card violations. Employee time records are often altered to reflect fewer hours of work than were actually performed. Drew Pooters, who had been an MP in the Air Force, encountered this when he worked as head of the electronics department at a Toys"R"Us store in Albuquerque, New Mexico. One day he went into the manager's office to check on some paperwork and saw a senior manager at a computer changing the records of hours worked. Drew supposes that the store's management stood to get a bonus if the store's labor costs were kept down. Still, he was shocked by what he saw.

I saw someone's time change from eight hours and twenty-three minutes to seven hours and fifty-nine minutes. I watched the manager a good long time while waiting to ask him a question. I even saw him editing my name, and I said, "That's not exactly legal."

He said, "It's none of your business," and that's when the threats started. . . .

He said, "Mind your own business. You didn't see this. Right? If you say a word about this, I'll kick your damn ass."

I backed down and said, "You're right. I'll do whatever I need to do."

He said, "You damn well better."[23]

Drew was nevertheless demoted from head of the electronics department to someone who unloaded trucks and stocked shelves, so he eventually quit. He was then hired as manager of a Family Dollar store. The Family Dollar chain has a computer-generated plan that managers are supposed to follow, but the plan didn't allow for enough work hours to cover all of the store's need for labor. According to the plan, called Matrix, payroll was supposed to be only 5 percent of gross receipts at the store. The rate at which Matrix expected trucks to be unloaded and items shelved allowed only 22 seconds per item. Lacking the help he needed, Drew worked extra hours.

When headquarters further reduced the paid hours he was allowed at the store, Drew told the district manager that he couldn't get by with the store so undermanned. He recalled:

She said, "Just delete the hours."

I said, "You can't do that. That's a violation of company policy. . . ."

She started rejiggering the hours right in front of me. I was looking over her shoulder when she did it. I said, "But that worker didn't take a lunch that day," and she said, "Now she did."[24]

Drew moved to Indiana and started working at a Rentway store just across the border in Michigan. Within two months he found his own work hours shaved. His pay slip for one week indicated that he'd taken a half-hour lunch each day when he hadn't. When he told the manager that he wouldn't sign an inaccurate pay slip, the manager told him that signing was the only way he would get paid.[25] Complaints of similar time-card violations have been reported of Walmart and Pep Boys.[26]

Barbara Ehrenreich encountered another way of cheating hourly workers out of pay. Instead of altering records in the computer, just insist that people be at work off the clock in the first place. At Merry Maids, a housecleaning service where Ehrenreich worked in Maine, she recalls, "We're told to get to work at 7:30, but the meter doesn't start running until about 8:00, when we take off in the cars, and there's no pay for the half hour or so we spend in the office at the end of the day, sorting out the dirty rags before they're washed and refilling our cleaning fluid bottles."[27] Similar complaints of hourly workers being forced to work when they knew they weren't on the clock have been lodged against Taco Bell, (the ever-present) Walmart, Family Dollar, A&P, and SmartStyle, the country's largest hair salon company [located in Walmart stores].[28]

A study conducted in early 2008 just before the recession got bad shows that illegal employer behavior is rampant, according to Steven Greenhouse in the *New York Times*.[29] A survey of 4,387 low-wage workers in Chicago, New York, and Los Angeles—workers in such fields as apparel and textile manufacturing, repair services, retail stores, restaurants, hotels, and home health care—"found that 26 percent . . . had been paid less than the minimum wage the week before being surveyed and that one in seven had worked off the clock the previous week. In addition, 76 percent of those who had worked overtime the week before were not paid their proper overtime. . . ." As a result of such violations, the researchers found, "the typical worker had lost $51 the previous week . . . out of average weekly earnings of $339. That translates into a 15 percent loss in pay." Of the 20 percent of workers who complained about wages or who tried to form a union, 43 percent reported illegal retaliation, such as firing or suspension. The prevalence of such retaliation may explain why only 8 percent of workers who suffered serious injuries on the job filed workers' compensation claims.

Nik Theodore, one of the study's authors said, "The conventional wisdom has been that to the extent there were violations, it was confined to a few rogue employers or to especially disadvantaged workers, like undocumented immigrants. What our study shows is that this is a widespread phenomenon across the low-wage labor market in the United States."

You might think that such blatantly illegal acts, brazenly performed, would be rare because most managers, even if tempted by bonuses, would be too frightened of law enforcement; they'd be afraid of getting caught. But the chances of getting caught and punished are astronomically small. Workers don't have the wherewithal to sue and there's not enough money at stake in any given provable case to motivate a lawyer to spend years battling a large corporation. So discovery of such practices through private lawsuit is next to impossible. And the chances of getting caught by the government are not much better. Over the last generation, the workforce has grown from 90 to 145 million workers but the number of wage-and-hours investigators has fallen. There are now only 788 of them to monitor the legal compliance of 8.4 million businesses.[30] Even if an inspector looks at falsified records, she won't know that they're falsified unless employees trying to keep their jobs tell her so. The only bright spot is that, responding to the findings of the study done in 2008 and released in 2009, Labor Secretary Hilda Solis said she was about to hire 250 more wage-and-hour investigators.[31]

$ $ $

The meat industry keeps consumer prices down and profits up at the workers' expense by switching from union to nonunion labor. At one time the meat industry was highly unionized, paid good salaries, and was concentrated in big cities such as Chicago and Kansas City. Now, much of this dangerous work takes place in remote locations, far from any city, in Kansas and Arizona. The workers are largely immigrants from Latin America or Southeast Asia. Their pay is so poor that trailer parks dot the landscape in the western Kansas towns of Garden City, Liberal, and Dodge City, writes Thomas Frank in *What's the Matter with Kansas?* The work is so hard, one angry worker told Frank, "After ten years, people walk like they're sixty or seventy years old."[32] But beef prices are low and corporate profits high.

Workers tend to work more hours to make ends meet when their wages are low. This development belies the claim of philosopher John Hospers that labor-saving machinery has brought not only many conveniences to the average person, but also more free time in which to enjoy them. Low wages have deprived people of leisure time.

In the 1950s and 1960s many men earned a living wage for the entire family. But as wages have stagnated since about 1973, work hours for men have increased and an increasing proportion of married women with children now work full time outside the home. In 1992 Harvard economist Juliet Schor described the resulting decline of leisure in our society. At that time, about two-thirds of adult women were employed, including women with children. Schor writes:

Many working mothers live a life of perpetual motion, effectively holding down two full-time jobs. They rise in the wee hours of the morning to begin the day with a few hours of laundry, cleaning, and other housework. Then they dress and feed the children and send them off to school. They themselves then travel to their jobs. The three-quarters of the employed women with full-time positions then spend the next eight and a half hours in the workplace.

At the end of the official workday, it's back to the "second shift"—the duties of housewife and mother. Grocery shopping, picking up the children, and cooking dinner take up the next few hours. After dinner there's clean-up, possibly some additional housework, and, of course, more child care.[33]

Schor cites studies estimating that the average employed mother puts in over eighty hours a week of housework, child care, and employment. Men are affected by this trend as well. Instead of getting home at 5 p.m. to have dinner with the family, many men arrive home in the middle of the evening. Sometimes they're at a second job; sometimes they work overtime at time-and-a-half. A twenty-eight-year-old factory worker in Massachusetts told Schor:

Either I can spend time with my family, or support them—not both. I can work 8-12 hours overtime a week at time and a half, and that's when the real money just starts to kick in. . . . If I don't work the OT my wife would have to work much longer hours to make up the difference, and our day care bill would double. . . . The trouble is, the little time I'm home I'm too tired to have any fun with them or be any real help around the house.[34]

These problems are worst at the lowest end of the pay scale among people earning less than twice the minimum wage. Twenty years ago many low-wage workers, such as those at nursing homes, already worked two full-time jobs to make ends meet,[35] and the situation has gotten worse since then. Imagine what this does to family life. The point is that the relentless pursuit of less labor cost to keep consumer prices down without sacrificing investor income requires people to work more hours. This harms not only workers but also their families. On average, Americans now work more hours per year than people in any other industrialized country. In 1950, Americans worked fewer hours than people in Japan, Britain, Germany, and France, but by 1998 Americans worked more hours than people in any of these other prosperous counties.[36]

$ $ $

Free-market theory dictates that workers prosper when their productivity increases. When each worker makes more per hour of what they and other consumers want, more products are available in society and people can work fewer hours while enjoying higher standards of living. But that's not what has been happening in the United States. On average, the productivity of American workers has increased greatly since World War II, and for the first generation after the war the result of additional productivity showed up in higher standards of living for most people. However, since the early 1970s, productivity increases have not been matched by greater affluence for, or fewer hours worked by, average Americans.

This means that the stories told in this chapter and in earlier chapters are not just anecdotes that give a false impression of how the free market in the United States works. Rather, they represent the general trend; they illustrate the big picture. The illustrations include stories of invented diseases and ineffective treatments that enhance corporate profits, stories of CEOs receiving extraordinarily high compensation abetted by conflicts of interest, and stories of pseudoscientific disinformation campaigns conducted by major industries to continue their high profits and give their shareholders great returns. We also have stories of ordinary workers being required to work off the clock or having the record of the time they worked altered to cheat them out of pay and save money for corporations, stories of people unable to afford decent housing or health care, stories of people having to work so many hours to make ends meet that they can't interact meaningfully with their children, stories of companies cheating employees out of the workers' compensation and unemployment insurance they are legally due, stories of people earning so little from full-time employment that they qualify for government assistance for food and housing, and stories of companies discouraging unionization by legal and illegal means.

Statistics show the aggregate effects of scenarios like these. Economist Paul Krugman writes, "The value of the output an average worker produces in an hour, even after you adjust for inflation, has risen almost 50 percent since 1973. Yet the growing concentration of income in the hands of a small minority has proceeded so rapidly that we're not sure whether the typical American has gained *anything* from rising productivity."[37] This situation contrasts markedly with opinions in 1973 about productivity gains since World War II. No one doubted that the average worker and family had gained enormously from those productivity gains. But since 1973, the rewards to average workers are in dispute.

One way to make it appear that average people have gained from increases in worker productivity is to look at *average* earnings. But the *average* goes up whenever someone who is already rich becomes even richer. As Krugman points out, "If Bill Gates walks into a bar, the average wealth of the bar's clientele soars, but the men already there when he walked in are no wealthier than before."[38] The way to assess how most people are doing is to look not at the average but at the *median* worker or family, the one whose income or wealth is greater than that of half the population and less than that of the other half. When Bill Gates walks into a bar, the median doesn't change.

Adjusted for inflation, median household income increased about 16 percent between 1973 and 2005. But this overstates the gains of representative workers because, on average, more members of the family were working, and they were working more hours in 2005 than in 1973. In particular, more women with children were working outside the home. This isn't a bad thing in itself but when women with children earn money working outside the home, the household often incurs additional expenses that households with a stay-at-home parent don't incur. Childcare is the largest additional expense, but eating out more or buying prepared food because no one is home to cook can also add to household expenses. So the extra income of both spouses working outside the home can't all be put on the plus side of household economic well-being.

Second, we don't usually think that our pay has gone up when our hourly wage stays the same but we work more hours. The pay check is larger, but that's because more hours are worked, not because the rate of pay has increased. That's our situation. Because increases in household income result merely from more hours worked, Americans aren't getting paid for the 50 percent additional productivity of their labor each hour. In fact, Krugman reports, "The median inflation-adjusted earnings of men working full-time in 2005 were slightly lower than they had been in 1973."[39]

That might seem bad but the reality is actually worse. In 1973, as a result of the postwar baby boom, the workforce was relatively young compared to today. People generally earn more as they age, so to get a fair comparison of earnings in 1973 and 2005 it's necessary to compare the earnings of people of similar ages in these two different years. "If we look at the earnings of men aged thirty-five to forty-four—the men who would, a generation ago, often have been supporting stay-at-home wives—we find that inflation-adjusted wages were 12 percent *higher* in 1973 than they are now."[40]

Where has all the money gone? Most of the money has gone to corporate big wigs and wealthy shareholders. This represents a change from the past. In the 1970s I taught in a management program that featured stakeholder analysis. Management decisions were supposed to be sensitive to the needs of workers and managers, to the welfare of communities where workers and managers lived, to the health of the environment, and, of course, to shareholders. Shareholders were only one of the constituencies of management concern. The founder of our program, James C. Worthy, a retired vice president of Sears and a former undersecretary of commerce in the Eisenhower administration, used to emphasize the difference between making a profit and maximizing profit. Making a profit was, of course, essential, but maximizing it was not. As long as a corporation provided investors with a reasonable rate of return it could use some resources to meet the needs of its other stakeholders. It could improve wages or benefits for employees, contribute to community projects, and so forth.

Former labor secretary Robert Reich claims that the rules have changed. Now investors want the greatest rate of return and move their money quickly if they are disappointed. Reich writes, "In the 1990s, the average investor held on to a share of stock for a little more than two years. By 2002, the average holding period was less than a year. By 2004, it was barely six months, a new record."[41] High-level managers are under great pressure to keep investors happy, including institutional investors, and receive huge bonuses when they succeed, Reich claims:

Just as Walmart has squeezed its suppliers for better deals, so have the managers of America's largest pension funds and mutual funds squeezed companies for higher profits, which translate into (not always directly, but with sufficient predictability that such squeezes are typically rewarded) higher share prices. Before 1980, Wall Street had been the handmaiden of industry, helping large oligopolies raise capital when necessary. After 1980, industry became the handmaiden of Wall Street.[42]

As a result, according to Reich, there is "no longer a place for corporate statesmen who viewed their role as balancing the interests of all parties, including their employees, the citizens of communities where they did business, and the nation as a whole."[43]

Reich dismisses current praise for and claims of "corporate social responsibility." Where it exists, he says, it's mostly PR lauding actions that make good old-fashioned free-market sense. For example, McDonald's more humane slaughter techniques save the corporation money by reducing worker injuries. Walmart's "green" packaging is cheaper than what it replaced. Alcoa saves $100 million a year from its energy-saving and environmental initiatives.[44] In the current investor climate, Reich maintains, corporations have to focus completely on profit maximization.

Jack Welch, who took the helm at General Electric in 1981, epitomizes the new perspective, which gives heed only to investors. Welch's goal was to maximize profit, thereby generating maximum returns to investors in the forms of dividends and elevated stock prices. He came to be called "Neutron Jack" because, like a neutron bomb, he made people disappear. Steven Greenhouse gives the numbers: "Under Welch, Schenectady, New York, GE's original headquarters, lost 22,000 jobs. Louisville, the home of appliances, lost 13,000. Evendale, Ohio, which made lighting, lost 12,000; Pittsfield, Massachusetts, home to GE's plastics division, 8,000; Erie, Pennsylvania, which made locomotives, 6,000." Welch's biographer, Thomas F. O'Boyle, thought it particularly notable, as I do, "that [Welch's] actions [were] taken not to curtail losses but to enhance profitability, and in that regard, they presaged a change in philosophy that would become the prevailing attitude of the 1990s."[45] He was not trying to make a profit; he was trying to maximize profit. He behaved as if shareholders were his only constituency.

The effect on the price of GE stocks was spectacular. When Welch took over GE in 1981, GE's market capitalization, the worth of all its stocks, was $13 billion. When he retired from GE twenty years later, it was $500 billion. But Welch had eroded job security, leaving many displaced workers to find alternative work, most often at lower pay, an illustration of why hourly pay has declined for men since the 1970s. He impoverished communities, which lost support for their charitable institutions. These communities also lost many local businesses as the local economy no longer had the spending power to sustain them. It's a case of Wall Street harming Main Street; shareholders, high corporate executives, and many highly paid corporate managers and workers did very well indeed at the expense of most workers and communities. Not a win-win situation.

Investors quickly recognized the benefits to themselves of corporations ignoring all considerations other than shareholder value. *Business Week* called Welch "the gold standard against which other CEOs are measured." *Fortune* called him "the manager of the century," adding, "Welch wins the title because in addition to his transformation of GE, he has made himself far and away the most influential manager of his generation."[46] Given this new set of values, it's no surprise that when Sears unexpectedly laid off 50,000 workers, one-seventh of its workforce, its shares climbed 4 percent. Xerox stock climbed 7 percent when it announced letting 10,000 people go, more than 10 percent of its workforce. Kodak announced reducing its workforce by 10,000 also, but its stock continued to decline until it announced the elimination of an additional 6,600 jobs.[47]

The tendency of the economy to reward investors more than workers continues in the new century. Steven Greenhouse and David Leonhardt reported in the *New York Times* in 2006 that the median hourly wage of American workers had declined 2 percent in the previous three years in spite of the fact that worker productivity had increased. "As a result," they write, "wages and salaries now make up the lowest share of the nation's GDP since the government began recording the data in 1947, while corporate profits have climbed to their highest share since the 1960s. UBS, the investment bank, recently described the current period as 'the golden era of profitability.'"[48] Economists at the investment bank Goldman Sachs add, "The most important contributor to higher profit margins over the past five years has been a decline in labor's share of national income."[49]

Here's a case in point. We saw in chapter 4 that failed CEO of ConAgra, Bruce C. Rohde, walked away with $45 million in compensation during his eight years as CEO, as well as a generous severance and retirement package. By contrast, James P. Smith had worked for ConAgra for twenty-nine years when Eric Dash interviewed him for the *New York Times*. Smith (his real name) works at a plant in Omaha running a machine that crushes 3,600 pound blocks of pork and beef. His shift begins at 3:30 a.m. When he started at ConAgra in 1977 he earned $6.40 an hour. His wage in 2006, a year of prosperity when unemployment hovered around 5 percent, was $13.25 an hour. After inflation, this represents a decrease of over 30 percent in real income.[50] In other words, his pay in 2006 covered the cost of a package of consumer items that was 30 percent smaller than the package he could afford in 1977. And median pay in the United States has declined an additional 10 percent since the start of The Great Recession.[51]

Again, the stories told here are not unrepresentative anecdotes; they illustrate the main trend in the development of the free market in the United States. That trend belies the claim of free-market enthusiasts that there is no conflict between workers and owners because workers gain when owners and managers make business investments and decisions that increase worker productivity. The notion that we now have a fair game and a win-win situation is an illusion.

The question is what to do about this. Progressive taxation that takes more from the rich than the poor is one way to return to workers the share of national wealth generated by their increased productivity. It's also a way to finance a new progressive agenda. More general recognition of these facts is one way to place tax increases on the wealthy and a new progressive agenda at the center of practical political discussions. Chapter 6 adds another reason for progressive taxation. Many government programs favor wealthy people and therefore tend to concentrate income and wealth at the top. Progressive taxation is justified to counteract the effects of such government programs by taking from the rich some of the gains they enjoy at public expense.

6

Corporate Welfare

Business people in the United States often think of themselves as favoring a small government that allows the business community to operate within a free market to produce what consumers want. In fact, however, businesses often seek and receive government help at taxpayer and consumer expense to increase profits beyond what the free market would allow. The prevalence of such government favors, which enrich the already affluent, justifies progressive taxation. Revenues from such taxes could enable the government to return some ill-gotten gains to ordinary Americans.

Consider, for example, the sugar industry. The United States Department of Agriculture (USDA) lends money to sugar processors that must be repaid within nine months either in cash or in an amount of sugar of equivalent value. The sugar is valued at $.18 for a pound of cane sugar and almost $.23 for beet sugar. These prices are far above world prices. To maintain the domestic price of sugar at these high prices, so that repayment of loans in sugar instead of cash will fulfill the sugar processors' commitments without the federal government losing money, the federal government does two things. It sets a quota on the amount of sugar that can be exported to the United States, enforced by a prohibitively high tariff on exports above the quota, and it limits the amount of sugar that domestic processors are allowed to sell. The artificially high price of sugar helps domestic sugar growers and processors but hurts American consumers and workers, as Jason Lee Steorts explains in the *National Review*:

Each time you buy sugar or a product made with sugar, the difference between the price you pay and the lower price you would pay absent the sugar program . . . can be thought of as a sugar tax. Unlike most taxes, this tax never finds its way to government accounts. Instead, it passes directly from your pocket to the sugar industry's profit statements.

A GAO [Government Accounting Office] study found that, between 1989 and 1991, the sugar tax cost American consumers an average of $1.4 billion per year. By 1998, that number had risen to $1.9 billion.[1]

American jobs are lost because the high cost of domestic sugar influences manufacturers of products containing sugar, such as confectioners, to either shut down or relocate to Canada, where sugar prices are lower. The Sweetener Users Association estimates that Americans lost between 7,500 and 10,000 jobs between 1997 and 2003 as a result of the sugar subsidy.

The American sugar industry has influenced legislation with campaign contributions. Although they employ only 62,000 workers and comprise only 0.5 percent of the American agricultural sector, their political campaign contributions between 1990 and 2004 comprised 17 percent of all such contributions from the agricultural sector of the economy. The Fanjul brothers of Florida, whose Flo-Sun company produces sugar cane, contributed $573,000 to candidates, both Republican and Democratic, in 2004. A sugar beet cooperative in the Red River Valley of North Dakota, American Crystal, outdid Flo-Sun with $851,000 in contributions that year. But these contributions are small compared to the returns. Of the approximately $2 billion a year that Americans pay extra for sugar as a result of the USDA's sugar program, at least $1 billion lines the pockets of a relatively few American sugar companies.[2]

A host of other industry-inspired agricultural subsidies have the same effect of harming consumers. In a moment of candor, Trent Lott, while still a U.S. senator said, "I've been in the unholy agricultural alliance for 33 years. I've voted for every damned ridiculous agricultural program and subsidy conceived by the minds of men."[3] He was nearing retirement.

If businesses are trying to maximize profit, this is the way to go. A couple million dollars in campaign contributions yield a billion dollars in additional profit. But society is harmed. The profit motive is tied to the public good, Adam Smith argued in *The Wealth of Nations*, only under conditions of an ideal free market. Under those conditions, he writes,

Every individual . . . endeavours as much as he can . . . to employ his capital . . . so . . . its produce may be of the greatest value. . . . He intends only his own gain, and he is in this . . . led by an invisible hand to promote an end which was no part of his intention. . . . By pursuing his own interest he frequently promotes that of the society more effectually than when he really intends to promote it.[4]

Smith realized, however, that greedy business people would try to subvert the free-market system by obtaining government favors because profits tend to be low in a really free market. He wrote that in a well-developed free market, "competition . . . would every-where be . . . great, and consequently the ordinary profit as low as possible."[5]

Smith thought that if business people are really trying to maximize profit, any praise they have for a free market will be insincere or misinformed because their actual interest is to create monopolies, restrict competition, gain government favors, and in other ways avoid the discipline of the market that keeps profits low. Smith wrote of business people that their "interest is never exactly the same with that of the public. . . . [They] have generally an interest to deceive and even to oppress the public, and . . . accordingly have, upon many occasions, both deceived and oppressed."[6] This chapter looks at several ways that businesses in the United States have sought and received government help in avoiding the discipline of the market. Some of these are practices that Adam Smith warned against; others have been invented more recently. The net result of these government actions has been to concentrate wealth toward the top at everyone else's expense. Progressive taxation is justified as a means of returning some wealth to its rightful owners.

Many free-market conservatives side with Adam Smith against business interests on these issues. For example, the *National Review*, where the sugar subsidy is decried, was started by conservative William F. Buckley and remains a bastion of (mostly free-market) conservatism. Many free-market conservatives recognize that corporate welfare violates their principles.

$ $ $

One form of corporate welfare against the interests of the consuming public is, as we've seen in the case of the sugar industry, import restrictions. Adam Smith put it this way:

In every country it always is and must be in the interest of the great body of the people to buy whatever they want of those who sell it cheapest. . . . [The interest of] merchants and manufacturers . . . is, in this respect, directly opposite to that of the great body of the people. . . . It is the interest of the merchants and manufacturers of every country to secure to themselves the monopoly of the home market.[7]

Import restrictions are designed to give domestic producers that "monopoly of the home market."

The pharmaceutical industry's opposition to the importation of prescription drugs from Canada is another example of corporations increasing their profit by reducing competition through government-imposed import restrictions. Actually, in some cases the restrictions applied to reimportation because the drugs in question were ones that these same pharmaceutical companies had manufactured in the first place and then exported to wholesalers in Canada. With restrictions on (re) importation in place, prices for the same set of drugs averaged 67 percent more in the United States than in Canada in 2002, giving consumers a powerful incentive to buy their drugs in Canada instead of in the United States, which many people did.

Responding to complaints from drug manufacturers, in 2002 the United States Congress sided with the pharmaceutical industry and disallowed the importation of prescription drugs from countries where they are cheaper. One rationale was this: the extra profits that pharmaceutical companies make in the United States by charging higher prices here serve the public good because these profits are used for drug research, from which everyone will benefit in the long run as new drugs help people fight disease, disability, and death. However, in the light of the extraordinarily high profits in the pharmaceutical industry (noted in chapter 4), it's hard to believe that they need more profit to fund necessary research.

A second rationale is given by Gardiner Harris, writing in the *New York Times*:

Drug makers . . . argue that imported drugs can be dangerous, noting that neither American nor Canadian health authorities assure their quality. Indeed, the Food and Drug Administration has repeatedly cited the risks from imported drugs, and regulators in recent months have sought to shut down small stores springing up across the country that help Americans buy imported drugs.[8]

Does this strike you as reasonable? I find it hard to believe that drugs would be tainted by crossing the border between Canada and the United States, but not by crossing all the state borders between Connecticut and California. Most likely, similar to the sugar industry, the drug companies were maximizing their profits, as Adam Smith would expect, by enlisting the government's help to maintain a monopoly in the domestic market that resulted in higher prices for their products than true free-market competition would allow. As Smith put it:

Consumption is the sole end and purpose of all production. . . . In the restraints upon the importation of all foreign commodities which can come into competition with those of our own growth, or manufacture, the interest of the home-consumer is evidently sacrificed to that of the producer.[9]

Most Americans didn't have to read Adam Smith to figure out that restrictions on the importation of prescription drugs from Canada was mostly a case of competition between the profit motive and consumer welfare. It 2002 the government decided to help wealthy corporations against its own citizens.

$ \$ \ \$ \ \$ $

A more complete monopoly results, and therefore even higher profits can be obtained, when the government grants people a patent on what they produce so that no one can legally compete with them for customers in that product. This isn't to say that patents are bad. They generally serve the public by giving people the incentive to invent new products from which society benefits. But patents do confer a monopoly, which means that *eventually* it will be in the public interest to end the patent-created monopoly. However, it's still in the producer's interest to extend the patent and retain the monopoly. The extension of patents to unreasonable lengths is a form of corporate welfare that free-market conservatives should oppose, just as they oppose unnecessary import restriction.

Dr. Marcia Angell, former editor of the *New England Journal of Medicine*, notes that the Hatch-Waxman Act of 1984, designed to make it easier to bring generic drugs to market, also extended the period of patent protection. Additional acts in the 1990s had the same effect. "The result," she writes, is that the effective patent life of brand-name drugs increased from about eight years in 1980 to about fourteen years in 2000. For a blockbuster—usually defined as a drug with sales of over a billion dollars a year (like Lipitor or Celebrex or Zoloft)—those six years of additional exclusivity are golden. They can add billions of dollars to sales—enough to buy a lot of lawyers and have plenty of change left over. No wonder big pharma will do almost anything to protect exclusive marketing rights.[10]

In 2004, for example, Pfizer was awarded a six-month extension of its patent on the antifungal drug, Diflucan, against a challenge from Ranbaxy Laboratories of India.[11] It was obvious to Pfizer that competition lowers profits because it forces the company to lower prices. In patent law, as in all situations of monopoly on Adam Smith's understanding, there is no invisible hand that makes actions in the business person's interest conform to what is most helpful to society. Instead, after patent protection has done its proper job of stimulating innovation, what's good for business conflicts with what's good for society. In the light of the pharmaceutical industry's extraordinarily high profits (discussed in chapter 4), there's no reason to think that patent extensions on its products are needed to generate profits that serve society by stimulating innovation. Instead, such extensions seem to be a form of corporate welfare through government interference with competition.

$ $ $

Government harms taxpayers also when it allows businesses to use public property at below-market rates. David Bollier, journalist and public policy analyst, writes,

Not many Americans realize that they collectively own one third of the surface area of the country and billions of acres of the outer continental shelf. The resources are extensive and valuable: huge supplies of oil, coal, natural gas, uranium, copper, gold, silver, timber, grassland, water, and geothermal energy. The nation's public lands also consist of vast tracts of wilderness forests . . . [and] sweeping prairies.[12]

One way to maximize profit is for businesses to convince government to allow them to use these resources at below-market rates. Mining is a case in point. The Mining Act of 1872 was designed originally to encourage the development of the West. It stays on the books today, long after the West has been developed, because it favors mining companies who give large campaign contributions to legislators who keep the act in place. It works this way. If a mineral company makes a find, it can get a "patent" on the land, which entitles the company to buy the land for either $2.50 or $5 an acre, depending on the mineral in question. Through this process, a valuable land area the size of Connecticut has gone from federal to private hands. One estimate is that the Mining Act's federal give-away to mining interests since 1872 totals $245 billion. Phelps Dodge, for example, bought the land over its Morenci copper mine for $5 an acre and has since extracted billions of dollars of copper from the mine. The company estimates that $10 billion worth of copper remains to be extracted. The companies that benefit from these fire-sale prices at public expense say that they need this government support to make mining worthwhile, but they nevertheless pay much higher, market-based royalties to private parties when they discover minerals on private land.[13]

Another give-away to mining interests is that taxpayers often pay to clean up abandoned mining sites where extraction processes used acids, cyanide, and other toxic substances. These substances endanger wildlife and human life when they enter streams and rivers where they can travel more than one thousand miles. According to the Environmental Protection Agency, cleaning up abandoned mining sites could cost taxpayers between $32 and $72 billion.[14]

The mining industry does pay for its privileges but most payments go to campaign coffers instead of to taxpayers. Between 1993 and 1998, for example, mining lobbies, including the National Mining Association, gave almost $40 million to candidates and to political action committees that support candidates who are pledged to keep the federal subsidy in place. In view of the amount of federal subsidy the mining industry received during this period, the return on their investment was 30 to 1.[15]

For years, but no longer, oil companies were actually able to evade part of the royalties they owed to the federal government for pumping oil on federal property. How? Oil companies pay royalties of 12.5 percent for onshore extraction and between 16 and 33 percent for offshore extraction. The scam concerned the price of the petroleum on which these percentages were computed. It's called the *posted price,* which companies kept artificially low, as much as $4 a barrel lower than they would be in a free market, in order to reduce the royalties they had to pay.

The scam was ended in 2000 after some oil-state senators blocked the Interior Department's efforts to make the posted price more realistic. During the controversy it was revealed that Texas Senator Kay Bailey Hutchison, who was instrumental in blocking the new Interior Department rules, had received $1.2 million in campaign contributions from oil and gas interests between 1994 and 1998. All told, the industry had spent $93 million on lobbying in 1997 and $14 million in campaign contributions during the 1997–1998 election cycle. These expenditures made perfect sense if the industry goal was to maximize profit. The industry gave to lobbyists and candidates much less than it got back in the form of favorable treatment from the government.[16]

Livestock grazing on public land is another example of corporate welfare. In 1999, the federal government charged $1.35 per head of cattle per month for grazing on its (our) land, whereas on state-owned and private land, ranchers had to pay an average of $11.10, which should therefore be considered the market price. At the market price, the federal government would have collected about $750 million, whereas in fact it collected only $93 million. Thus, ranchers were allowed to shortchange the federal government, and so the federal taxpayer, to the tune of hundreds of millions of dollars in just that one year.[17]

The pharmaceutical industry also profits from public property. Most of its new drugs, especially breakthrough drugs, are actually developed by academic researchers working at taxpayer expense, often under the auspices of the National Institutes of Health (NIH). Before 1980, technologies developed with taxpayer money were part of the public domain; there were no exclusive patents on them that prevented manufacturers from using them as they saw fit. But in 1980 Congress passed the Bayh-Dole Act, which allowed publicly funded research institutions such as universities and small businesses to apply for patents on the discoveries of its researchers. The idea was to engage the entrepreneurial spirit among researchers and their institutions so they would more effectively bring to light and then to market new ways of helping humanity. The law may well have worked as intended to some extent. However, an unintended result was that large pharmaceutical companies can now buy patents that stem from publicly funded research, thereby relieving themselves of the need to conduct the kind of fundamental research necessary for significant pharmaceutical breakthroughs.

In general, big pharma lets the taxpayer fund the fundamental research and then piggybacks on these discoveries by creating and marketing similar drugs for the same conditions. These are called *me-too drugs*. When a patent runs out on one of its drugs, the pharmaceutical company just changes the formula a bit, calls it a new drug, and gets a new patent. This is why we have, for example, six different statin drugs for lowering cholesterol—Mevacor, Lipitor, Zocor, Pravachol, Lescol, and Crestor. Dr. Sharon Levine, associate executive director of the Kaiser Permanente Medical Group, explained:

If I'm a manufacturer and I can change one molecule and get another twenty years of patent rights, and convince physicians to prescribe and consumers to demand the next form of Prilosec, or weekly Prozac instead of daily Prozac, just as my patent expires, then why would I be spending money on a lot less certain endeavor, which is looking for brand new drugs?[18]

Dr. Marcia Angell sums up the extent to which large pharmaceutical companies depend on research at public expense:

Of the seventy-eight drugs approved by the FDA in 2002, only seventeen contained new active ingredients, and only seven of these were classified by the FDA as improvements over older drugs. The other seventy-one drugs approved that year were variations of old drugs or deemed no better than drugs already on the market. In other words, they were me-too drugs. Seven of seventy-eight is not much of a yield. Furthermore, of those seven, not one came from a major US drug company.[19]

Here, again, private profit is made at taxpayer expense. Drug companies depend on public money for basic research and then piggyback with me-too drugs sold at high prices.

$ $ $

The financial industry benefits tremendously from special treatment by the federal government. The industry is enormous. Ray Dalio of Bridgewater Associates, a large Connecticut money-management firm, put it this way: "The money that's made from manufacturing stuff is a pittance in comparison to the amount of money made from shuffling money around. Forty-four percent of all corporate profits in the U.S. come from the financial sector compared with only 10% from the manufacturing sector."[20]

Bailouts are a major way that the federal government supports financial institutions with taxpayer money. Since 1980 the federal government has bailed out financial institutions more than a dozen times.[21] Between 1982 and 1992, for example, the Federal Reserve provided money to Mexico, Argentina, and Brazil to avoid these countries defaulting on their debt commitments, that is, to avoid their failure to repay loans, many of which were to American banks. Again, in 1994–1995 Americans came to the rescue of the Mexican peso to avoid investors in high-risk and high-yield Mexican debt losing their shirts, as they would have done if the peso kept losing value.

There are several reasons for these bailouts. There's the humanitarian reason of helping people in poor countries by propping up their economies. There's a foreign policy rationale of not wanting chaos in these countries to destabilize the hemisphere's international community. And there's the realistic worry concerning our domestic economy that if banks lose too much money, they won't be able to lend domestically to the extent that American businesses and consumers need in order for our economy to thrive. However, whatever the nature and cogency of the rationales, these bailouts used taxpayer money to ensure that American (and other) banks don't lose money on loans that they should never have made in the first place.

Because we will continue to need banks to lend money, the rationale of saving banks to keep credit markets open will apply to almost any situation when banks lose enormous amounts of money for any reason, including their own greed and incompetence. The general message of bailouts, then, is that banks no longer have to be responsible for their own failures. If their risky loans work out, they win, making a good profit; if they don't work out they don't lose, as free market theory would dictate, because the government will use taxpayer money to

bail them out. The profit is private but the risk that would justify the profit in a free market is borne by the public. Thus, bailouts transfer (often taxpayer) money to predominantly wealthy
institutions and investors. Ultimately, bailouts tend to further
concentrate the wealth.

To be fair, it must be said that most bank bailouts don't use
taxpayer money. For example, the $4 billion used in 1984 to
bail out Continental Illinois Bank and the $4 billion used to
bail out the Bank of New England in the early 1990s came
from the Fed, Treasury Department, and Federal Deposit Insurance Corporation (FDIC). Those entities got the money from
fees that banks are required pay into the FDIC and the Federal
Reserve to meet such emergencies. In larger bailouts, however,
taxpayer money is used, as in the massive $250 billion bailout
of savings and loan institutions from 1989 to 1992 and the
Bush administration's $700 billion bailout of a host of banks
and other financial institutions in 2008.

Most of the immediate beneficiaries of these bailouts were
depositors, not shareholders, and most depositors are probably
members of the middle class. Still, the entire system is designed
to allow risky behavior from which lending institutions can
reap great profits without having ultimate responsibility for
failure because no federal administration wants to preside over
the collapse of the nation's financial system.

Institutions deemed too big to fail reap additional gains
from the system. Because depositors and investors know that
the federal government will not allow them to fail, these unusually large banks can borrow money and attract depositors
at lower cost than smaller banks can. During normal times,
such as from 2000 to 2007, Gretchen Morgenson reports in
the *New York Times*, "the cost of funds for small institutions
averaged 0.29 percentage point more than that of banks with
$100 billion or more in assets. But from late 2008 through June

2009, when bailouts for large institutions became expected, this spread widened to an average of 0.78 percentage point."[22] This change in spread results in $34.1 billion extra profit per year to the nation's eighteen largest bank-holding companies. Because the spread usually increases anyway during a recession, the extra profit that accrues to the largest banks at taxpayer expense may be as little as $6.3 billion. But this is still a huge annual subsidy from the public treasury.

Given the public need to keep major financial institutions afloat, which justifies these bailouts, it would make sense for the government to regulate these institutions more rigidly. The government is in effect acting as an insurer of financial security, and insurance companies commonly require those it insures to act with prudence. No one complains when a private insurer requires the companies it insures to install sprinkler systems to put out fires and institute accounting practices to reveal risk.[23] However, until the great bailout of 2008, regulation of the financial sector had been on the decline since 1980 despite the need for repeated bailouts during the 1980s and 1990s.

One of the most significant regulation reductions was the repeal of the 1933 Glass-Steagall Act. That act disallowed banks that accept deposits from engaging in investment banking and brokerage activities. Its repeal in 1998 allowed banks to put depositors' money at risk in ways unheard of since the Great Depression. Paul Volcker, former chairman of the Federal Reserve, would reinstate Glass-Steagall, but his view has not prevailed in the Obama administration's deliberations about how to reform the system.[24] The Obama administration was unwilling also to require large financial institutions to break up into smaller ones so that none is too big to fail. If the new regulations contained in the administration-endorsed Dodd-Frank Wall Street Reform and Consumer Protection Act (2010) prove inadequate to prevent another collapse, as many observers believe they are,[25] taxpayers will again pay the cost of saving organizations that reaped enormous profits while taking financial risks that eventually caught up with them.

$ $ $

The federal government's seemingly deliberate failure to enforce immigration laws is another way that it helps money move from poorer to richer Americans.

Some free-market conservatives claim that our immigration laws as currently written lead inevitably to illegal immigration because the laws don't allow enough immigrants into our country to meet our economic needs. The government shouldn't be blamed for failure to enforce laws that really can't be enforced because they run afoul of economic logic. This is the view of Frank Sharry, executive director of the National Immigration Forum. He claims that the United States'

labor market demands an estimated 500,000 full-time low-skilled service jobs a year. . . . More than half the new jobs created in the American economy require hard work, not multiple diplomas. . . . Young native-born workers are smaller in number, better educated than ever, and more interested in office work than in manual labor. Consequently, much of the nation's demand for housekeepers, childcare workers, landscapers, protein processors, busboys, cooks, janitors, dry wallers, and construction workers is met by a steady flow of some 500,000 undocumented migrants who enter and settle in America each year.[26]

From this view, immigration is needed for economic growth. We have illegal immigration because current quotas don't allow enough legal immigrants to enter our workforce to do jobs that native-born Americans are unwilling to take.

Against this view are statistics and common sense. The statistics, according to Mark Krikorian, executive director of the Center for Immigration Studies, belie the claim that illegal immigration responds to the need for more workers as the economy grows. He writes,

If we examine the four years before and after 2000, we see that the first period, 1996–2000, was a time of dramatic job growth and rapid expansion, while 2000–2004 saw slower economic growth and weaker labor demand. Immigrant unemployment grew significantly during that period. . . . And yet immigration actually increased slightly, from 5.5 million arrivals [both legal and illegal] during the first period and 6.1 million new immigrants during the second.[27]

Common sense tells us that Americans will take any job if the pay is high enough. Illegal immigrants do dry walling, construction, cooking, childcare, and landscaping, all pursuits that many Americans engage in simply for pleasure. Ordinary Americans often garden, build additions on their houses, have children that they care for, and cook for themselves and others without any pay at all. Few people, by contrast, floss their teeth simply for fun. In fact, it's difficult to get people to floss their teeth at all even though flossing has health benefits. Yet, there's no shortage of people willing to take jobs as dental hygienists and spend days on end flossing other people's teeth. Why do enough people apply for distasteful work while there's a shortage of people to do the kind of work that many Americans like so much that they do it in their spare time? Common sense tells us it's the money.

We have plenty of applicants to do an inherently distasteful job but too few applicants for work that can be personally pleasurable because the one pays much more than the other, and when people are trying to make a living they usually go for what earns them a living wage. Given a decent wage, there will be no shortage of Americans willing to cook, build, landscape, and take care of children. Nor will there be a shortage of house cleaners, busboys, or protein processors. In fact, a study by Steven Camarota of the Center for Immigration Studies compared the increased availability of foreign-born workers to the increasing unemployment of native-born Americans who could take the same jobs. Between 2000 and 2005 the immigrant population with only a high school diploma or less increased by 1.5 million, whereas unemployment among Americans with similar credentials increased by 3.2 million.[28] We have the workers.

The big difference is pay. Although the matter is debated, the weight of evidence supports the view that the extra number of immigrants represented by illegal immigration is needed not to get work done but to drive down labor costs and thereby improve employer profits. *New York Times* columnist Nicholas Kristof cites a study to this effect: "The most careful study of this issue, done by George Borjas and Lawrence Katz and published by the National Bureau of Economic Research, found that the surge of immigration in the 1980s and 1990s lowered the wages of America's own high school dropouts by 8.2 percent."[29] Eduardo Porter gives this example in the *New York Times*:

Starting about 30 years ago, as illegal immigration began to swell, building maintenance contractors in big immigrant hubs like Los Angeles started hiring the new immigrant workers . . . to drive down labor costs. Unions for janitors fell apart as landlords shifted to cheaper nonunion contractors to clean their buildings. Wages fell and many American-born workers left the industry.

Between 1970 and 2000, the share of Hispanic immigrants among janitors in Los Angeles jumped from 10 percent to more than 60 percent. . . .

The pattern repeated itself as immigrants spread throughout the rest of the country. By 2000, Hispanic immigrants made up nearly 1 in 5 janitors in the United States. . . . Janitors' median earnings fell by 3 percent in real terms between 1983 and 2000. . . .

In New York City, janitors cleaning commercial buildings make $19 an hour. . . . The union never lost ground in the city, and it is still unusual to find illegal immigrants cleaning office buildings there.

In Southern California, by contrast, unions were decimated in the 1980s, and [now] unionized janitors earn between $8.50 and $11 an hour.[30]

Economist James Galbraith agrees that immigrants depress wages but thinks that the cycle starts not with immigrants showing up to work for less, but with employers lowering wages to a point that discourages Americans from taking the jobs. After the wages are lowered, employers find immigrants to do the work. He writes that employers drive down wages through

outsourcing, or an anti-union campaign, say, or perhaps a legislative maneuver that blocks a rise in the minimum wage and so causes its real value to fall. Now for native workers the worst jobs no longer provide adequate pay. Immigrants may *then* be recruited, directly or through the grapevine, to fill them. They will flood the regions (Los Angeles, Texas) where sweatshops flourish, while remaining scarce in union towns like Detroit. And they will come from low-wage countries like Mexico.[31]

Galbraith gives this example. After 1994, Harvard University lowered its janitorial wage from $11 an hour to $9.55. Only then did it start to hire immigrant workers. The presence of immigrants in the community can't account for the lower wages because the wage for the same work stayed high at MIT only a few miles away.[32]

Whichever way the causal arrow points—from immigrant employment to lower wages or from lower wages to immigrant employment—the federal government is implicated in the lower wages of the working poor (and the consequent higher profits of their employers) because it fails adequately to enforce laws against illegal immigration. The main reason that illegal immigrants come to the United States is to find work at higher pay than they could get in their home country. Cut off the supply of jobs available to illegal immigrants and most will decide to stay home. That's why immigration from Mexico to the United States, legal and illegal, plummeted when the recent recession in the United States made jobs scarce, according to Julia Preston in the *New York Times*. The Mexican government released data showing that even as early as August 2007 to August 2008, Mexican migration to the United States slowed as the US economy slowed. Preston writes,

Mexican and American researchers say that the current decline, which has also been manifested in a decrease in arrests along the border, is largely a result of Mexicans deciding to delay illegal crossings because of the lack of jobs in the ailing American economy.

The trend emerged clearly with the onset of the recession and, demographers say, provides new evidence that illegal immigrants from Mexico, by far the biggest source of unauthorized migration to the United States, are drawn by jobs and respond to a sinking labor market by staying away.[33]

This has long been known: a good way to discourage illegal immigrants is to deter would-be employers from giving them jobs. That's why a 1986 immigration law criminalizes employers giving jobs to illegal immigrants. But the law gives employers a big loophole. They aren't allowed *knowingly* to employ illegal immigrants. For the most part, employers can claim that they were fooled by the identification papers shown to them by prospective employees and were therefore not knowingly employing illegals. Employers were thus usually let off the hook, a dodge that a lot of bar owners probably wish was available to them when they illegally admit underage patrons. Bar owners are usually held to account by local and state authorities when they improperly assess IDs but employers are not held to the same standards by the federal government. In addition, writes Eduardo Porter,

The penalty for knowingly hiring illegal immigrants includes up to six months in jail—or up to five years in particularly egregious cases—and fines that range from $275 to $11,000 for each worker. Yet fines are typically negotiated down, and employers are almost always let off the hook. Only 46 people were convicted in 2004 for hiring illegal immigrants; the annual number has been roughly the same for the last decade.[34]

Mark Krikorian adds:

Enforcement of the ban on hiring illegal aliens . . . has been all but abandoned. We might date the abandonment from INS [Immigration and Naturalization Service] raids in Georgia during the Vidalia onion

harvest in 1998, which caused large numbers of illegal aliens . . . to
abandon the fields to avoid arrest. By the end of the week, both of the
state's senators and three congressmen had sent an outraged letter to
Washington complaining that the INS "does not understand the needs
of America's farmers," and that was the end of that.

So . . . , rather than conduct raids on individual employers, Operation Vanguard in 1998–99 sought to identify illegal workers at all
meat-packing plants in Nebraska through audits of personnel records.
The INS then asked to interview those employees who appeared to be
unauthorized—and the illegals ran off. The procedure was remarkably
successful, and was meant to be repeated every two or three months
until the plants were weaned from their dependence on illegal labor.

Local law enforcement officials were very pleased . . . , but employers and politicians vociferously criticized the very idea of enforcing the
immigration law. Gov. Mike Johanns organized a task force to oppose
the operation; in Washington, Sen. Chuck Hagel (R-Neb.) pressured
the Justice Department to stop. They succeeded, the operation was
ended, and the senior INS official who had thought it up in the first
place was forced into early retirement.[35]

Most employers of illegal workers, even if only to create the
appearance of not knowing that the workers are illegal, collect Social Security numbers from all of their employees; they
and their employees thus pay Social Security taxes. The Social
Security Administration (SSA), trying to make sure that contributions are attributed to the proper accounts, runs checks
to make sure that the name of the worker matches the social
security number on file. Mismatches can occur due to name
change, marriage, divorce, misspelling, and typographical error,
as well as to illegal workers using Social Security numbers that
are either fake or that belong to someone else of a different
name. Without any attempt to catch illegal workers, Krikorian
writes, the SSA

in 2002 sent out almost a million "no-match" letters to employers. . . .
Most of the problem was caused by illegal aliens lying to their employers, and thousands of illegals quit or were fired when they were found
out. The effort was so successful at denying work to illegals that business and immigrant-rights groups organized to stop it and won a 90
percent reduction in the number of letters to be sent out.[36]

If the government really wanted to curtail illegal immigration, it could further develop and employ the system of catching illegal workers and their employers by matching Social Security numbers to names and visiting all those without a proper match. Failure to do this is just another way that the government favors the relatively wealthy (employers) over the relatively poor (the undereducated Americans whom immigrants largely displace).[37]

$ $ $

We saw in chapters 4 and 5 that the free market system as it actually exists in the United States often gives rewards disproportionate to contributions. Chapter 4 shows how, on the whole, rich people get more rewards than they deserve, and chapter 5 shows that working people—the working poor and those in the middle of the income spectrum—tend to receive less than they deserve. This chapter shows that the federal government often augments rather than ameliorates such injustice. The government protects some industries from foreign competition, thus hurting consumers; it extends monopoly patents, thus hurting consumers; it gives away public property to profit-making enterprises without demanding a market price, thus hurting taxpayers; it bails out financial institutions, thus hurting taxpayers; and it fails to enforce immigration laws, thus hurting the working poor by lowering their wages as they compete for jobs with illegal immigrants.

These government misdeeds suggest to free-market conservatives that if the government were smaller and less involved in the economy the free market would work better, which would help everyone (except for those who reap unjust rewards through government favors). However, these free-market enthusiasts fail to consider the benefits we all reap today as a result of past progressive government policies, which included investments in science, technology, education, and physical infrastructure. Had such free-market conservative advice been followed in the past, that is, had we not had a post–World War II Progressive Era, there would have been no GI Bill and we wouldn't have a workforce educated enough for today's jobs. We wouldn't have the interstate highway system that facilitates free-market commerce across our nation. We wouldn't have the agricultural abundance that resulted from government investments in agricultural research and government agricultural extension programs, which conveyed the fruits of that research to farmers. We wouldn't have computers; we wouldn't have the Internet. Imagine how impoverished relative to today we would be without these and myriad other government interventions in the free market, many of which took place during the postwar Progressive Era.

The lesson to be drawn from mistaken or corrupt government involvement in the economy is not less involvement but better involvement, and a new progressive agenda that builds the country's human and physical infrastructure is an example of better involvement. It is the counterpart for today of the postwar progressivism that was at the center of American politics during "the greatest generation." The progressive taxation needed to pay for these government programs is justified because it returns to ordinary Americans what wealthy people have unjustly received through government favors. In addition, drawing attention to corporate welfare can move progressive taxation and the entire progressive agenda from the periphery to the center of American political thought.

7

Stealing from Our Common Heritage

I often get e-mails from my conservative friends to the effect that government programs for the poor are unjustified because working people shouldn't have to subsidize those who don't work. They often quote Margaret Thatcher, who championed the importance of people working for a living. She said, for example, "Pennies do not come from heaven. They have to be earned here on earth." She was not opposed to charity but maintained that people need money before they can be charitable. "No one would remember the Good Samaritan if he'd only had good intentions; he had money as well."[1] It was on this basis that she criticized socialism, which she saw as giving to some people the money that other people had earned. "Socialist governments traditionally do make a mess. They always run out of other people's money."[2]

I like to surprise these friends by agreeing completely that, gifts and charity aside, people should pay or work for the benefits they receive. I think that this is the mainstream view and that policies based on this view should not be marginalized; they should be at the center of our political dialog.

I am not alone among progressives in believing that, gifts and charity aside, people should pay or work for the benefits they receive. Political economists Gar Alperovitz and Lew Daly write, "Nothing is more deeply held among ordinary people than the idea that a person is entitled to what he creates or his efforts produce." And people who don't work to produce anything of value don't deserve any reward. They add, "In the workplace, a person who shirks all day at his job will not be tolerated for long. His fellow employees, forced to work more to make up for his shirking, will say that he is 'not earning his keep.' The employer simply says 'I am not paying you for nothing.'"[3]

A realistic understanding of the implications of this view, however, may startle my conservative friends, because among those implications is justification of steeply progressive income taxes for extremely wealthy households.

Alperovitz and Daly argue that rich people should be subject to progressive taxation because society, rather than any individual, generates most of the progress that creates extraordinary wealth. If society is primarily responsible for productivity-improving innovations that enrich entrepreneurs, society should reap the greatest rewards. When individuals use what society has produced over generations and centuries primarily to enrich themselves and their families, they are appropriating to themselves what belongs to society in general. They are reaping benefits for which they have neither paid nor worked and should therefore have to forfeit much of their income and wealth through progressive taxation.

Consider, for example, society's large role in the development of the light bulb. Thomas Edison's invention depended in part on the British desire in the 1820s to collect more taxes from their Irish subjects. The British believed that if they surveyed the Emerald Isle more accurately and completely, their tax assessments could be more thorough. However, their survey method using triangulation from hilltop to hilltop was ineffective when the rainy and misty Irish weather made it difficult for surveyors to see from one hilltop to the next. The surveyors needed a more powerful light that could penetrate the soupy atmosphere.[4]

In 1825, Thomas Drummond invented limelight to solve this problem. Oxygen was pumped through a nozzle that had been soaked in alcohol and then set on fire. The alcohol burned fiercely amid the oxygen and heated a ball of lime that was less than an inch in diameter. When heated the lime gave off a brilliant white light that could be directed by a parabolic mirror placed behind the flame. Drummond claimed that his new light was eighty-three times as bright as the light of a gas flame.[5]

Repeated attempts to use limelight in lighthouses were frustrated by great expense and by leaks in the gas lines needed to provide the flame that heated the lime.[6] Limelight, which had its greatest successes in theaters, advanced civilization toward the incandescent light bulb by showing that more light can be produced from the glow of a substance heated by a flame than from the glow of the flame itself.

The next step was to use electricity instead of a flame to heat the substance that glows. In 1849, Belgian physicist Floris Nollet enlarged and improved the method of generating electricity, first discovered by Michael Faraday by 1831, of rotating a metal disc between the poles of a horseshoe magnet. After Nollet's death, Englishman Frederick Holmes, who had worked with Nollet, adapted this increased source of electricity to make an arc light. Electricity was sent along carbon rods that were placed so that they nearly touched. When the electricity jumped from one carbon rod to the next, it created a spark that made the rods incandescent.[7]

Additional electricity was made available for arc lights in 1870 when French engineer Zenobie Gramme, also a former associate of Nollet's, adapted the ideas of the Danish inventor Søren Hjorth to produce much more electricity through a positive feedback loop. Gramme knew that an iron bar would become magnetized when an electric current was passed through a wire that was wrapped around it. When this magnetized bar is turned within the electrical field, it produces electricity (just as a metal disc produces electricity when it's rotated between the poles of a horseshoe magnet). If the additional electricity is then fed into the wire that's wrapped around the metal bar, the magnetism increases, which increases the electricity that results from rotating the iron bar, which increases the electricity in the wire, which further increases the magnetism in the bar, and so on. This device came to be known as a dynamo. It supplied the first source of really continuous electricity and made the arc light a success.[8]

One limitation of the arc light, however, was that the carbon tended to burn away. The solution, it was generally thought, was to place the carbon, or whatever other substance would serve as a filament by glowing when electricity was passed through it, in a vacuum where it couldn't burn. But no one had produced a vacuum complete enough for this purpose.[9]

In 1878, Thomas Edison joined the search for filaments that wouldn't burn up. He tried metal filaments, such as platinum, which were either too expensive or which burned out quickly. He returned to carbon with carbonized paper, which he produced by heating strips of paper in a kiln along with carbon. But those filaments burned out, too. Then he acquired a better pump, recently produced by Hermann Sprengel in Germany, which allowed him to create an almost perfect vacuum in glass bulbs.[10]

Working in his Menlo Park, New Jersey, laboratory, where he had his own glass-blowing shed to make the bulbs, Edison tried thousands of different filaments, including carbonized versions of all the plants he could think of, such as bay wood, boxwood, hickory, cedar, flax, and bamboo. He had biologists send him samples of wood from around the world. In his own words, "Before I got through, I tested no fewer than 6,000 vegetable growths, and ransacked the world for the most suitable filament material."[11] By the end of 1880, he had developed a carbonized cotton thread into a filament that lasted for 1,500 hours, and he began marketing the invention.

The company that Edison formed in the United States, Edison General Electric Company, eventually merged in 1892 with Thomason-Houston Electric Company to become General Electric. It's the only company currently on the Dow Jones Industrial Index that was on the original Dow Jones Index when it was formed in 1896.[12]

Edison became wealthy as a result of his hard work, and he deserved great rewards for his inventive genius that resulted in more productive workers and more satisfied consumers. However, as the story of the invention of the light bulb indicates, he doesn't deserve all of the credit because he didn't do all of the work. The work of many people of his own and of previous generations was necessary to make the light bulb possible. Edison didn't invent glass or the glass blowing that he used in his work. Edison didn't discover electricity; Otto von Guericke produced the first generator of static electricity in 1660. Robert Boyle experimented with electric transmission in a vacuum. Benjamin Franklin showed that lightning was a form of electricity. Henry Cavendish experimented with electric conductivity. Michael Faraday developed the electric motor, electric generator, and electric transformer in the 1830s. Other pioneers of electricity on whom Edison's work depended included Floris Nollet, Zenobie Gramm, and Søren Hjorth. Thomas Drummond's limelight brought to fruition the idea of generating light by heating a substance to incandescence, and Hermann Sprengel invented the pump needed to create a vacuum powerful enough to keep Edison's filament from burning out too quickly.

Developments after Edison invented the light bulb also added to the invention's value. In 1888 Nikola Tesla invented a generator of alternating current, which is more efficient than direct current. George Westinghouse got a contract to generate electricity at Niagara. Without the work of such people, we wouldn't have electricity as we now know it, and all of the inventions and processes that use electricity, including Edison's light bulb, but also including telephones, computers, and the entire array of electric appliances from refrigerators to blenders to washing machines wouldn't be possible or commercially viable.[13]

When current inventors and entrepreneurs improve or market these products to make life more pleasant for consumers, they deserve rewards for their work, but they don't deserve to be rewarded for all the work of their predecessors that made their work possible. The work of predecessors belongs to society in general, because it's part of society's cultural and technological legacy. So the rewards from the use of this work should accrue to society in general. A convenient way for society to receive its just compensation is for successful entrepreneurs to pay progressive taxes.

Society's extensive role in technological development is the near-universal norm. For example, if we didn't have electricity in abundance, we wouldn't have aluminum. This light metal is referred to in ancient documents and was identified and named in 1808 by Sir Humphry Davy. In 1821, Pierre Berthier discovered aluminum-rich bauxite in France, but the metal cost more than gold so there was no commercial use for it until a cheap method was available for extracting aluminum from bauxite. Friedrich Wohler started experimenting with methods of refining aluminum in 1827. These experiments were known to one of Wohler's students, Frank F. Jewett, who communicated that information to Martin Hall who, simultaneously with Paul L.

T. Heroult, discovered in 1886 how to use electricity to refine aluminum. Dissolve aluminum oxide in molten cryolite and then put a current of electricity through it; molten aluminum settles to the bottom. This is still the basis of all aluminum smelting. No electricity; no aluminum.[14]

Without aluminum there would be no commercial air travel as we know it. It was the first metal that was light enough and could be produced cost effectively to be used in commercial airplanes. Many additional discoveries were also necessary for air travel, of course. There's the whole history of scientific theories and discoveries behind the invention of the internal combustion engine. There's the history of experiments with gliders, as well as the history of theories of air and of vacuums. There's the development of special kinds of aluminum, such as heat-treated aluminum, which was used in the first all-metal air ships, including dirigibles such as the Hindenburg.[15]

Computer development required a lot more than just electricity. Computers as we know them today depend on solid-state circuitry, which in turn depends on knowledge of semiconductors. This goes back at least to the discovery of silicon by the Swede Jacob Berzelius in 1824. Michael Faraday showed in 1833 how conductivity varies with temperature. In 1879, Charles Hall showed that an additional electric force is produced when a wire containing electricity passes through a magnetic field, which inspired Julius Lilienfield, who was interested in using semiconductors for sound amplification, to gain patents for a layered semiconductor structure that may be considered the first solid-state circuitry. The software development by Bill Gates Jr. depended on all this history of electricity and semiconductors, not to mention the history of binary mathematics.[16]

Scientists have been able to gain inspiration and insight from predecessors and contemporaries owing to the development of communication technologies. First there was the invention of writing and then of alphabetical writing, which made literacy potentially available to the masses. The invention of movable type and the printing press increased greatly the realistic possibility of disseminating knowledge widely. The more recent inventions of telephones, computers, and the Internet made possible communication that is faster and cheaper. Without these techniques to serve first as preservers and then as "transmission belts" of knowledge, scientists and inventors would be too intellectually isolated from one another to benefit from each other's experiences and insights. The pace of discovery and development that enriches our lives would be much slower.[17]

Entrepreneurs inherit these developments as part of society's general culture. We saw, for example, how Jack Welch increased shareholder value at General Electric tremendously and earned hundreds of millions of dollars in the process. But consider this rhetorical question posed by political scientist Robert Dahl: "Who has made a larger contribution to the operation of General Electric—its chief executives or Albert Einstein or Michael Faraday or Isaac Newton?" And Newton said, "If I have seen further it is by standing on the shoulders of giants."[18] Warren Buffett, one of the wealthiest people in the world, expressed a similar sentiment when he said in 2004, "society is responsible for a very significant percentage of what I've earned."[19] Accordingly, in 2011, anticipating congressional efforts to reduce federal budget deficits, he proposed higher taxes on what he called "the mega-rich."[20]

$ $ $

Unless much of the riches of wealthy entrepreneurs and executives are taxed heavily and returned to the public treasury, the productive efforts of the government and the contributions of its taxpayers are being ignored. This is because much of the infrastructure and technologies that make workers so productive and some entrepreneurs so wealthy today stems from government support.

As early in American history as 1798 the federal government was responsible for initiating the machine-tool assembly line by ordering muskets from Eli Whitney. The fledgling United States didn't have as many skilled craftsmen as did the Europeans to make handcrafted, high-quality machines and implements, including muskets. To be militarily competitive, Americans needed a way to make implements of war with relatively few master craftsmen. The solution was interchangeable parts produced en mass, parts that craftsmen of average ability could assemble. Although Whitney delivered only five hundred muskets (a year late), his contract with the government started the machine-tool manufacturing industry and led to the eventual predominance of the United States in mass production with interchangeable parts, which is the backbone of modern industry.[21]

The Hatch Act of 1887 gave federal money for the establishment of agricultural experimentation stations where research was done to increase agricultural productivity. Such government research was central to the development of improved fertilizers, pesticides, and hybrid varieties of grains, especially corn. In 1914 the federal government passed the Smith-Lever Act, which funded cooperative extension services in each state to transmit the fruits of new agricultural knowledge to ordinary farmers. As a result, by the turn of this century, 95 percent of American corn was a hybrid variety and yields per acre were up from 25 bushels in 1930 to 130 bushels in 2000. Also, the Department of Agriculture's Agricultural Research Service developed more than 70 percent of the varieties of citrus grown in the United States.[22] Wealthy owners of citrus groves, of grain-producing farms, and of feeding facilities where corn is fed to cattle, hogs, and chickens all owe their riches in part to far-sighted government-funded research and outreach.

The aviation industry was developed by government funding as well. Primarily for reasons of national defense, the federal government established the National Advisory Committee on Aeronautics in 1915 to "investigate the scientific problems involved in flight and to give advice to the military air services." They constructed and used wind tunnels and found out how to reduce engine drag by nearly 75 percent. They developed retractable landing gear. During World War II the government funded General Electric's development of jet engines.[23]

The National Science Foundation contributed $90 million that resulted in development of commercially viable magnetic resonance imaging technologies. The Office of Naval Research funded studies that resulted in the invention of lasers, which are used in today's CDs, DVDs, data storage systems, precision metal cutting, and surgical procedures. We saw in chapters 4 and 6 that most of the blockbuster drugs that earn billions for pharmaceutical companies had been developed at public expense. Alperovitz and Daly give this additional example, Taxol:

The General Accounting Office estimates that the National Institutes of Health spent a total of $484 million on the development of this drug between 1977 and 2002. Bristol-Myers Squibb—the firm that obtained the patent and marketing rights—achieved world-wide sales of $9 billion between 1993 and 2002, but the government received only $35 million in royalties from these earnings. . . . The story is similar for . . . Prozac (for depression), Xalatan (for glaucoma), and most of the leading HIV and AIDS drugs.[24]

The Internet was also developed at public expense, beginning with the Defense Department's Advanced Research Projects Agency (ARPA) in the 1960s. By 1970 they had developed ARPANET, a system that facilitated the free flow of information among academics and others who were working on problems related in some way to national security. The thought behind the project, in the words of Joseph Licklider, the first director of ARPA's computer offices, was that "when minds interact, new ideas emerge."[25] In the 1950s and 1960s, most computer-related research and development (R&D) came from the federal government.[26]

Government funding also has launched the careers of most researchers in many fields, including those who eventually work in the private sector, according to a study done in 1995: "In electronics 85 percent of researchers surveyed did government-funded work prior to getting private funding. In chemicals, the rate was 86 percent, and in information processing it was 62 percent."[27] And government funding is still prominent in new fields such as nanotechnology. In 2003 the government committed itself to spending $3.7 billion in this area over four years.[28]

There's really no alternative in our market-oriented economy to the government taking the lead in basic R&D whose benefits are too diffuse and its payoffs are too uncertain to justify private investment. Research in a space program can result in materials to make better running shoes. ARPANET, which was designed originally to facilitate scientific research, was the basis for the Internet, which has turned out to be a platform for selling those running shoes. When people can't predict the commercial applications of research, it makes no sense for commercial enterprises in the free market to provide funding. In addition, the time frames for commercial applications of the research are often impossible to determine or they are simply too long. An expensive project that won't make money for at least five or ten years is not within the horizon of possibility for firms whose management and directors depend on shareholder reactions to quarterly reports.

So we should expect taxpayer money to fund basic and even not-so-basic research in the future as it has in the past. According to Alperovitz and Daly, in 2004 federal government funding accounted for nearly two thirds of all basic research done in the United States. Federal obligations for . . . R&D and R&D plant and equipment topped $110 billion in 2005; included in this was more than $26 billion for basic research. Over the last decade and a half the federal government allocated more than $1.3 trillion to R&D and related R&D plant and equipment, and nearly $290 billion to basic research.[29]

Many new technologies, new industries, new products, new jobs, new fortunes, and improved efficiencies will depend on public investment in the future as they have in the past. On the principle that people should pay or work for what they receive, it would seem that those who benefit most from these government efforts—the captains of the new industries and their investors—should pay much more than others into public coffers because they have received so much more than others from these public expenditures.

$ $ $

Free-market conservatives might reply that at each stage of scientific, technological, or commercial development the genius of some great individual is essential, regardless of how far back the chain of contributing individuals goes and regardless of how much public money was used. Each of these geniuses should be rewarded accordingly as a great benefactor of humanity. Because there's little we can do for geniuses of the past, we should concentrate on rewarding the extraordinarily productive individuals alive today. These movers and shakers don't owe anything to society; society owes its comfortable affluence to them.

This reply ignores the fact that when the culture has developed to a certain stage, the next step in the development of science, technology, design, or commerce almost never requires someone with *unique* genius. If unique genius were required, we wouldn't have so many discoveries that are simultaneous.

Here are some examples: Sir Isaac Newton and Gottfried Wilhelm von Leibniz discovered calculus in such temporal proximity that it's difficult to know who did it first. Charles Darwin published his theory of natural selection in great haste when he learned that Alfred Russell Wallace had come up with essentially the same idea. (To his enduring credit as a human being, Darwin always referred to the theory as "Mr. Wallace's and my theory" even though Darwin certainly was the first to formulate the idea in his mind and notebooks.) Francis Crick and James Watson published their double-helix model of DNA in haste because they were sure someone else, perhaps Linus Pauling, was about to discover it independently. The X-ray crystallographic photography of Maurice Wilkins and Rosalind Franklin and Pauling's already-published model of the alpha helix structure of some proteins made the discovery of the double helix imminent, even before the discoverer's identity was certain.[30]

Patent disputes are another indication of simultaneous discovery. Alexander Graham Bell and Elisha Gray filed patent applications on devices to transmit vocal sounds telegraphically on the same day but Bell was first. However, his idea didn't really work and Gray's did, so Bell got all the credit only because he was allowed to revise his patents. Ten years earlier immigrant Italian-American Antonio Meucci tried to get a patent on a device that would have worked but he didn't have the $10 necessary to secure his patent.[31] Thomas Edison was sued successfully in England for infringing on the light bulb patent that Joseph Wilson Swan had been issued in 1878, the year that Edison first started working on the light bulb problem. As part of the suit's settlement, Edison was required to make Swan a partner in his British electric works.[32]

Writing in the early 1920s, William Fielding Ogburn and Dorothy Thomas noted that besides the calculus, simultaneous discoveries in mathematics include, in Alperovitz and Daly's words, "the law of inverse squares, logarithms, the decimal point, the principle of least squares, the method of indivisibles, and non-Euclidian geometry (a cornerstone of Einstein's general theory of relativity.)"[33] In addition,

many advances in chemistry have also occurred simultaneously, including the law of gases; the discovery of oxygen, boron, and other elements; the periodic law itself; molecular theory; and the hypothesis of the arrangement of atoms in space. . . . Key developments in electrification such as the Leyden jar (the ancestor of today's capacitors), incandescent electric light, the induction coil, the self-exciting dynamo, electric motors, and electric trains were simultaneously discovered or invented, as were many other important instruments and devices, including the pendulum clock, telescope, thermometer, microscope, telegraph, typewriter, sewing machine, phonograph, [and] microphone.[34]

The germ theory of disease, anesthetics, the theory of color, molecular theory, and the law of the conservation of energy can be added to the list. Another example is the very theory we're discussing, the theory of simultaneous discovery. It was itself discovered independently by Auguste Comte, Thomas Macaulay, Francis Galton, Friedrich Engels, and Albert Einstein.[35]

In short, society isn't beholden to unique individuals without whom we'd lack modern conveniences. Just about all discoveries combine genius with social preparation, and there's always enough genius in society to turn social preparation into discovery. Bill Gates did a great job with Microsoft but the essential insights were there for anyone of genius, and in fact Gary Kildall did invent a similar system and is thought by some scholars to be the primary inventor of software for personal computing. Alperovitz and Daly write,

Whether it was Gates or Kildall or Tim Paterson (among other competitors) who "won the race" for marketable PC operating software in the 1980s, it is clear that *this technology would have emerged anyway, in roughly the same time frame, because the available knowledge and the existing computer culture made it feasible and the growing market demand made it profitable.*[36]

So we don't owe to Bill Gates alone that books like the one I'm writing can be composed on PCs. Social, technological, and commercial developments up to that time determined that authors would soon have PCs at their disposal.

Still, it might be said, even if the development is inevitable, and many people had the chance to take the next step and complete the process, the person who actually does take that next step should be rewarded handsomely. The fact is that it was Bill Gates, not someone else, who established a contract with IBM to supply software for personal computers.

Fair enough. Gates deserves a lot of credit and has justly reaped great rewards. But he doesn't deserve *all* the credit, nor should he keep *all* the rewards. Much of the credit belongs to scientists, inventors, and entrepreneurs going back centuries who set the stage for Gates's achievement. On the principle that people should pay or work for what they receive, Gates should compensate society for the productive efforts of these forebearers who were themselves products of a society that encouraged inventiveness. Gates should also compensate the government and its other taxpayers for their investments in R&D and their development of infrastructure that underpin the success of personal computing. To his credit, Gates is in fact returning the vast majority of his wealth to society through the Bill & Melinda Gates Foundation, to which Warren Buffett is also a major contributor. In 2010, thirty-eight other billionaires joined Gates and Buffett to pledge more than half of their wealth to charity.[37]

$ $ $

But how much of an entrepreneur's wealth should go to the government and through the government to society in general?

Nobel Prize–winning economist Robert Solow calculated in the 1950s that between 1909 and 1949 about 88 percent of increased worker productivity was due to general "technological change," not to capital investment for which entrepreneurs and investors can take credit.[38] (This discovery was the basis for Solow receiving the Nobel Prize in economics.) Studying the period from 1929 to 1966, economists Moses Abramovitz and Paul David calculated the general social input responsible for increased productivity at 84 percent. John Kendrick put the social input at 85 percent for increased productivity between 1929 and 1948 and at 70 percent for increased productivity between 1948 and 1969. Edward Denison of the Brookings Institution developed a method of "growth accounting" that puts the figure at 72 percent for the period 1929 to 1982.[39] From these figures it seems safe to say that according to highly regarded, mainstream economists, at least 70 percent of productivity increases in the past, and therefore of current productivity that augments affluence in our society, are attributable to society's general improvements in technology and education, not to innovations and investments for which individual entrepreneurs, investors, or corporations can take credit.

These findings, combined with the principle that, gifts and charity aside, people should pay or work for the benefits they receive, suggest that wealthy entrepreneurs and rich investors owe a larger percentage of their income and wealth to the public than do members of the middle class. Taxes should be steeply progressive. Here's the reasoning.

The 70 percent of current productivity that results from general improvements in technology and education belong to everyone equally *as an inheritance (or gift from the past)*. So, in the $15 trillion US economy, over $10 trillion belongs to society's workers in general, the rest to individuals for the particular work that they do. Because there are about 120 million households in the country, the yearly income per household attributable to general improvements in technology and education (which belongs to everyone equally) is over $83,000.[40] Yet the median (gross) household income in the United States is under $50,000.[41] Of this amount, about 30 percent ($15,000) is attributable to individual productivity rather than to productivity that results from general social evolution. So, of the $50,000 median income, the household is, on average, receiving only about $35,000 of the $83,000 it should get from income gains that belong equally to everyone in society. This means that more than half of the households with the equivalent of at least one full-time worker don't receive even half of their share of income that stems from improvements in technology and education attributable to society in general.

Now consider households with (gross) incomes of $150,000 a year. These are also usually considered middle class even though they are well within the top 10 percent of households by income. Thirty percent ($45,000) of this income can be attributed to individual efforts and 70 percent ($105,000) to productivity gains that belong to society in general. These households clearly owe society some taxes for the part of their income that comes from social input, as they are receiving more than the $83,000 that is their fair share of wealth attributable to social evolution. Their taxes should be a much larger percentage of their income than the taxes of people at the median and below because the poorer households don't even get half their share of social wealth in their gross income, whereas these $150,000-per-year households get more than their share. By the same reasoning, the richest one-hundredth of 1 percent of households (earning millions of dollars per year) should pay a much larger percentage of their gross income in taxes because the disproportion between what they receive of social wealth (millions of dollars) and what is theirs if social wealth were shared equally ($83,000) is much greater. Whereas a 28 percent marginal tax rate may be fair for households with gross earnings of $150,000 per year (the rate typically paid by that group during the Clinton administration), a rate closer to 65 or 70 percent seems reasonable, on this reasoning, for the richest households. Households between these two should have marginal rates between 28 and 65 or 70 percent, whereas households with less than $150,000 gross income should have rates less than 28 percent.

The exact tax rates for particular incomes aren't as important here as the conclusion that *steeply progressive taxation is needed for social justice.*[42] Regressive and flat taxes are unjust because they fail to return to the public the percentage of income that wealthy households receive as a result of public expenditures and of social, cultural, and economic evolution whose fruits rightfully belong equally to everyone in society.

$ $ $

The steeply progressive taxation justified by this reasoning could raise a great deal of revenue. Simply abandoning the Bush-era tax decreases, which are set to expire at the end of 2012, would raise an additional $3 trillion dollars over a ten-year period, according to the *Washington Post.*[43] Increasing by merely one-half the federal income taxes paid by the top 1 percent of households over the levels that prevailed during the Clinton years would raise an additional $2 trillion during the coming decade.[44]

The federal government could get some additional trillions over the next ten years by closing loopholes that enable some wealthy corporations to avoid paying taxes altogether. In 2010, for example, Verizon earned $11.9 billion in pretax United States profits, but rather than pay taxes, the company actually received a $705 million refund from the federal government.[45]

General Electric earned $14.2 billion in 2010, $5.1 billion from its operations in the United States, and rather than pay taxes, received a whopping $3.2 billion in tax benefits.[46] For many such companies, off-shore tax havens, which are perfectly legal under current law, deprive the federal treasury of billions of dollars every year.

Additional federal earnings could be realized by doubling the tax rate on capital gains from 15 percent to 30 percent. Warren Buffett doesn't think that such an increase would discourage investors.[47] What is more, according to figures cited by Peter Orszag, former director of the White House Office of Management and Budget, Social Security could be financed indefinitely without any reductions in benefits simply by making the payroll tax a flat tax.[48] Currently, the tax applies only to income below $106,800.[49] Making it a flat tax would have it apply to income above this level as well.

The additional revenue generated by these and other changes in our tax laws could and should be used to improve the lives of people in society (and, to a lesser extent, of people around the world) who are not receiving their fair share of the productivity increases made possible by government expenditures and by our common cultural heritage. Most benefits should be retained domestically because our country is a unit of sharing within which productivity-enhancing public investments were made. In addition, Americans were responsible for many of the social, technological, and cultural developments that enhance American productivity and enrich our entrepreneurs. However, some developments that improve productivity originated overseas. So, the American public owes something to the rest of the world, which justifies using some of the extra tax revenues collected with steeply progressive taxation for foreign aid.

But the bulk of that extra tax revenue should be used to improve the lives of working Americans who don't currently get their fair share of our common heritage. We've seen that poor Americans are shortchanged most; they receive less than others of the approximately $83,000 that would be theirs if common social wealth were shared equally. But this applies only to working Americans. Accumulated social wealth improves *worker productivity*, which implies that working is a prerequisite (among those capable of work) to qualify for the benefits of affluence that accumulated social wealth makes possible. Another consideration is this: we don't want to discourage productivity and invite personal and cultural degeneration by giving healthy adults money for doing nothing. We need to maintain the standard that adults who are able to work but who remain idle by choice do not get taxpayer help. Such people, those who are unproductive simply because they are lazy, should be allowed to suffer whatever poverty may result. And when these people take jobs and display unproductive laziness on the job, we won't condemn employers who fire them.

However, as we have seen in earlier chapters, there are millions upon millions of workers in the United States who work full time or average more than forty hours per week by holding down two or more part-time jobs who don't receive a living wage. The increase of the minimum wage in 2009 to $7.25 an hour provides a yearly income for people who work forty hours per week fifty weeks of the year of just $14,500 before deductions for payroll and other taxes. This is clearly not a living wage.

Jack Newfield, senior fellow at the Nation Institute, reported in 2003 on low-income workers in New York City:

Some 56 percent . . . have no health insurance for their families, 52 percent have no pension or 401(k) and 37 percent of these workers fell behind in rent payments during the past year, 18 percent had their utilities shut off and 14 percent had to postpone necessary medical treatment. This low-wage world includes busboys, waitresses, janitors, food-service workers, store clerks, security guards, porters, maids, home health aides, day laborers and deliverymen.[50]

These people, more than six hundred thousand of them in New York City at the time, are not deadbeats. "Six out of ten have a high school diploma; and more than one in ten is a college graduate. . . . They are not teenagers working part-time jobs or subsidized members of middle-income households. More than 90 percent of those trapped in low-wage jobs are adults. More than 75 percent are now working full-time. They are not substance abusers, alcoholics or the mentally ill."[51]

Writing in the mid-1990s about households with yearly incomes of $25,000 or less, political scientist Andrew Hacker notes that because their elementary and high schools are so poor, only one in ten of the children go to college. The children become discouraged early on and recognize that the American Dream is not meant for them. "And from this realization results much of the behavior that the rest of society deplores."[52]

In most parts of the United States today, a family with one or two children needs at least $37,000 a year to make ends meet, and in some areas, where real estate prices and rental costs remain above average, the figure is higher. I reach this number by adjusting for inflation the results of studies done in 1995. Two polls in 1995, one by Roper-Starch and another by Gallup, found that most respondents thought that $25,000 a year was the bare minimum for a family of three.[53] Increase this for inflation between 1995 and 2011 and the figure is $37,000 a year.[54]

You can confirm this figure for yourself by just working out your own budget for your own family, keeping your expenses at or below a gross yearly income for the family of $37,000, from which you must deduct payroll and other taxes. If your employer supplies health insurance, deduct the employee's portion and remember the copayments when you need health care. Deduct also whatever you think you owe each month for car payments, car insurance, health insurance, rent or mortgage, and so forth. If you bought this book you've probably already blown the budget. In order to live within a household income of $37,000 or less, most readers of this book would have to alter their lifestyles radically. They would have to find different housing and drive different cars. At a yearly income much less than $37,000 for a family of three you might find that, like many working poor people who can't afford rent, you have no choice but to move in with relatives or be homeless.

Currently, as we saw in the case of Walmart, society has a host of programs to subsidize low-wage workers and, indirectly, the businesses that pay them less than a living wage. These programs enable the working poor to scrape by, supplementing wages with food stamps and section 8 housing assistance, providing health care through Medicaid, and much more. Without such subsidies we would have many times the current number of people living in public parks or in cardboard boxes under highways; of children with no schooling because they have no address and inadequate clothing to attend school; and of children damaged permanently by inadequate nutrition, many dying before the age of five as is common in some third world countries.

It's important to realize that programs for the working poor subsidize businesses as much as employees because without these programs minimum-wage workers wouldn't be available. People who live in parks or in cardboard boxes under bridges are too preoccupied with staying warm, keeping out of the rain, and getting food for themselves and their children to prepare themselves to greet customers at Walmart, stock shelves at a supermarket, or serve as maids, security guards, waitresses, busboys, or delivery people. In this sense, businesses that pay little more than the current minimum wage are not viable in a true free market. A business is viable only if it can pay wages that attract and maintain the workers it needs and businesses such as Walmart are not doing this at present.

Unfortunately, raising the minimum wage to a living wage might harm the working poor more than it helps them. If we take $37,000 a year as a minimum, and recognize that many families today, as during the 1950s, rely on a single wage earner, the minimum wage would have to be $18.50 an hour to ensure that every family with a full-time worker reaches the minimum annual income. Even economists who favor increasing the minimum wage worry that such a drastic hike would cause unemployment among the very poor people whom the minimum wage is supposed to help. Many employers who find that it makes economic sense (under present conditions) to hire workers at $8 or $10 an hour would lose money hiring the same people for $18.50 an hour because many $8- and $10-an-hour employees simply don't add $18.50 of value to the business each hour. Employers would therefore fire many employees if the minimum wage were increased to $18.50 an hour. Many of the working poor would go from low wages to no wages.

Yet the low income of the working poor deprives them of their fair share of American prosperity. Imagine yourself in this situation. You would never be able to own your own home, never be able to buy a new car, never be able to save money to send your children to college, never be able to travel internationally no matter how hard you worked because the wage scale for the work you do wouldn't provide enough money to realize these basic elements of the American Dream. If the minimum wage can't be raised to lift the working poor out of this demoralizing situation, an alternate means is necessary.

Fortunately, there is such an alternative means—the EIC. It was started as the earned income tax credit (EITC) in 1975 during the Ford administration and was considerably expanded in 1986 under Ronald Reagan, who was an enthusiastic supporter. Under the EIC, the government not only returns to low-wage workers the federal income tax that was withheld during the year, but it also adds additional money to lessen the poverty of households with low incomes. For the tax year 2010, for example, a household with a single full-time worker earning $7.25 an hour, which is $14,500 a year, would receive $3,050 if there was one dependent child in the household, and $5,036 if there were two or more dependent children.[55] Total income for a three-person household could by this means be elevated to over $19,500 a year. This is better than merely $14,500 a year, but certainly inadequate; no one can properly raise two children decently on $19,500 a year. The EIC is a great idea because it encourages people to work but it is entirely inadequate as currently funded because it fails to lift tens of millions of hard-working Americans out of poverty.

As we've seen, a decent American lifestyle requires that households with two dependent children and a single wage earner working full time at the minimum wage receive a supplement that brings household income up to at least $37,000 a year because that seems to be the minimum for an adequate family life in the United States. Thus, the EIC for a household with a $14,500 yearly income and two or more children should be at least $22,500. In households with only one dependent child the subsidy could be reduced by perhaps 20 percent, and where no dependent children are present it could be reduced by perhaps 50 percent. The exact figures aren't as important here as the principles agreed upon by Republicans and Democrats since the 1970s: (1) that people should be encouraged to work and (2) that the federal government should supplement low wages. The only novelty here is recognition that a decent life is denied to families with two or more children if household income is below about $37,000 a year.

These principles and facts imply that the federal government should grant enormous subsidies to supplement the inadequate pay of the working poor. Large as they are, however, these subsidies would not distort labor markets and cause increased unemployment because the money would be coming from the public treasury, not from employers.[56] The treasury would get the money from steeply progressive taxes on incomes and investments like those we had from World War II until the 1980s, taxes already justified by commonly accepted principles about work and rewards.

Consider how these subsidies might work. As we've seen, for households with two or more children and a yearly income of $14,500, the subsidy would be $22,500. As household income increased from $14,500, the subsidy might decrease by, say, 50 percent of increased income.[57] So, a household with $15,500 would receive a subsidy of $22,000 instead of $22,500 for a total household income of $37,500 instead of just $37,000. At this rate the subsidy would disappear when household income reached $57,500. Above that income people would start paying income taxes instead of receive money from the treasury. Again, these subsidies would be less for households with only one child and still less for households with no children.

If the subsidies are high enough, the government could save a lot of money (although not achieve net savings) by reducing a host of programs designed to help poor people, such as food and housing assistance. Such programs would still be needed for those unable to work or unable to find sufficient employment even at the minimum wage, but millions of households that now receive food and housing assistance would, given the increased EIC, no longer qualify because their household incomes would be too high.

The net cost of such a robust EIC would be paid for by the progressive taxation that rich people owe to society as a result of having appropriated more than their share of our common heritage. Other programs funded by higher taxes on the wealthy could help the middle class as well as the poor. For example, in chapter 8 we'll look at improving public education and in the Conclusion we'll discuss public investments in health care and in transportation infrastructure that can help middle-class as well as poor Americans. All such public expenditures, we'll see, ease the financial plight of most Americans and promote a robust work ethic while taking from the rich only what our commonsense moral principle requires: gifts and charity aside, people should have to pay or work for the benefits they receive. Because this principle appeals to the center of American opinion, following its implications to their logical conclusion is another way of taking back the center for a new progressive agenda.

8

The Social Contract

High in the crow's-nest of the new White Star Liner *Titanic*, Lookout Frederick Fleet peered into a dazzling night. It was calm clear and bitterly cold. There was no moon, but the cloudless sky blazed with stars. The Atlantic was like a polished plate glass; people later said they had never seen it so smooth.

This was the fifth night of the *Titanic*'s maiden voyage to New York, and it was already clear that she was not only the largest but also the most glamorous ship in the world. Even the passengers' dogs were glamorous.[1]

So begins *A Night to Remember*, Walter Lord's classic account of the sinking of the *Titanic*. At about 11:40 p.m. on Sunday, April 14, 1912, the ship's fate was sealed. The ship was going over 22 knots in an effort to reach New York in record time.

Suddenly Fleet saw something directly ahead, even darker than the darkness. At first it was small (about the size, he thought, of two tables put together), but every second it grew larger and closer. Quickly Fleet banged the crow's-nest bell three times, the warning of danger ahead. At the same time he lifted the phone and rang the bridge.

"What did you see?" asked a calm voice at the other end.

"Iceberg right ahead," replied Fleet.

"Thank you," acknowledged the voice with curiously detached courtesy. Nothing more was said.

For the next 37 seconds, Fleet . . . stood quietly . . . watching the ice draw nearer. Now they were almost on top of it, and still the ship didn't turn. The berg towered wet and glistening far above the forecastle deck. . . . Then, miraculously, the bow began to swing to port. At the last second the stem shot into the clear, and the ice glided swiftly by along the starboard side. It looked to Fleet like a very close shave.[2]

Of course, the ship hadn't actually avoided collision with ice beneath the sea; instead, she received fatal damage that helped to alter received ideas about social justice.

The White Star Line's *Titanic* was not just the largest ship to sail the seas, she also had fully half again the tonnage of the Cunard Lines' *Mauritania* and *Lusitania*, which, when completed only five years earlier, were the largest and fastest vessels to date.[3] The *Titanic*'s luxury was commensurate with her size and her first class clientele commensurate with her luxury. She carried some of the cream of American society, including John Jacob Astor, Ben Guggenheim, Martin Rothschild, Mr. and Mrs. George Widener (Philadelphia banking and street-car interests), Henry Sleeper Harper (of the publishing family), Robert W. Daniel (another Philadelphia banker), and J. Bruce Ismay (managing director of the White Star Line). These people didn't travel light. The Ryersons, for example, thought nothing of traveling with sixteen trunks. In addition:

The 190 families in First Class were attended by 23 maids, eight valets, and assorted nurses and governesses—entirely apart from hundreds of stewards and stewardesses. These personal servants had their own lounge on C Deck, so that no one need suffer the embarrassment of striking up a conversation with some handsome stranger, only to find that he was Henry Sleeper Harper's dragoman.[4]

Although Fleet, standing way up in the lookout, could feel no crash, some first class passengers could feel it. To Major Arthur Godfrey Peuchen, it felt like a heavy wave striking the ship. Lady Cosmo Duff Gordon thought it was "as though somebody had drawn a giant finger along the side of the ship," whereas Mrs. E. D. Appleton could hardly feel any jolt at all, but could hear a ripping sound "like someone tearing a long,

long strip of calico."[5] In steerage, by contrast, there was no subtlety about the crash. People berthed far below deck on the starboard side heard a tremendous noise and felt a jolt that tossed them out of bed.[6]

The distinction between first and third class became more apparent when the ship was sinking and people were being loaded onto lifeboats. In keeping with the safety requirements of the time, the *Titanic* didn't have enough lifeboat capacity to accommodate all passengers. Given her size, she was required to be able to accommodate only 962 passengers but to the White Star Lines' credit, her lifeboats could actually accommodate 1178. Even this larger figure, however, was only 52 percent of the 2207 people on the ship that night, and only 30 percent of the ship's full capacity. Choices had to be made.

The most general directive was, "Women and children first!" But this didn't necessarily mean all women and children any more than the phrase "All men are created equal" meant *all* men in 1776. When in 1908 the White Star Lines' *Republic* sank, Captain Sealby told those approaching the lifeboats, "Remember! Women and children go first; then the First Cabin, then the others!"[7] The *Titanic* had no such rule but class distinctions accepted at the time produced similar effects. The crew blocked some of the passageways between steerage and the boat deck, often by locking steel gates. At other points the gates were open, but no one was informed. Many third class passengers used their own initiative to survive, some "crawling along the crane from the well deck aft . . . , others climbing vertical ladders to escape the well deck forward."

In many cases, crew members and others actively helped to guide third class women and children up from steerage and on to lifeboats. Colonel Archibald Gracie, a West Point graduate and amateur historian, was among these people. Just when he thought he had loaded all the women on to lifeboats, however, dozens of women appeared on the boat deck, apparently released after having been confined below during the crucial period of boat loading.

Numbers reveal the big picture. Only 4 of the *Titanic*'s 143 first class women perished, and 3 of these were by choice, whereas 15 of 93 second class women died, as did 81 of 179 third class women, nearly half. As for children, only one of the first and second classes' 29 children died, whereas 23 out of 76 steerage children perished.[8] The death rate among third class children, and even more significantly among third class women, was greater than that among first class men.[9]

Initially, the failure strictly to observe the rule that women and children go first was not even noticed because few third class passengers were interviewed by the major newspapers covering the story of the *Titanic*'s demise. A United States Senate inquiry into the disaster included testimony from only three third class passengers. The British Court of Enquiry exonerated the ship's company and crew from discrimination against people in steerage without hearing from a single third class passenger and despite testimony from the only surviving steward from third class that men in steerage were forcibly kept below deck for more than two hours after the crash. The New York *Sun* charitably reported that survivor J. Bruce Ismay, managing director of the White Star Line, "behaved with exceptional gallantry. . . . No one knows how Mr. Ismay himself got into a boat; it is assumed he wished to make a presentation of the case to his company."[10]

But the tide turned quickly. Within days people were wondering why Mr. Ismay wasn't among the 1,502 people who perished, and he was lambasted in the press. Although third class passenger Olaus Abelseth considered access to the boat deck a privilege properly reserved for first and second class passengers, even as the ship was sinking,[11] such sentiments were on the wane then and find few adherents today. Writing in the mid-1950s, Walter Lord comments on the fact that the percentage of third class children lost was greater than that of first class men: "It was a contrast which would never get by the social consciousness (or news sense) of today's press. . . . A new age was dawning. . . . [The *Titanic* disaster was] the last time the special position of First Class was accepted without question. . . . Never again would First Class have it so good."[12]

Lord was right. Today we distinguish between privileges that we think money should be able to buy and privileges that we think should be outside of commercial relationships. In general, we think that people should be able to use their money to buy luxuries, such as large houses close to the seashore, cars with extraordinary performance, and huge diamond rings. But when it comes to life-and-death situations, we typically think that money should not be used to determine who lives and who dies. This is why we don't allow people legally to buy vital organs for transplant but insist instead that scarce organs be allocated according to considerations that exclude the recipient's income or wealth. In situations of medical triage no attention is supposed to be paid to the social standing of those in need of scarce medical resources. When we had universal military subscription to fight World War II, the Korean War, and the war in Vietnam, it was illegal for a family to buy their son's way out of the draft, in contrast to an earlier time when it was perfectly legal during the Civil War for wealthy families of northern men to pay someone to serve as a substitute for their son's active participation.

In early 2009, a commercial aircraft made an emergency landing in the Hudson River in New York City with no loss of life. If the pilot had been less skillful, the plane would have broken apart and sunk quickly. Had that occurred, would we consider it right if first class passengers were saved first? I don't think so. We expect equal treatment regardless of income, wealth, social standing, or ticket price in life-and-death situations. This is a change in our thinking since the Civil War and the *Titanic* disaster. The question is this: what justifies such a change? Why do we now, at least in theory, think we should exclude considerations of income and wealth from decisions about who lives and who dies?

$ $ $

Philosopher John Rawls gave an attractive answer to this question, and many others, in his seminal work, *A Theory of Justice*.[13] This work didn't influence people to change attitudes toward class distinctions. Rather, it provides a reasoned rationale for a change in attitude that had already taken place before the book's publication. The book justifies and follows the implications of views about fairness that occupy the center of American political and social thought.

Rawls looks at social rules as if they were the products of a contract because contracts in a free-market setting have the potential to satisfy the individualistic, selfish desires of all concerned; they can create win-win situations. For example, my wife and I want to have vinyl siding on our house. We consult two or three contractors and decide to engage the contractor with the best combination of low price and good reputation. We would rather have a sided house than the money needed to pay for having the house sided. The contractor, by contrast, would rather have the agreed amount of money than the materials and free time that he has to give up to side our house. It's a win-win situation; the contractor gets what he wants and we get what we want. Similarly, the people employed by the contractor would rather give up their free time to work for the contractor in order to be paid rather than keep their free time and receive no pay. The contractor would rather give the workers their pay than do all the work himself. These are all win-win situations. All participants get what they prefer to have. Contracts, faithfully adhered to in a free-market setting, have the potential to satisfy the individualistic, selfish desires of all the contracting parties.

If society were set up this way, our basic social relationships might also be mutually beneficial. This is the fundamental thought behind the social contract tradition in political philosophy from the time of Thomas Hobbes and John Locke in the seventeenth century to Jean Jacque Rousseau in the eighteenth century to John Rawls in the twentieth century. The idea is to think of the state and its government as depending for its legitimacy on a contract that creates a win-win situation among citizens and between the citizens and the government.

Of course, we know that explicit contracts are not ordinarily entered into when a state is founded. And even when a state does originate in something like a contract—the United States began with the Articles of Confederation—some helpful elements of true free-market contracts are missing. For one thing, individuals don't have veto power over the social or political contract the way they do in the free market, where anyone who doesn't like the deal can walk away unharmed before signing. With the social contract, the best that can be done is to require a majority, or perhaps a super majority of 60 percent or 75 percent, before the contract goes into effect. People who vote against the contract that receives the required votes are nevertheless stuck with it, so it's not purely win-win; there can be losers. Such losers could include minority groups whose distinctive religions, ways of life, or tastes are outlawed by a contract geared to the wishes of the majority.

Losers could also result from great disparities of wealth or power among the contracting parties. Wealthy and powerful people could use their riches and influence to mount public relations campaigns that convince many citizens to vote for a constitution that is really more in the interest of the ruling elite than in the interest of most voters. The majority could end up as losers because, like Walmart employees convinced that unionization would harm them, they were misled as to their true interests.

John Rawls addresses these concerns by suggesting that the contract in question be merely a *hypothetical* contract, a contract that results from a thought experiment rather than from a real vote. The social contract will be the one agreed to under the conditions of the thought experiment. To eliminate the possibility that the strong would take advantage of the weak, the rich take advantage of the poor, or the majority take advantage of a minority, Rawls asks everyone taking part in this thought experiment to pretend to be ignorant of his or her true identity. Participants should imagine that they are choosing the basic rules of society without knowing whether they are male or female, rich or poor, religious or secular, blue collar or white collar, members of a racial or ethnic minority or members of the majority, lovers of opera or of tractor pulls, and so forth. He calls this condition being *behind a veil of ignorance*.

I like to picture this by imagining the inhabitants of the Starship *Enterprise* planning to inhabit an unpopulated planet (because the series has been canceled). As many of you know, people enter (and exit) the starship by entering a machine that reduces them to their elementary particles. These particles are beamed up (or down) to the intended destination, after which they are reassembled at the other end of the journey according to the mathematical formula that is unique to each individual. In order to place the citizens of the *Enterprise* behind the veil of ignorance that Rawls recommends for the process of choosing society's basic rules, imagine that people on the ship are told that after they enter the machine to be beamed down to the new planet, the mathematical formula for their reassembly will be chosen among all such formulae of the starship's inhabitants. No one has any way of knowing which formula will be used for his or her reassembly. Anyone could be turned into anyone else through a random process resembling the Wheel of Fortune.

Under these conditions—behind the veil of ignorance—Rawls thinks self-interest dictates that people choose basic rules for society that treat everyone fairly. Behind the veil of ignorance each person reasons that if any person or any group is treated unfairly, he or she may turn out when the veil is lifted to be an individual or a member of a group that suffers. The only way to protect oneself from this possibility is to support rules that treat everyone fairly. In other words, in this hypothetical situation, people will care about everyone as much as they care about themselves and do so out of self-interest. There's no problem of the rich oppressing the poor, the powerful oppressing the weak, or the majority oppressing a minority.

An interesting aspect of this hypothetical situation is that no one will be outvoted by others. Everyone is in exactly the same position, so what seems good to one person should seem good to others as well. In theory, and we're talking about a theory, the vote on the basic rules of society should be unanimous. What is more, the group's decision should, like typical contracts in a free-market situation, serve the interests of all concerned; it should be a win-win situation.

Although Rawls doesn't address this specific issue, it seems that people deciding on the basic rules of society from behind a veil of ignorance would not put their lives in jeopardy by allowing wealth, income, or fame to influence who gets help in life-and-death situations, such as occurred on the *Titanic*. They would want emergency services to help people on the basis of other social rules and priorities that society holds dear. One of these is efficiency, the goal of saving as many people as possible.

While the *Titanic* was sinking, for example, lifeboats were deployed before they were at full capacity. Lifeboat no. 1 had a capacity of 40, but carried only 12;[14] no. 2 was about 60 percent full; nos. 5 and 6 could each hold 65 people, but contained only 40 and 28.[15] If third class passengers had been allowed on the loading deck when these boats were launched, their underuse might have been avoided and more people might have been saved. People behind the veil of ignorance would realize that the improved efficiency of ignoring social rank in emergency situations could increase their chances of survival.

But individual survival isn't the only goal in life, even in emergency situations. In the aftermath of the *Titanic* disaster, much chagrin centered on failure to save women and children first because the ideal at the time (and perhaps still today to some extent) was not to treat everyone equally but to give priority to women and children. Attention to social rank interfered with realization of this ideal.

Today, when resources are inadequate in life-and-death situations of transplant surgery, for example, we favor treating those in the greatest need who are most likely to benefit from the transplant. This is again a matter of efficiency. But in addition to considerations of efficiency, our ideals oppose ranking patients by social status and, when all medically relevant criteria are met equally, we prefer cueing, random selection, or other criteria that don't involve wealth or social position. Our practice may reflect an ideal of social solidarity or stem from a religious tradition that claims that everyone is equal in the sight of God.

People behind the veil of ignorance will opt for equality regardless of social position also because, apart from life-and-death situations, they will want equal freedom to pursue their dreams. This will lead them to favor, Rawls thinks, freedom of speech, freedom of religion, and, more generally, the fundamental freedoms contained in the Bill of Rights, the first ten amendments to the Constitution of the United States, which guarantee freedom from intrusive government interference in people's private lives. Not knowing whether their desires will resemble those of most other people or instead be somewhat eccentric, they will want the freedom to pursue their dreams in their own ways as long as they aren't interfering with others doing the same. In exchange for having this freedom themselves, they will be willing to grant a like freedom to all others.

Recognizing that some matters must be decided for everyone through a political process—laws will be needed to establish rules for driving, the conditions of military service, attendance at school, funding for schools, and myriad other matters—the people behind a veil of ignorance will want to be able to participate in government decisions on an equal basis with every other adult citizen. They will want the right to vote and to have their votes counted equally with the votes of everyone else. In other words, they will support some form of democracy and will reject measures that disenfranchise large segments of the population affected by electoral outcomes.

Finally, people behind the veil of ignorance will opt for equality regardless of social position because they know that free-market economies produce the greatest wealth by having people compete with one another for jobs, customers, income, and prestige. Meritocracy promotes efficiencies and economic growth that enrich society generally. Giving advantages to people based on unearned social position compromises efficiency and threatens to make everyone poorer. In short, allowing people to compete without regard to gender, race, sexual orientation, and so forth gives everyone the best chance of living a comfortable life in a wealthy society.

This doesn't mean, however, that people behind a veil of ignorance will opt for strict equality of income, wealth, or possessions. They realize that societies become wealthy only when talented people have some personal incentives (selfish motives) to work hard, as they generally do in free-market contexts. Societies that try to enforce complete economic equality usually fail at achieving that goal and, in the process, discourage entrepreneurial behavior. The result in the former Soviet Union, in China under Mao, and in Cuba under Castro was economic stagnation that impoverished almost everyone, depriving these societies of the affluence that we take for granted. So, denying talented people significant rewards for their extra work impoverishes them and the rest of society; it's a lose-lose situation. Talented people who would be rich if properly motivated by personal gain are poor and people of modest talents are poorer than they need be because they lack the share of material wealth that would have been theirs as members of a more affluent society.

This lose-lose situation, however, can be transformed into a win-win situation in the following way. Allow some people to become richer than others on the condition that the rich improve the wealth of society in ways that benefit society's poorest members and everyone else. Behind the veil of ignorance, people don't know if they will be talented and rich or not talented and relatively poor. Under Rawls's proposal, if you discover that you are among the talented people, you get to be richer than others, which is a win. If, however, you turn out to be less talented, you also win; you benefit from letting some people be richer than you are because they are required to share some of their riches with you.

If you are hedging your bets behind the veil of ignorance, you will want the poor (and therefore everyone between the poor and the rich) to gain as much as possible from inequalities granted to the rich because you want the worst thing that can happen to you to be as good as possible. So, you will favor steeply graduated taxes that place as much burden as possible on the wealthiest households and will want some of the resulting additional tax revenue redistributed so that the working poor receive a living wage that supports a decent life. Thus, Rawls's reasoning reaches the same conclusion as the reasoning in chapter 7. Steeply progressive taxation on the wealthy should fund a robust Earned Income Credit (EIC).

People behind the veil recognize, however, that they can't tax the rich so heavily that talented people are discouraged from maximizing their economic output. Looking at economic history to determine how high taxes on the rich can be without impairing economic growth, they find that the top tax bracket in the 1950s, a time of considerable economic growth, was 91 percent. They note also that in the prosperous 1960s the top tax bracket was consistently 70 percent or more. Corporate and capital gains taxes were also high in those decades. These figures suggest that a top tax bracket of 65 or 70 percent poses no risk of stalling the economy.

This social contract argument for progressive taxation with a top marginal tax rate of 65 or 70 percent reaches the same conclusion as the argument in chapter 7 but the bases of the two arguments are entirely different. In chapter 7 the conclusion follows from the uncontroversial principle that generally speaking people should pay or work for the benefits they receive. In light of the contributions to our affluence—and so to the great wealth of some individuals and corporations—of general social evolution and of government-funded R&D, progressive taxation is needed to ensure that rich people return to society that portion of their wealth that they owe to the work of others. This line of argument doesn't rest at all on a social contract, hypothetical or actual, and therefore remains sound even if Rawls's argument is rejected. By the same token, rejection of the principle in chapter 7 or of the historical account of social and government contributions to individual and corporate wealth doesn't affect at all the soundness of Rawls's reasoning. These are two completely independent lines of thought that support the same conclusion. And it takes only one, not both, for the conclusion to be fully supported.

$ $ $

Rawls's approach endorses using some of the additional government revenue that steeply progressive taxation would generate to improve public education so that everyone has fair equality of opportunity. As we've seen, people behind the veil of ignorance would allow some inequality of income and wealth. But they'd want a fair shot at the better-paying positions and would realize that freedom to compete for these positions isn't enough. Those with inferior educations wouldn't have a realistic chance of success. So, from behind the veil, people want the government to support high-quality, affordable education that's available to everyone, resulting in an equal educational opportunity that promotes fair equality of opportunity.

Unfortunately, educational opportunities are and always have been extremely unequal in the United States, as the following two stories illustrate. The first is about competition for slots in prestigious *preschools* in New York City:

The race begins at 9 a.m. the day after Labor Day, as parents speed-dial the city's elite nursery schools in hopes of just getting an application.

Reports last week that former Wall Street analyst Jack Grubman may have elevated his rating of AT&T stock so Citigroup chief Sanford Weill would help Grubman's twins get into a top nursery school show how cutthroat admissions can be among the City's privileged.

The prize—admission to the 10 or so best schools in the city for 2- and 3-year-olds—is perceived as the first step to the best kindergarten, the best college, the best connections.

The children are "really with New York's best and brightest," said Victoria Goldman, author of *The Manhattan Directory to Private Nursery Schools....* "It never hurts to rub elbows with the right ones."

Some speak up to three languages already and are taught by teachers with master's degrees in early childhood education. . . . Annual tuitions can top $15,000.[16]

The other story shows how poor the educational opportunities are at the other end of the socioeconomic spectrum. It's the story of Anna, a single parent of two children, and her twelve-year-old daughter Sarah. They lived in

a Boston public housing tenement. . . . The foyer, which smelled of urine, had two rows of mailboxes, all long ago rifled and mangled so far out of alignment that the metal doors would no longer lock. . . .

Anna rose every day at 5:30 a.m., . . . ate toast made of day-old bread, roused her two children, and leaving them to fend for themselves, headed out in darkness by 6:30 a.m. to catch a train and two buses in order to arrive on time at her place of work.

In the winter, Anna arrived home after dark.

It would be seven o'clock before she would ask both [children] about their homework assignments. Her questions were perfunctory. Having left school at 16, Anna had little if any capacity to help her children with schoolwork they couldn't understand. . . .

By nine o'clock, Anna would climb into bed and lie sleepless with nameless worry. . . . She was . . . concerned . . . about whether Sarah would become pregnant in high school as Anna had, and lose what small chance she had of getting *out*.

Anna was very tired. . . . She wanted her children, above all, to get an "education," though for her the word was little more than a mantra. . . .

Anna did not own a car. She did not own a clothes washer or a dryer or a vacuum cleaner or a dishwasher. . . . Every necessary ordinary little task required a trip. A trip required a bus. A bus took time. Time she did not have. Her building had no washing machines, so she had to take a bus to the Laundromat.[17]

Because Sarah was falling behind in reading, she qualified for extra help under the Title I program, which gives schools extra money for specialists and tutors to spend additional time with children having difficulty with basic skills, such as reading and math. But the program requires that parents be actively involved in their children's education. Lawyer and social critic Randall Robinson comments, "The people in Washington who wrote the laws had time to spend in their children's schools. They must have thought that Anna too could make time to spend in her children's. But, as was the case with the vast majority of the working poor, time was not Anna's to make. It was her supervisor's, and he was not sympathetic." Robinson describes what happened when Anna finally did meet with school officials on a Saturday:

"How many times have you been able to come to the Title I parent meetings at school in the last year, Mrs. Brown?" asked one of the white lawyers. . . .

"Well, I come when I can." This was an evasion. . . .

"But just how many times?"

"I have never been to one."

Anna told them about her life, in the idiom of her world, with no embarrassed fakery. She told them about the long hours spent on her job and at the Laundromat and cooking. . . . She told them about struggling to make it on a minimum-wage paycheck. . . .

"Do you read with Sarah at home?" asked the other white lawyer.

"Yes, as often as I can," answered Anna wearily. *Are these people Crazy? Have they listened to nothing I've said?* Anna looked at Ms. Cooper [Sarah's teacher]. . . .

Anna did not know that Sarah had been assigned to Ms. Cooper's class by computer. She also did not know that the school's principal considered Ms. Cooper to be one of the weakest teachers and that, computer assignments notwithstanding, students with parents likely to complain were never assigned to teachers like Ms. Cooper.[18]

Robinson concludes:

Give a black or white child the tools (nurture, nutrition, material necessities, a home/school milieu of intellectual stimulation, high expectation, pride of self) that a child needs to learn and the child *will* learn. . . .

Sarah was failing. She was failing when she should not have been. . . . Sarah was not failing because she was black. She was failing for the same reasons that Appalachian white children fail. Grinding, disabling poverty.[19]

Statistics support the claim that poverty reduces children's academic success. Research done by Karl Alexander, for example, on the progress of Baltimore students from first through fifth grade on the California Achievement Test shows the effects of socioeconomic difference. On average, students from families of low socioeconomic status started first grade 32 points behind children in the most affluent group, but finished fifth grade 73 points behind.[20] Richard Kahlenberg, senior fellow at the Century Foundation, writes,

Despite innumerable experiments and extensive research designed to identify the keys to educational success, no other variable can compare in importance to the economic-class composition of the student body. . . . The best teachers are drawn to the schools with the highest socioeconomic levels. Teachers in middle-class schools are more likely to teach in their field of expertise, more likely to have higher teacher test scores, and more likely to be experienced. Their expectations are higher. The curricula they use are richer and more demanding.[21]

In short, one way to provide more equal educational opportunity in the United States, and thereby promote fairness as well as economic efficiency, is to reduce the grinding poverty of Anna and her daughter Sarah so that Anna would have the time and resources to be more involved in her daughter's education. Again, a robust EIC would be very helpful.

Public expenditures specific to education can help as well. Karl Alexander's research on school children in Baltimore yielded a surprising result, which came from comparing changes in the students' scores during the school year with changes that took place during summer vacations. Alexander tested students at the beginning of each school year and then again near the end to determine their progress during the year. A by-product of testing this way is the availability of information about what happened during the summer, which is determined by comparing the children's scores just before school lets out in spring with their scores in the fall when they first come back to school.

On average, children from the lowest socioeconomic families lost some points, usually 2 or 3, during the summer, whereas children from the highest socioeconomic group tended to gain 10 or 15 points during the summer. It seems that they had engaged in enriching activities outside of school. In fact, whereas the poor kids fell 41 points further behind the rich kids from the beginning of first to the end of fifth grade, they didn't fall behind at all during the school year. The school was not failing these children. They lost a total of more than 52 points during the four summers between first and fifth grades, which more than accounts for their falling behind the rich kids by a total of 41 points between the beginning of first and the end of fifth grade.[22]

This research suggests, Malcolm Gladwell points out in *Outliers*, that we would serve poor children better if we had more school days and much, much shorter summer vacations. The school year in the United States is typically just 180 days, whereas in South Korea it is 220 days and in Japan 243.[23] Of course, a matter that Gladwell doesn't raise, extending the school year to that extent would cost a lot of money. But it would be integral to a new progressive agenda because competition for prestigious academic preparation for lucrative careers would be fairer if more money were spent on education. As with the expanded EIC, funding could come from the increase in progressive taxation that we've seen fairness requires anyway.

In addition to lengthening the school year, expenditures on early childhood education and kindergarten would be justified by the same principle of fair competition. The poor kids in Alexander's study entered first grade significantly behind the children of more affluent families. This deficit could be reduced greatly (although probably not eliminated entirely) by making early childhood education of three- to five-year-olds and kindergarten universally available at public expense. Steven Greenhouse concludes his review of the effectiveness of Head Start, an early childhood education program:

In light of the studies showing that child readiness programs lead to better results in school and lower dropout and incarceration rates, the nation should guarantee Head Start places to all three- and four-year-olds in families earning less than $50,000 a year. At present, just 40 percent of the three- and four-year-olds in households earning $20,000 to $30,000 are in preschool programs, half the rate for families earning $100,000 or more.[24]

Higher education also needs additional government funding to create conditions of fair competition for lucrative positions of power and prestige. It is extremely rare for people to move up the socioeconomic ladder very far without a college degree and, increasingly, without some sort of graduate diploma as well. Yet the cost of higher education has been increasing faster than the rate of inflation, making university education unaffordable to many people at or below the median household income. One reason for higher tuition, fees, and housing costs at public universities, traditionally the most affordable four-year institutions, is the decline of state support over the last three decades. On average, states now fund only one-third the cost of education at these institutions. With declining state funds, the universities cover costs by charging students more for tuition, fees, and housing, which now average more than $15,000 a year, an increase of about 40 percent since the 2002–2003 school year.[25]

The major federal government program designed to help students and their families meet the high costs of higher education is the Pell Grant program. But it has failed to keep up with inflation. In the school year 1975–1976 these grants covered 84 percent of expenses at the average state university, whereas for 2007–2008 the highest grant covered only 32 percent of these expenses. As a result, among students who enter four-year institutions, a Department of Education study found in 2004, only 41 percent of low-income students managed to graduate within five years, whereas 66 percent of high-income students had done so.[26] And many middle class students don't even enter four-year colleges in the first place. More than 400,000 high school graduates each year who are qualified to enter a four-year college fail to do so for financial reasons. Many of these attend two-year colleges, but 170,000 don't go to college at all.[27]

Students at two-year colleges can typically complete the first two years of a four-year degree. However, although in one survey 75 percent of such students said they planned to transfer to a four-year institution to complete a bachelor's degree, another study showed that among students who entered two-year colleges in the mid-1990s, only 17 percent had made the transfer to a four-year institution within five years.[28]

Unequal access to higher education, like unequal early-childhood education, unequal funding for public schools, and unequal educational enrichment during school vacations, puts people from poor families at the kind of permanent disadvantage in a competitive society that no one behind the veil of ignorance would endorse. The government should use some of the additional revenue raised through progressive taxation to increase teachers' salaries, to fund more days in the school year, to hire more teachers so that classes can be smaller, to improve and expand school facilities, to provide preschool and kindergarten for all children, and to provide loans and grants on a needs basis so that no qualified student is denied the opportunity to study at a four-year college. Only then will our society be as affluent as possible. And only then will the American Dream be truly available to all talented individuals who are willing to work for it.

Unfortunately, owing to the antigovernment-antitax ideology that guides the most influential members of the Republican Party, the United States is moving in the opposite direction. According to *New York Times* correspondent Sam Dillon, thousands of school districts across the nation, reacting to reduced support from taxpayers, were slashing school budgets in 2011. They were "gutting summer-school programs, cramming classes into four-day weeks or lopping days off the school year,"[29] just the opposite of what needs to be done to give people equal educational opportunity and to train our workforce for increased productivity. At the same time, students in higher education, not states, are now paying more to cover costs at public universities,[30] with the unsurprising result that average college debt continues to grow.[31]

Taking back the center for progressive policies in education is therefore essential at this time. Progressive taxation, a robust EIC, and massive investments in education are also needed to maintain and promote democracy, which is our next topic.

9

Democracy

The New York State Senate was in turmoil in June 2009 when two Democratic senators, Pedro Espada Jr. and Hiram Monserrate, decided to switch parties and give Republicans a majority. The new majority quickly voted to make Senator Espada its president pro tempore, which made him first in line in case anything happened to Governor David Paterson because the state lacked a lieutenant governor at the time.

All this happened because a billionaire became upset with the Democratic majority in the senate. Tom Golisano had bankrolled the Democrats, thereby helping them to gain control of the senate, but became upset within months of their victory when senate Democrats favored a bill raising taxes on the wealthy. When he first heard of the senate Democrats' plan, Golisano went to Albany to meet with then majority leader Malcolm Smith about the matter but he found Smith inattentive. Golisano complained that Smith just played with his BlackBerry. "I said, 'I'm talking to the wall here.'" So he decided that the senate needed new leadership. He persuaded two Democrats to switch parties to oust Mr. Smith.

On June 9 both Senator Smith and Republican Senate leader Dean Skelos claimed to be the majority leader. The Democrats locked the Senate chamber and refused to turn over the keys to the Republicans, who vowed to hold a Senate session in a nearby park if necessary. But in the end the Republicans had the votes and a key, so they had the Senate.[1]

It's uncertain exactly what Mr. Golisano promised Senators Espada and Monserrate but it may be related to what billionaires can offer more of than most of us—money. Mr. Espada has a history of misconduct regarding campaign finances. *New York Times* columnist Jim Dwyer explains that Espada "owes the city $61,750 in fines for fraudulent campaign fund-raising going back to 2001. He has failed to file 41 reports with the State Board of Elections, and has racked up $13,553 in penalties since 2002."[2]

His disputes about money extend also to his request for a total of $2 million in earmarked taxpayer money for two nonprofit corporations that were brought into being shortly before the requests were made. Democrats refused to allocate the funds because they were uncertain if these were legitimate nonprofits doing the kind of work that will benefit citizens of New York.[3]

Uncertain also is whether Mr. Espada even lives in the Bronx district that he represents. Dwyer explains:

His cars are registered at a house in Mamaroneck [which is outside his district]; his bank statements go to Mamaroneck; he has said that's the home his wife wants to live in. However, last year, when he ran for the State Senate and his Bronx residency was challenged, a court-appointed referee ruled that all his Mamaroneck connections did not amount to proof that he did not intend to return to the apartment in the Bronx, the standard under the election law.[4]

Local activists claim that they would protest Senator Espada's representation of their district when he doesn't live there, except they don't know where to protest. The normal place would be outside the Senator's district office, but he doesn't have one.

Mr. Monserrate, the other defecting senator, is tainted as well. A former marine and twelve-year veteran of the New York City Police Force, he was under indictment for having (allegedly) stabbed his companion with a broken glass. He retired from the city police after a finding that he suffered from a psychological disability.[5] He finally became a power broker in the state senate, which is less likely than ever to pass legislation that increases taxes on wealthy people.

The ousted Senator Smith claimed that the Republican coup was "illegal and unlawful." Columnist Dwyer comments, "How come? Apparently, it was unfair of the Republicans to buy two senators whom the Democrats had already paid for, fair and square."[6]

This case illustrates how extremes of wealth can influence politics and detract from the democratic ideal. People who value democracy should favor policies that reign in great wealth. Campaign contributions, lobbying, and public relations campaigns by and on behalf of moneyed interests often deflect elected officials from their proper role of serving the public good.

If anything is central to American political ideals it is the importance of democracy. One way to take back the center for a new progressive agency is to show people how that agenda, by reducing disparities between the super-wealthy and the rest of society, helps to protect democracy from rule by the rich.

Consider some other examples of money deflecting politics from a democratic path that serves the majority of Americans toward laws and policies that serve primarily to further enrich the already wealthy. In 1990 US Senator Richard Bryan introduced legislation to increase CAFE (corporate average fuel economy) standards on cars and SUVs by 40 percent, thereby curtailing air pollution, improving the US balance of trade, and reducing our dependence on foreign sources of oil—worthy goals that would improve our economy and protect our health. But the legislation would have cut into automobile company profits that stem from the sale of gas-guzzling SUVs. Auto industry campaign contributions influenced enough senators to kill the bill by filibuster.[7]

In 1999 the chair of the Republican Party told the CEO of a large pharmaceutical company that a $250,000 donation to the party would "keep the lines of communication open [so that they could] keep passing legislation that will benefit your industry." After the companies spent about $262 million on lobbying and campaign contributions before the 2000 elections, Congress favored the companies with lucrative extensions of patent monopolies on popular drugs.[8] US consumers suffered higher prices for drugs as drug company profits soared.

US taxpayers suffer as well. The pharmaceutical lobby's influence is given credit for a controversial provision in legislation authorizing Medicare Part D, a prescription drug benefit. The provision disallows the government from bargaining with drug companies to get lower prices for drugs covered by Medicare and paid for largely by taxpayers.

The Airline Passenger Fairness Act was introduced in the US Senate in 1999 to make airline companies more responsive to customer needs. Within weeks of its introduction the industry made over $400,000 in political contributions and all of the provisions that the airline companies didn't like—the teeth of the legislation—were removed.[9]

During the 2000 campaign, oil and energy companies contributed heavily to the Republican Party. After the election the heads of contributing companies were invited by Vice President Cheney to help him write a national energy policy that relaxed regulations on energy development permits and helped increase company profits.[10]

During the 1997–1998 election cycle the financial services industry spent $200 million on lobbying and contributed more than $150 million to secure repeal of the Glass-Steagall Act, the New Deal legislation that required separation of commercial banking, investment banking, and insurance. This repeal is believed by many to have contributed to the financial meltdown of the next decade, which cost taxpayers one or two trillion dollars. Taxpayers were tapped because the failure of major financial institutions could spark another great depression. Also possibly influential, however, is the fact that the financial industry uses some of its great profitability (four times that of manufacturing when neither is melting down) to lobby continually and bankroll sympathetic politicians. The financial industry gave more than $1.3 billion to political causes between 1990 and 2002.[11] Given the bailout, the recession, the deficits, and the increase in unemployment in 2008–2009, it's hard to argue that the financial sector's political influence advances the public interest.

The influence of big money on politics was satirized in 2000 by a group calling itself billionairesforbushorgore.com. They posted this on their former website:

While you may be familiar with stocks and bonds, currency speculation, IPOs and all the rest, there's a new investment arena you should be aware of: *legislation*. If a mutual fund returns 20% a year, that's considered quite good, but in the low-risk, high-return world of legislation, a 20% return is positively lousy. There's no reason why your investment dollar can't return 100,000% or more.

Too good to be true? Don't worry, it's completely legal. With the help of a professional legislation broker (called a Lobbyist), you place your investment (called a Campaign Contribution) with a carefully selected list of legislation manufacturers (called Members of Congress). These manufacturers then go to work, crafting industry-specific subsidies, inserting tax breaks into the code, extending patents or giving away public property for free.

Just check out these results. The Timber Industry spent $8 million in campaign contributions to preserve the logging road subsidy, worth $458 million—the return on their investment was 5,725%. Glaxo-Wellcome [now GlaxoSmithKline] invested $1.2 million in campaign contributions to get a 19-month patent extension on Zantac worth $1 billion—their net return 83,333%. The Tobacco Industry spent $30 million in contributions for a tax break worth $50 billion—the return on their investment: 167,000%. For a paltry $5 million in campaign contributions, the Broadcasting Industry was able to secure free digital TV licenses, a give-away of public property worth $70 billion—that's an incredible 1,400,000% return on their investment.[12]

One result of this influence of big money on legislation is that some issues of importance to public welfare are ignored. Former labor secretary Robert Reich points out that when pharmaceutical companies lobby for legislation that extends their lucrative patents, and manufacturers of generic drugs lobby against such legislation, the debate centers on profits for the companies involved:

Left out of this debate are the fundamental questions of whether drug companies ought to be advertising and marketing prescription drugs to the general public when it is doctors who should be making decisions about medications; how much of the costs of drugs go to advertising and marketing them; and whether there's enough difference between nearly identical drugs to justify the expense of bringing them to market in the first place.[13]

Over the years, Democratically controlled congresses have paid decreasing attention to issues of social inequality that might be addressed by increasing the minimum wage or providing skill training for the unemployed. In 1963 the Democratic congress passed six of ten such bills; in 1979 four of seven; and in 1991 two of seven.[14] As money gains influence in politics through the ascendency of the super-rich, effective concern about the plight of people with little money decreases. Yet, such people constitute a large part of the demos in our democracy.

Robert Kuttner, coeditor of the *American Prospect*, gives this example:

You have a politics in which . . . high-quality child-development programs—early childhood, pre-kindergarten, after-school—are not an option, despite the fact that, according to every social scientist who has studied the question, they make a crucial difference in whether children grow up to be productive citizens. For about $60 billion a year you could have a comprehensive, universal, development-oriented childhood program. But when money shapes the agenda, the policies that would inspire ordinary people to get involved don't even make it into the discussion, and people tune out.[15]

Some evidence of their tuning out is that in most elections, most of the Americans eligible to vote don't show up at the polls.

Big money has this extraordinary influence in American politics because few politicians have the financial resources to run an effective campaign to gain or remain in elective office without massive campaign contributions. The amount of money needed for political campaigns has been increasing for decades. In 1976, incumbents in the US Senate spent an average of $610,000 on their races for reelection. The figure grew to $3 million in 1986 and $4.4 million in 2000. By 2000, the average winner of a US Senate seat spent $7.7 million.[16] Imagine having a job that you love but that you can keep only if you can raise from sources outside your official employment sums in the neighborhood of ten or twenty or thirty *thousand dollars a week*. That's the position of most incumbent US senators.

The situation in the US House of Representatives is better but not good enough for the average American to mount a campaign. No successful challenger for a seat in the House spent less than $850,000 in 2000.[17] By 2010 Democrats in contested House races, including incumbents, were spending over $1 million each.[18] The largest increase in spending, however, came from outside special-interest groups,[19] because early in 2010 the Supreme Court removed restrictions on corporate campaign expenditures that directly endorse or oppose a given candidate.[20] This increases the pressure on representatives to please these moneyed interests.

The general trend can be seen most clearly in presidential races. Total spending by and for *all* candidates was $500.9 million in 2000, $820.3 million in 2004, and $1.7 billion in 2008.

The Obama campaign alone spent $740.6 million in the 2008 race, which was more than the combined expenditures of the George W. Bush and John Kerry campaigns four years earlier.[21]

This money can't come from most Americans, economist Joel Magnuson points out. "Less than one tenth of one percent of the American population has the willingness or financial ability to donate more than $1,000 to political candidates." As a result, "this minute fraction of the population composed mainly of wealthy individuals and powerful corporations dominates U.S. political institutions."[22]

During his bid for the Republican Party's presidential nomination in 2000 Senator John McCain, a member of the sane center, called the campaign finance system "an elaborate influence-peddling scheme by which both parties conspire to stay in office by selling the country to the highest bidder." He said of Republican proposals for tax code changes that benefit the wealthy, "Now we're going to see this big thick tax code on our desks, and the fine print will reveal another cornucopia for the special interests and a chamber of horrors for the taxpayers."[23] He was right, of course, as the Bush tax cuts of 2001 and 2003 demonstrated.

I look at it this way. You have senators who need to raise campaign funds of, say, $20,000 per week every week of their political lives. If they aren't independently super-rich, they're somewhat like drug addicts who don't make enough money to feed their habit. One reason (not the only reason) most people are reluctant to hire drug addicts to handle their finances is the fear than when drug addicts needed more money for their habit than their salaries provide they are tempted to steal from their employers. The same danger exists with political junkies. Their political habit requires a lot more money per week than almost any drug habit, yet we let them handle the country's finances and are surprised when billions upon billions of dollars are misappropriated. So, we complain about government waste and often vote to "throw the bums out" because they haven't kept their campaign promises. (They may well have kept the promises they made to their rich benefactors.) Thus, we sometimes exchange one set of cash-starved political junkies for another set. Is this really what we have in mind when we say we're a democracy?

Charles Lewis, president of the Fund for Independence in Journalism, thinks not. He sums up the situation this way:

For more than 200 years, the United States has been an ongoing experiment in democratic government, a system in which each person has a theoretically equal say in collective decisions, the workings of government are transparent for all to see, and the will of the majority prevails over narrow factional interests. Today we appear to be launching a new experiment—one in which access to power is rationed by money, politicians can choose to reveal only what will benefit them, and each industry and special interest sets its own rules. Such a system can be called many things, but democratic isn't one of them.[24]

$ $ $

When great disparities of income and wealth prevail, moneyed interests can hijack the political process indirectly (as well as directly) by influencing what appears on mainstream media as news. A generation ago, a host of news organizations provided what they considered to be important news. These organizations were geared more toward informing the public than maximizing profit. The potential for greater profit led larger corporations to acquire them in mergers that started in the 1980s. So today a mere dozen or so corporations control the major broadcast television networks, cable networks, major newspapers, and magazines. These large corporate conglomerates contain a host of financial and commercial enterprises geared toward maximizing profit. The goal of profit maximization results in the replacement of news that citizens need in order to perform their duties in a democracy with entertaining human interest stories. A lot of "hard news" is replaced by coverage of the funeral of a pop star, the rehab of a starlet, the legal troubles of a football player, the marital infidelity of an elected official, and a plethora of heartwarming stories about ordinary people overcoming great odds to help others. Such coverage tends to improve ratings because people enjoy these mini–soap operas. Improved ratings increase advertising revenues. This all makes sense from a business perspective.

The problem is that such practices deflect attention from issues that people need to be aware of to petition their legislators and vote intelligently. If properly informed, how many voters would want to pay more for drugs, pay more taxes for drugs bought under Medicare Part D, pay more for sugar than necessary, subsidize mining companies and cotton growers, and so forth? As Thomas Jefferson put it, "If once [the people] become inattentive to the public affairs . . . you and I, and Congress and Assemblies, Judges and Governors, shall all become wolves."[25] He didn't foresee that instead of wolves government officials would become pliant advocates of special interests against the common good.

In addition to distracting attention from pressing matters, the profit motive applied to the media results in reductions in investigative reporting. It's much cheaper to interview politicians, report their views, cover political or personal disputes among politicians, and treat political races as if they were sporting events than to spend months of investigation finding out what politicians and their corporate sponsors would prefer that voters not know—such as how politicians are helping corporations to raid the public treasury or soak the consumer. What is more, reporters who insist on digging deep into issues that affect public welfare may find that the easier sources of ordinary news—interviews with noted politicians or their staffs—are denied to them. This lets everyone know that intrusive investigative reporting will not be tolerated. When insistent reporters lose vital access to newsmakers, their successors are likely to be more cooperative.[26]

More insidiously, corporate public relations directly infiltrate the news. PR firms and the PR sections of major corporations produce broadcast-ready audios and videos that appear to be news items that radio and television stations have produced. The videos often come in two versions, one that is fully edited with voice-overs and another that includes all the video footage and a script that the television station can use to make its own audio accompaniment. All of this is free to stations, which, pressured by time and money constraints, simply put on the air what they have received.[27] The public, which still gets most of its news from television,[28] receives as news what is actually an exercise in public relations.

Even the most prestigious news organizations have done this. On June 24, 1994, for example, the *New York Times* ran a story on the name change of Federal Express to FedEx. The *Times* simply passed along the text and the photo (of a FedEx jet), attributing the photo to the Associated Press. In fact, the photo was taken by a FedEx employee and then FedEx paid the Associated Press to distribute it as if it were news rather than an advertisement.[29]

Deliberately sown conflation of biased corporate sources of information with more (usually) neutral sources in science is one of the strategies behind what we saw in chapter 4 with regard to cigarette smoking and climate change. The industry disputing what scientists had established trotted out experts of its own to give the appearance of a meaningful scientific debate on the matter. The media, operating on the habit of presenting corporate PR as news, allowed the corporate experts to pose as neutral investigators rather than expose them as corporate operatives.

Robert Reich points out that corporate PR can forestall needed legislative measures. When two bills were pending in Congress to combat increasing childhood obesity by regulating the way that food companies market their products to children, Kraft Foods proclaimed that it would stop marketing some of its products to children under twelve. General Mills, McDonald's, and Coca-Cola soon followed suit, pledging to spend half their child-oriented advertising dollars promoting "healthy lifestyles." Because these pledges convinced much of the public that the problem was being addressed responsibly, public pressure for legislation waned, allowing legislators to do what their large corporate sponsors wanted—absolutely nothing. Instead of legislation that would have resulted in specific mandatory standards, the public was left with vague corporate promises of voluntary behavior that could be abandoned as soon as the public turned its attention to other issues.[30]

News Corporation advertised a campaign to help teenage girls avoid predatory men they might meet online at News Corporation's MySpace. This move put a stop to efforts to require the corporation to give parents free software to block access to MySpace from home computers.[31]

British Petroleum (BP) started in 2002 to advertise itself as earth friendly, concerned about global warming, and dedicated to leading society to a postpetroleum future. But its promised expenditures on research toward this end were meager compared to its profits from petroleum, which soared as oil prices increased. The energy bill that Congress passed in 2006, which provided little money for nonfossil-fuel-based energy but provided a lot of money for oil exploration and development, may have been influenced, Reich thinks, by public perceptions that energy corporations like BP were already taking care of the problem of providing renewable energy for the future.[32]

Corporate PR also deflected attention from sweatshop abuses in the third world. In the mid-1990s it seemed that consumers would pressure legislators to limit the importation of goods from the third world that were made by workers who were too young (child labor), too poorly paid, or exposed to too many workplace hazards. Apparel manufacturers assured the public that they were taking care of these problems, thereby mollifying the public and precluding legislation. However, subsequent investigation indicates that many third world factories have a double set of books, one for their own use and the other for international auditors.[33]

When there is pressure for higher CAFE standards for cars and trucks, automotive companies declare that they are going to increase the average fuel economy of their fleets voluntarily. For example, when there was such pressure in 2000, Ford announced that it would improve the mileage on its SUVs by 25 percent. But after the threat of legislation had passed Ford found that selling gas-guzzling SUVs was too lucrative to curtail, so they withdrew their pledge. Then, when oil prices increased again in 2005, Ford pledged to increase tenfold its production of hybrid vehicles.[34]

The cumulative weight of corporate PR can influence a large percentage of ordinary people to lose all sense of reality on issues that affect corporate profits. Corporations fund conservative think tanks designed to convince average Americans that the government can't do anything right. The message is that private enterprise is the only way to get good results, a message that corporations spread so as to avoid government competition, oversight, and regulation. The resulting loss-of-reality orientation among many Americans was well illustrated in the 2009 debate over health-care reform.

Some senior citizens, misled by the propaganda of antigovernment-antitax extremists, were afraid that health-care reform would interfere with Medicare. It seems that bias against government is so strong that when people like a service it doesn't occur to them that it's provided by the government. In reality, of course, Medicare is a government program.

A *Wall Street Journal*/NBC poll in August 2009 found that 45 percent of respondents believed that President Obama's health-care plan would authorize "death panels," a group that decides whether a patient should be treated or left to die. The notion that this is part of anyone's proposed reform of health care is so ludicrous that even Georgia Republican Senator Johnny Isakson said that such a belief is "nuts." The poll found that 55 percent of Americans thought that reformed health care would extend publicly provided health care to illegal immigrants and 50 percent thought it would involve the use of federal money to fund abortions. Three bills had passed out of House committees at the time the poll was taken and none had any such provision.[35] However, this fact didn't stop e-mails with these and other bizarre claims from reaching me. As we've seen, many activists on the right have no respect for facts in their crusade against "big government."

Yet, it's hard to believe that even they would want to live in the kind of country that they are trying to create in America. Imagine a country in which rules to ensure the environmental safety of oil extraction in the Gulf of Mexico were drawn up by the corporations doing the extraction. Oops! It seems we had something close to that in April 2010, which resulted in massive pollution from a leaky well owned by BP. Self-imposed safety standards and self-monitoring of adherence to those standards makes no sense in our current free market because companies today are supposed to be maximizing profits to maximize shareholder value. This gives them incentive to cut corners on public safety. Without government to set standards and monitor compliance, the public is at great risk of accidental catastrophes.

With the BP experience behind us, and recognizing the chicanery in the pharmaceuticals industry (as described in chapter 4), how many of us really want the government removed from the health-care business? Do you want to trust big pharma to test the safety and effectiveness of new medications without any government oversight? You'd have to be crazy to forgo Food and Drug Administration protection. In addition, if "big government" had left health care alone in the past, we wouldn't have most of the currently available health-preserving and life-saving medications and technologies (such as laser surgery) because they are the result of research at (or funded by) the National Institutes of Health and other government agencies. The same is true of basic R&D in other fields, such as communications. Without government involvement we wouldn't have computers or the Internet.

Do you want government out of the transportation business? Then I guess you wish we didn't have the interstate highway system and other elements of the transportation infrastructure that an advanced industrial society needs, because these were government projects. Do you dislike government regulation of private firms installing the transportation infrastructure? Then just let the companies that make highway bridges design the bridges however they want and inspect the bridges themselves to ensure their continued safety.

How about energy? We could let companies produce electricity in nuclear power plants with only the safety measures that company directors and shareholder who live far, far away consider necessary. Talk to people in Japan about that.

Maybe we could let one state secede from the United States where all the antigovernment-antitax enthusiasts could live with minimal government "intrusion" in their lives. All industries would have to do their own basic R&D as well as create and maintain the physical infrastructure necessary in an industrial society. At the same time, these industries would all be completely free to make up and monitor their own safety standards. Financial institutions could make up their own rules, too, with no possibility of government bailout (because that would be unwarranted intrusion of the government in free enterprise). It's difficult to know whether people in that state would be killed off by environmental pollution, toxic medications, tainted food, or collapsed buildings and bridges before their economy failed and depression ensued because of crumbling infrastructure, inadequate technological innovation, or implosion in the financial sector. The antitax-antigovernment crowd is totally out of touch with reality because they've been misled by self-serving corporate propaganda.

$ $ $

The power of large moneyed interests to distort debate on important matters is one reason that democracy can't survive indefinitely if some people become enormously rich. Other reasons, as we've seen, include the ability of moneyed interests to choose which topics enter public debate and which politicians have enough campaign funds to be serious candidates.

Countries with great inequality tend to have authoritarian governments. Rich people pool their resources to ensure that political decisions benefit the upper class. Using their wealth in this way for political advantage yields even more wealth to the already wealthy and allows rich people to control the political process even more thoroughly for their own benefit. Because, as has been said, "you can't fool all the people all the time," the wealthy class uses some of its resources to buy police power to suppress dissent. When persuasive propaganda doesn't secure their program, force does the trick.

The danger of inequality to the maintenance of democracy can be seen by looking at democratic and authoritarian

countries through the prism of the Gini Index, which was developed in 1912 by Corrado Gini to measure equality and inequality in the distribution of a society's income. In a society
that receives a score of 1 on the index, a single individual earns
all of society's income. At the other extreme, in a society that
receives a score of 0 on the index, everyone has the same income. As a society's income becomes more equal, its score on
the index goes down; as income is distributed more unequally,
the score goes up.[36]

The United States had a Gini Index rating of slightly over
0.50 in the early days of the Great Depression. In the early
1960s our rating was slightly under 0.40, indicating greater
equality of income distribution. It's now up to 0.47. Among
the thirty countries in the Organization for Economic Co-op-
eration and Development (OECD), the world's "developed"
countries, the average Gini Index rating is 0.31. The Gini Index
rating of the United States (0.47) more closely resembles that of
countries with less secure democratic traditions and practices,
such as Mexico (0.52), El Salvador (0.51), Malaysia (0.49),
Philippines (0.46), Ethiopia (0.49), and Guyana (0.45).[37] The
danger that inequality poses to democracy has been noted even
by conservative former chairman of the Federal Reserve, Alan
Greenspan. Commenting in 2005 on the increasing concentration of income in the United States, Greenspan said, "For the
democratic society, that is not a very desirable thing to allow it
to happen."[38] Democratic President Woodrow Wilson made the
same point more forcefully in 1913 when he wrote, "If there
are men in this country big enough to own the government of
the United States, they are going to own it."[39]

One way to improve the Gini Index rating of the United
States is for taxes to be more steeply progressive, as they are
in most other OECD countries, because the revenue generated from these additional taxes can be used to expand such

programs as the Earned Income Credit (EIC), which increases the income of the working poor. Such tax measures not only improve the economic position of the working poor and expand membership in the middle class but they also improve democracy by increasing voter participation. Poor people vote less often than people of greater means. For example, more than half of Americans eligible to vote live in households with incomes below $50,000 a year, but less than 40 percent of those who actually do vote live in such households. In general, voter participation increases with income.[40] Tax measures, such as progressive taxation and the EIC, which increase the income of the majority of Americans, will increase voter participation and thereby strengthen our democracy. The promotion and preservation of democracy is thus another reason, independent of the reasons given in prior chapters, to adopt these tax policies.

$ $ $

Another measure helpful to improving the United States' rating on the Gini Index is support for unions. A survey of twenty OECD countries revealed that every country with a Gini Index rating of less than 0.30 had a workforce that was more than 45 percent unionized (seven countries). The average unionization in these countries was about 60 percent and their average Gini rating was 0.26. Of the remaining thirteen countries in the survey, with Gini Index ratings over 0.30, only one country had more than 40 percent union participation and the average union participation was under 30 percent.[41] International comparisons suggest that union participation increases economic equality.

The same conclusion can be drawn for the United States by comparing union membership with inequality of income across several decades. Inequality, as we've seen, has been increasing in the United States since about 1973. Union participation has declined significantly during this same period, hitting

11.9 percent in 2011, the lowest percentage in over seventy years.[42] A decade of dramatically increasing equality, by contrast, 1935 to 1945, saw union membership increase from 12 percent to 35 percent.[43] Consider these figures from the League of Women Voters:

Between 1947 and 1973, a period of high union density, worker productivity and median worker income both doubled. In the 25 years between 1980 and 2005, a period of rapidly declining union density, worker productivity increased by 71 percent, while the median compensation of U.S. workers (wages and benefits) increased only 19 percent. During those same years the top 1 percent of earners (about 1.4 million tax filers) increased their share of national income from 8.2 percent to 17.4 percent.[44]

Even though union members have never been a majority in our economy, when they constituted more than a quarter of the workforce their contracts influenced what nonunion employers offered to their workers. My father, working as an engineer at Grumman Aircraft in the 1960s, believed that Grumman was good to its workers because they didn't want the workers to unionize, which they might well have done if Grumman hadn't approximated the pay and benefits that unionized workers were getting nearby.

Starting in the 1970s, however, many employers adopted a different tactic to avoid unionization: they increasingly contested union elections. Whereas in 1962 42.1 percent of union elections took place with the consent of employers, in 1977 only 8.6 percent went uncontested. Employers also started increasingly to harass and fire union organizers, which is illegal. According to the National Labor Relations Board, illegal firings took place in only one of twenty union elections in the 1950s. The figure rose to one in four in the 1990s.[45] Attacks on unions intensified in 2011 as several states, most notably Wisconsin, moved to remove collective bargaining rights from unions representing state workers.[46]

Unions promote American democracy not only by improving the country's rating on the Gini Index but also, more directly, by promoting voting. Paul Krugman writes:

Unions explicitly urge their members to vote; maybe more important, the discussion of politics that takes place at union meetings, the political messages in mailings to union members, and so on, tend to raise political awareness not just among union workers but among those they talk to, including spouses, friends, and family. . . . One recent statistical analysis estimated that if the share of unionized workers in the labor force had been as high in 2000 as it was in 1964, an additional 10 percent of adults in the lower two-thirds of the income distribution would have voted.[47]

One approach to strengthening unions and thereby increasing equality and strengthening democracy is contained in the Employee Free Choice Act. If enacted, this bill will allow a union to represent workers whenever more than 50 percent of the workers have signed a card requesting that union's representation. The idea is to circumvent employer harassment, intimidation, and sometimes illegal firings during union elections. Opponents of the bill, if they aren't simply antiunion, worry that merely checking a card may not represent a worker's true sentiments. Union officials and others may harass and intimidate workers to get them to sign. However, it's hard to know if this is a realistic danger. Given the well-known and well-documented increase in employer intimidation and illegal behavior, the greater danger at the moment would seem to be from employers, not from union officials.

$ $ $

Estate taxes are paid when people die and leave money to their heirs (except spouses, who are exempt from the tax). Only a small percentage of American families have ever been subject to the tax, which began in 1916. Since then the tax has sometimes been an effective way of combating large concentrations of wealth. When the tax was only 20 percent, it had little effect on wealth concentration, but then it was raised to 45 percent, to 60 percent, to 70 percent and finally to 77 percent before being reduced to 55 percent, then to 45 percent, and now to 35 percent. Currently, the first $5 million dollars per individual ($10 million for a married couple) are exempt from the tax altogether.[48]

In 1929, before inheritance taxes and income taxes on the rich were high, the top tenth of 1 percent of households owned more than 20 percent of the country's wealth. Higher taxes reduced their ownership to just 10 percent by the mid-1950s.[49]

Some conservatives would like to eliminate the estate tax. They say it's unfair because it taxes the same income twice. People paid income or capital gains taxes to build up their estates and then, with the estate tax, the same money is taxed again when they die. During his last debate before the 2000 election, George W. Bush expressed this view: "I just don't think it's fair to tax people's assets twice regardless of your status. It's a fairness issue. It's an issue of principle, not politics."[50]

But as philosophers Liam Murphy and Thomas Nagel point out, "Multiple distinct taxes often tax people's assets 'twice,' as when a sales tax is imposed on the expenditure of someone's after-tax income, or a property tax is collected on an asset that was bought with income subject to tax."[51] This is true, but only part of the story. In fact, for the most part in our economy taxes are levied whenever money changes hands. When money changes hands from my employer to me, I pay income taxes. But that's far from the end of taxation on my paycheck. I use some of what is left after the tax to pay a contractor to put siding on my house. The contractor gives some of that money to laborers who pay income taxes on what they receive. The contractor also uses some of my money to buy materials from wholesalers who use part of the money to pay their workers who pay income taxes. When the contractor and wholesaler make a profit on some of the after-tax money they received from me, they pay income taxes on that profit. And so it goes. Taxation applies as money circulates throughout the economy. There's no obvious reason why the transfer of money from the deceased to his or her heirs should be an exception to this rule.

Here are some relevant considerations regarding the fairness of the tax. First, it doesn't deprive anyone of gains from their own work; it applies only to wealth that people inherit, in most cases, because they were born into a very wealthy family. In other words, the tax applies primarily to what most inheritors never did a thing to earn in the first place. Second, before the Bush tax cuts of 2001 only 2 percent of families were subject to the tax.[52] Since then the threshold of an estate's size before it's subject to the tax has been raised. A couple's joint exemption from the tax was increased in stages from $1.35 million in 2000 to $7 million in 2009 and $10 million in 2011. As a result of these increases, by 2011 the tax applied to about one half of 1 percent of estates that were inherited in the United States.[53]

The controversy over retention of the estate tax illustrates the power of big money to confuse the public. Conservatives dubbed it a *death tax,* as if it applied to everyone who dies, and convinced a lot of Americans that they are harmed personally by the tax. Of course, nothing could be farther from the truth. More than 99 percent of Americans in 2011 enjoy the benefits of federal revenues that the tax generates without having to pay a dime for those benefits. The *Economist* reports that according to one study, the benefits are considerable. Complete repeal of the tax would cost the treasury $776 billion over the ten-year period 2012 through 2021.[54] This is three-quarters of what Obama's health-care reform may cost in the first decade of its operation. Fiscal conservatives are concerned about the cost of health-care reform. They should be more concerned about repeal of the estate tax because the general public gets no benefit from the repeal; all the benefits go to wealthy heirs. The average taxpayer, rather than seeing the estate tax as a death tax that harms them, should realize that it's a way to fund cheaper and more secure health care that benefits them.

The estate tax helps to preserve democracy because it breaks up large fortunes that might otherwise be passed down from generation to generation, resulting in a moneyed aristocracy taking permanent control of our nation's affairs. Thomas Jefferson wanted above all to avoid "the general prey of the rich on the poor." He observed, "The great mass of our population is of laborers; our rich, who can live without labor, either manual or professional [are] few . . . [and] know nothing of what the Europeans call luxury. They have only somewhat more of the comforts and decencies of life than those who furnish them. Can any condition of society be more desirable than this?"[55] Estate taxes hinder the rich from preying on the poor and help to preserve the desirable conditions of relative equality that Jefferson believed necessary to preserve a republican form of government.

In addition, estate taxes make economic sense for a growing economy, according to some of America's wealthiest citizens, including Warren Buffett, George Soros, and Bill Gates. Inheritors of great wealth are not necessarily innovators or entrepreneurs, so allowing wealth to accumulate in their hands may result in failure to put money to its most productive use.[56]

Finally, a steeply progressive estate tax, like an equally progressive income tax, encourages wealthy families to establish and support charitable institutions. Although many extremely wealthy people are extraordinarily generous under the present tax structure—Bill and Melinda Gates, George Soros, Warren Buffett, and Ted Turner are among the most famous—the incentive for wealthy people to make charitable contributions increases with the progressivity of the tax code. When charitable contributions are tax exempt and the marginal tax rate, whether income tax or estate tax, is 35 percent, giving a million dollars to charity actually costs the benefactor only $650,000 because $350,000 of the $1 million would otherwise belong to the government. When the marginal tax rate on extraordinarily large incomes and estates is 70 percent, by contrast, the cost to the benefactor of a $1 million charitable gift or bequest is only $300,000 because $700,000 of the $1 million would otherwise belong to the government. As the cost to benefactors decreases, wealthy people will probably contribute more of their money to charitable causes in such areas as health care, education, and environmental protection. So, steeply progressive taxation promotes social welfare through increased charitable donations in the private sector. This reason for progressive taxation is independent of any contribution such taxation makes to maintaining democracy.

A second independent reason for progressive taxation on estates and incomes is John Rawls's social contract view that was examined in chapter 8. People behind the veil of ignorance would want to participate in politics on a level playing field rather than have politics dominated by the kind of economic elite that Jefferson worried about. They would also want equal opportunity for society's preferred positions, and such equality is endangered if the elite can use money and connections to get better training and monopolize key positions. At the same time, however, people behind the veil would recognize that families should be allowed to keep some money in the family over the generations because the ability to pass wealth down to succeeding generations may motivate some talented people to work hard in ways that enrich society generally. So, like the income tax, the estate tax should never be 100 percent.

A third independent reason for progressive taxation, whether on incomes or estates, is the commonsense moral principle discussed in chapter 7. The estate tax, like the income tax, reduces the amount of money people are allowed to retain from cultural evolution and from government support of technological progress, neither of which the typical wealthy family or individual has paid or worked for to any extraordinary extent. The principle that people should pay or work for the benefits they receive justifies a 70 percent tax on large estates, just as it justifies a similar tax on large incomes. Thus, the consideration that estate taxes help to preserve our democratic institutions is but one of four independent reasons for supporting them.

When people realize that the new progressive agenda, which includes reductions in inherited wealth, is needed to preserve a functioning democracy for future generations, that agenda will no longer be marginalized. It will be at the center of political debate.

10

Conclusion: Economic Growth

George Will is an often insightful commentator on social and political issues from whom I've learned a lot over the years. For example, his insights into the relationship between character and country or, as he puts it, between statecraft and soulcraft, are illuminating.[1] He's generally part of the sane center, but when it comes to economics, he seems to have a learning aversion or a learning disability. In July 2009 his column entitled "The 'Tax the Rich!' Reflex: It Will Make the Investor Class Anemic" seemed directed against the new progressive agenda that I advocate in this book.[2] He writes, with characteristic disdain, which I'm happy to return on this subject, that we should forgive typical Democratic members of the House of Representatives for their impulse to tax the rich because it's just a reflex they can't control.

However, it's a dangerous reflex, he thinks. He claims that the goal of taxing the rich is to reduce inequality (which is true, but not the whole truth) and that this goal competes with economic growth. This chapter challenges the second of these claims. Far from competing with economic growth, I argue, when the additional government revenue that stems from progressive taxation is spent on public goods as part of a new progressive agenda, economic growth will increase in the United

States and jobs will become more plentiful. Because increased job opportunities and economic growth are almost universally valued in the United States—when was the last time a successful presidential candidate called for fewer jobs and slower growth?—the new progressive agenda will occupy the center of American discourse once it is recognized as the best means to expand the economy and increase job opportunities.

George Will invokes the authority of US Federal Appeals Court Judge Richard Posner whom he quotes: "As society becomes more competitive and more meritocratic, income inequality is likely to rise simply as a consequence of the underlying inequality—which is very great—between people that is due to differences in IQ, energy, health, social skills, character, ambition, physical attractiveness, talent, and luck."[3] This suggests that if our rating on the Gini Index is 0.47 now, it will inevitably top 0.50 in the near future and continue to climb from there. The reason is that a more competitive and meritocratic society is more productive than a less competitive and less meritocratic society, and productivity gains are essential to maintain our standard of living. Will concludes, "Policies, such as steeply progressive taxation, that are intended to increase equality are likely to decrease society's wealth. They reduce the role of merit in the allocation of social rewards—merit as markets measure it, in terms of value added to the economy."[4]

How much economic history does George Will know? Surely he knows that economic growth in the United States was considerably greater in the 1950s and 1960s when society was considerably more equal (Gini Index ratings below 0.40 at times) than it has been recently. And is he aware of international comparisons? The average Gini Index rating of all thirty OECD (developed) countries is 0.31, making them much more equal than the United States, yet their workers' productivity, on average, compares well with ours.[5] So there's absolutely nothing to an economic growth rationale for increased inequality through greater emphasis on competition and merit. There are no universal verities preventing the United States from becoming more like other OECD countries, which have more progressive taxation and much greater equality.

Will's second concern about taxing the rich relates to the Great Recession, as he calls it, which was gripping the country in 2009. The American economy had been strong in recent decades, he correctly notes, on the strength of consumer spending, which had increased from an average of about 62 percent of GDP for the first three decades after World War II to about 70 percent of GDP by 2007. The recession seemed likely to return consumer spending to the older level, representing a loss of consumption of about a trillion dollars a year. The economy will stall, Will correctly observes, unless some other spending takes up the slack. And now we have his great non sequitor: "It is especially risky," he writes, "to siphon away still more of the resources of the investor class [through more progressive taxation]. It is prudent to expect that business investment will have to play a larger role in fueling economic growth than it has played in the last quarter century."[6]

There's no hint of recognition here that the economic history of the United States since World War II belies the assumption that lower taxes on the rich mean more business investment. Harvard economist Benjamin Friedman writes,

in contrast to the 4.2 percent of the country's national income that American business devoted to investment in new factories and machinery (after allowance for depreciation) on average during the 1960s and 1970s, the net business investment rate since 1980 has averaged only 3.2 percent. During the latter half of the 1980s and the first half of the 1990s, net investment as a share of national income averaged just 2.7 percent. Even during the investment boom of the late 1990s, net investment never regained the average rate of the 1960s and 1970s. (The peak was 4.1 percent in 2000.)[7]

What Friedman doesn't note, but Will should know, is that taxes on the rich went down in the 1980s. As taxes decreased on the investor class (in the 1980s) so did business investment. And as taxes on the investor class increased (in the 1990s), so did business investment. Will is counting on investment increasing as taxes on the investor class decrease, exactly the opposite of American experience in recent decades.

But these are not the biggest flaws in Will's reasoning. Will assumes that taxes raised from the investor class won't be invested. This assumption is reasonable only if we believe that the US Treasury Department, rather than make the money available for some sort of investment, will burn, bury, or shoot into outer space whatever money they receive from additional taxes on rich people.

Will discounts the possibility that the government may use tax revenue wisely because, like many free-market conservatives today, he assumes that governments almost always waste whatever money they have. Although he is on most issues part of the sane center, he succumbs to unrealistic antigovernment-antitax propaganda in economics. He thinks that when governments take charge, fiscal mischief, such as the wasteful corporate welfare discussed in chapter 7, is inevitable, so the only way to curtail waste is to reduce the size of government and increase the economic role of the private sector.

I maintain to the contrary that governments can and often do use money wisely. This chapter shows that high taxes on wealthy people are justified in part by the excellent use that governments can make of the additional revenue that such taxes generate. Government investments in what economists call *public goods* are, up to a point that the United States is far from approaching, more economically productive than expenditure of the same money in the private sector, so they are central to the new progressive agenda.

$ $ $

Public goods are goods that no individual or company has a financial incentive to create or maintain because their benefits are available free to everyone. The classic example is national defense. If the country is defended against foreign enemies, everyone in the country is defended just about equally. Private goods, by contrast, aren't available to everyone equally. I can exclude others from using my car or my private swimming pool. This makes a big difference. It's reasonable for me to buy private goods with my private money because that's the only way I'm going to get to enjoy them (unless others voluntarily share their private goods with me, and I can't always count on that). But it makes no free-market sense for me voluntarily to use my private money to provide national security because, unlike a car or swimming pool, I will have it automatically as soon as other people pay for it. From a rational economic point of view, I should wait for other people to pay for the guns, tanks, aircraft, ships, uniforms, food, housing, and ammunition that our troops need to defend us. When they have done so, I'll have national security free of charge. Of course, almost everyone reasons this way, which is why we don't depend on voluntary contributions and bake sales to pay for national defense. We rely on compulsory contributions—taxes. If the tax system is fair, everyone pays a fair share.

Compulsory payment conflicts with the free-market ideal, which is that people should be able to spend their money however they want. But this deviation from the free market is necessary because of what economists call market failures. Generally speaking, where public goods are concerned, the market fails to provide what the society needs because everyone wants someone else to pay for the good. In the jargon of economics, everyone wants to be a *free rider*. Unless the government steps in, society will suffer.

This is not a new, left-wing, or anti-free-market observation, even if some of today's free-market conservatives don't recognize it. Adam Smith made the observation in *The Wealth of Nations* in 1776. (George Will has some catching up to do.) "The sovereign," Smith writes,

has the duty of erecting and maintaining certain public works and certain public institutions, which it can never be for the interest of any individual, or small number of individuals, to erect and maintain; because the profit could never repay the expense to any individual or small number of individuals, though it may frequently do much more than repay it to a great society.[8]

A generation ago, Nobel prize–winning, free-market conservative economist Milton Friedman, writing with his wife Rose Friedman, quoted this passage of Smith and agreed with it.[9]

In the 1940s, Nobel prize–winning, free-market conservative economist Friedrich Hayek made the same observation in his classic work *The Road to Serfdom*:

Where . . . it is impracticable to make the enjoyment of certain services dependent on the payment of a price, competition [the free market] will not produce the services; and the price system becomes similarly ineffective when the damage caused to others by certain uses of property cannot be effectively charged to the owner of that property. In all these instances there is a divergence between the items which enter into private calculation and those which affect social welfare; and, whenever the divergence becomes important, some method other than competition may have to be found to supply the services in question. Thus, neither the provision of signposts on the roads nor, in most circumstances, that of the roads themselves can be paid for by every individual user. Nor can certain harmful effects of deforestation, of some methods of farming, or of the smoke and noise of factories be confined to the owner of the property in question or to those who are willing to submit to the damage for an agreed compensation.[10]

In all such situations, Hayek thinks, the government must step in to promote helpful outcomes that the free market would never produce.

Sometimes regulation, which requires little public expenditure, solves the problem. For example, regulations sometimes limit deforestation on private hillsides to protect people living in nearby valleys from floods and mud slides. Farmers are restricted in the pesticides they use in order to protect the health of people who depend on groundwater supplies that the pesticides might pollute and make dangerous for human consumption. Utilities and factories that burn coal containing sulfur are required to install "scrubbers" in their smokestacks to lessen the amount of sulfur dioxide that enters the atmosphere and produces acid rain that kills forests downwind. Manufacturers are required to install catalytic converters on cars to reduce the air pollution that cars generate. In cases like these, the cost of regulation falls on private individuals or corporations, not the public treasury, because it is individual activity that is endangering the public by degrading goods on which the public depends, such as clean air and potable groundwater, or by creating hazards, such as mud slides.

There are often two sides to many of these regulations, just as there are two sides to law enforcement in general. Regarding the criminal law, it's often said that a conservative is a liberal who's been mugged and that a liberal is a conservative who's been arrested. The situation is similar regarding regulations to preserve public goods or avoid public harms. A conservative is a liberal whose business can't expand because nearby residents complain about noise or pollution, and a liberal is a conservative whose family has been exposed to carcinogens from a local factory. The point is that when it comes to public goods we need to take a societywide view, not just the view of our own special interests. The regulations are justified when society gets more out of them than individuals lose by having their liberty constrained.

Teddy Roosevelt's trust busting was a form of regulation that, like current antitrust regulation, was designed to preserve competitive markets, which are public goods on which people depend for the economic advancement of society in general. No individual can create competitive markets any more than they can create clean air or clean groundwater. But monopolies can destroy competitive markets just as polluters can destroy clean air and water. So even though competitive markets are human creations, not gifts of nature like clean air and water, it makes sense for the government to regulate business to constrain monopolies that would retard economic progress by stifling the kind of competition on which progress depends.

The Securities and Exchange Commission similarly protects markets in securities by disallowing practices such as insider trading, which could reduce people's incentives to invest. Without such regulations potential investors would legitimately fear that the investing game is rigged, that an inside group is going to make all the profit from investing, so they shouldn't put their own money at risk. This would deprive our economy of the investment capital needed to improve worker productivity and increase our standard of living. One reason for the near meltdown of the economy in 2008 was the government's failure adequately to regulate some of the newer financial instruments that were, ironically, designed to help corporations reduce their exposure to risk.

In all of these cases, government regulations protect public goods, whether natural assets or human practices, that the government sustains but didn't create. In other cases, however, the government actually needs to create the public good. Both Hayek and the Friedmans mention highways. For the most part, it's impractical (would cost more than it's worth) to charge people individually for their use of roads and highways, so people are charged taxes that supply the money governments need to build and maintain roads. This is nothing new. In the early nineteenth century the State of New York built the Erie Canal to improve transportation and commerce between New York and the upper Midwest. Without the canal, Chicago would not have developed when it did. Abraham Lincoln enthusiastically supported such government-funded infrastructure projects, which were then called *internal improvements*. The federal government promoted the nineteenth century development of rail networks in the United States by giving railroad companies land in exchange for the construction of railroads. The federal government began funding the interstate highway system in the 1950s. In all of these cases, the benefit to the general public, in the form of improved infrastructure required by commerce and economic growth, was considered greater than the cost to the public treasury. It was thought that the government would ultimately get its money back from taxes on the increased volume of commerce in a growing economy.

The importance of government investment continues. Nobel Prize–winning economist Joseph Stiglitz points out that "much of the New Economy which gave rise to the [economic] boom [of the late 1990s] rested on the Internet, which government research had created; on the myriad of other innovations derived from basic research; and on biotechnology, which was based on government-funded advances in medicine and biology."[11]

$ $ $

These considerations suggest that American prosperity depends on implementation of a new progressive agenda funded by the extra revenue flowing from increasingly progressive federal taxes. I can't go into the details of such an agenda in the areas of education, energy production, energy use, transportation, and health care because no one person can reasonably claim enough expertise in all of these areas to justify detailed recommendations. The specifics must be hammered out in reality-based discussion and debate among members of the sane center. All I will do here is indicate some of the considerations that make public investments in these areas a good deal for the American economy and society.

Consider education. When the public invests in education, the primary beneficiaries are the students, their families, and their eventual employers. But the public in general benefits as well because an educated workforce is essential in industrial societies. Imagine what the United States (or any other country) would be like without public education. No country has ever had a literate majority without public education. If we stopped taxing people in order to support education, many families would lack the time and competence to teach their children adequately and would lack the funds to have others do the teaching for them. Our international competitiveness would sink and we'd increasingly resemble a poor third-world country where it's difficult to find workers who can read or do math well enough to learn the skills that businesses need.

Most thinkers agree with philosophers Liam Murphy and Thomas Nagel that it's in the interest of better-off people to fund education for everyone. "A considerable support for universal education by the haves, even with minimal tax contributions from the have-nots, will produce on balance a result that is advantageous for the haves as well as the have-nots, in both social and economic terms."[12] After all, the haves need educated workers.

But how good an economic investment is public education? Economist Benjamin Friedman gives some figures. We assume that in our free market, wages have some relation to productivity. Of course, the relationship isn't perfect. At the upper end, as we've seen, the relationship is loose because conflicts of interest boost CEO salaries beyond productivity and at the lower end increases in worker productivity haven't always been fully translated into increased wages. But by and large, increased wages are a good sign of increased productivity. With this in mind, consider the fact that, as Friedman asserts, "each additional year of schooling increases a person's lifetime earnings by 7 to 8 percent . . . not just because they work more hours but because they are also more productive." When the median income of a man working full time is $41,500 a year, as it was in 2003, an extra 7 percent salary means an extra $2,900 income *each and every year*. Many people work thirty or forty years, so the cumulative extra earnings and productivity are enormous. Yet, on average, an extra year of high school costs just $6,500. It's hard to imagine a better public economic investment than a year in high school. In fact, Friedman writes, "most estimates of the rate of return on education calculated on an investment basis exceed 10 percent. . . . (Over long periods of time the after-inflation rate of return on investing in the stock market is about 6 percent.)"[13]

The positive effect on individual earning of an extra year of education is about steady from third grade through junior year in college and then increases. Friedman reports, "In 2003 the average hourly wage of Americans who had graduated from high school (but not gone to college) was 34 percent above what people made who had not finished high school. But college graduates made 73 percent more than high school graduates, and those with advanced degrees made another 26 percent beyond that."[14] By 2008 the economic advantage of education had increased again. The median income for full-time workers without a high school diploma was $24,300, whereas high school graduates made $33,800, a difference not of 34 percent, as in 2003, but of 37 percent.[15]

Yet the situation faced in 2009 by my own city's school district, District 186 in Springfield, Illinois, is common around the country. The city has three large public high schools serving its

115,000 residents. The oldest, Springfield High, began operation in 1917. I don't know the exact age of the newest, Southeast High, but I have a friend who attended Southeast and he's fifty-six years old. A report to the school board indicated that all three schools need extensive renovation, and some people want to replace Springfield High altogether with a new high school further west, closer to the city's newer McMansions. But a new high school would cost about $60 million, whereas renovation of the old school would cost only between $36 million and $42 million. Still, the price tag for all three renovations would be between $108 million and $126 million, which is about $1,000 per resident (not per family or per public school student, but per resident).[16] Many residents have no children, have children who are too young or too old for K–12 education, or send their children to private schools. How much is the average citizen willing to pay?

It's seldom that the average family of four with a median income of $50,000 or $60,000 a year has an extra $4,000 lying around to give to the school district just for the extra cost of high school renovation. Still, a referendum to get the money from local taxpayers seemed realistic in 2007 when planning began. However, in 2009, when the report was completed, prospects had dimmed. Education reporter Pete Sherman points out,

Two years ago . . . , the district was running budget surpluses, the Dow Jones average was 3,000 points higher than it is now and many Springfield residents hadn't lost their jobs, or weren't being asked to take unpaid furlough days. Discussion of . . . a voter-approved property tax increase seemed more reasonable at the time.

Now, with the economic downturn and district budgets running in the red, school officials are reluctant to talk about a referendum too early.[17]

Federal dollars acquired from steeply progressive income taxes would be an extremely attractive way to pay for these renovations.

Early childhood education benefits the economy as well. Friedman tells us that

students who have been in Head Start—and, even more so, those who have been in more intensive early-intervention programs like the Syracuse Preschool Program and the Perry Preschool Program . . . tend to stay in school longer than students from comparably disadvantaged family backgrounds who have not participated in these programs. While in school, they are less likely to have to repeat a grade, and less likely to require "special education." (They also have much lower crime rates in their teenage years, and girls have lower rates of teenage pregnancy.)[18]

Tax-supported universal early-childhood education is another investment of revenue from increasingly progressive taxation that yields excellent returns down the line by lowering government expenditures and contributing to economic growth.

The same can be said of increasing Pell grants for young adults from poor and middle-income families to study at universities. What George Will seems unable to appreciate is that these programs aren't just government giveaways. They're *investments*. Surely he knows this about higher education. The GI Bill after World War II, which helped so many veterans from poor families attend college, is commonly considered a major factor in America's prosperity in succeeding decades. However, as we saw in chapter 8, cost considerations today prevent millions of young people from attending college.

$ $ $

Consider energy production and energy use. When I use electric power in my home I really don't pay the full social cost. I pay the amount that I'm billed but the bill doesn't include the full cost of various negative "externalities," negative effects on others that I don't pay for but that are costly to society. For example, most of the electric power coming from my local utility—City Water, Light and Power (CWLP)—comes from burning coal.

Burning coal contributes to global warming, which won't affect me directly, but may, later in this century, decimate Illinois and other Midwest farming by making the area too hot and dry to grow corn and soybeans. This could jeopardize our country's food independence and cause precipitous increases in the price of food for everyone. Global warming, if left unchecked, is expected also to warm the oceans, creating more violent storms that will destroy oceanfront property. Global warming is expected also to raise sea levels and inundate such low-lying cities as New Orleans, Miami, and Galveston. In worst-case scenarios, Boston, New York, and many other cities would be jeopardized as well.

The costs of climate change are not just in theory or in the future. Evan Mills, a scientist at the Lawrence Berkeley National Laboratory, reported in *Science*:

It is widely recognized that the costs of weather-related natural disasters have been rising. The impacts include an elevated need for assistance from outside impacted areas and a shrinking gap between insurance premiums and losses. . . . To put the burden of these costs on insurers in perspective, recent average annual losses surpass those experienced in the aftermath of the 9/11 attacks in the United States. These costs are substantial for insurers and their customers, leading to industry-wide unprofitability in the worst years (even including investment gains), abrupt price increases, and isolated bankruptcies.[19]

The costs cited here don't include the enormous costs associated with Hurricane Katrina because Mills's article was published three weeks before the New Orleans disaster.

Future costs of continuing climate change are unknown, but an economic report sponsored by the British government concluded that the costs of climate change could top 5 percent of global GDP and would, in a worst case scenario, be as much as 20 percent of global GDP *each and every year*.[20] None of these costs are reflected in my utility bill in Springfield, Illinois. Besides adding to global warming, burning coal to supply me with eletricity adds to air pollution, which harms people's health. I don't pay the medical bills or increased insurance premiums of the people affected.

Because I presently escape paying so much of the cost of my electricity consumption, I'm tempted to use more of it than I probably would use if I had to pay the full amount. This means that I will be less inclined to spend money to reduce my use of electricity, such as by buying more energy-efficient appliances and light bulbs, than I would be if I had to pay for all the externalities. The same is true of my use of gasoline, which contributes not only to global warming and air pollution but also to American dependence on foreign sources of oil. This dependence harms our economy through a poor balance of payments (we import more from the rest of the world than we export), and through the need for huge military expenditures to ensure a continued supply of imported oil. Because society ultimately pays for these externalities, it makes sense for society to subsidize my conservation of energy, whether electricity or oil, in order to reduce the social costs of my energy use. Again, this is an investment with good returns.

The same logic justified the Obama administration's cash-for-clunkers program. The country will save more from the reduced gas consumption of newer cars compared to old ones than it spent ($3 billion) to get the gas-guzzlers off the road. Yet again, these are investments that, like most investments in a free market, improve the bottom line. But taxes are needed to make these government investments possible.

Energy-saving government expenditures create jobs. Just as the cash-for-clunkers program put some people back to work in the auto industry, retrofitting buildings for energy efficiency will create lots of jobs for people who can learn to use a caulk gun. Substituting clean, abundant sources of energy—wind and solar power, for example—for coal and oil will create even more jobs, Van Jones predicts in his popular book *The Green Collar Economy*:

If we are going to beat global warming, we are going to have to weatherize millions of buildings, install millions of solar panels, manufacture millions of wind-turbine parts, plant and care for millions of trees, build millions of plug-in hybrid vehicles, and construct thousands of solar farms, wind farms, and wave farms. That will require thousands of contracts and millions of jobs—producing billions of dollars of economic stimulus.[21]

$ $ $

Transportation is another area where public investment financed by progressive taxes on wealthy people can yield high returns to society. When you use your car, you not only degrade the environment, harm human health, compromise national security, and aggravate the country's balance-of-payments problem, little of which you pay for when you buy a gallon of gas, but you also contribute to road congestion, which has gotten dramatically worse over the last few decades. The Texas Transportation Institute report released in 2011 indicates nearly steady increases in the amount of time people spend stuck in traffic on U.S. roads. In the country as a whole, commuters spent 14 hours stuck in traffic in 1982 but 34 hours in 2010.[22] The situation is much worse in some urban areas, such as Washington, D.C. (74 hours), Chicago, Illinois (71 hours) and Los Angeles (64 hours). It's as if commuters in these cities were forced to work an extra week or two every year.[23]

These traffic delays consume (waste) a lot of gasoline, which just adds to all the problems associated with using oil. In addition, while sitting in congested traffic, barely moving with the engine on, people breathe concentrated doses of exhaust fumes, which is extremely harmful to health. What is more, the time lost in traffic subtracts from time people could be spending at work or with their families, thereby impairing commercial efficiency and family ties.

The situation would be worse today if the government hadn't invested in public transportation in the past. The Texas Transportation Institute (using constant 2010 dollars throughout) estimates that public transportation saved the country $6.9 billion in 1982 and $12 billion in 2000 but $16.8 billion in 2010. Even so, the cost of traffic delays in 2010 was $101 billion, up from $21 billion in 1982 and $79 billion in 2000.[24]

The 2009 American Recovery and Reinvestment Act allocates $8.4 billion for public transportation projects. In light of the savings generated by increasing and improving public transportation, this use of taxpayer money is fully justified. Individual families can gain in two ways. Public investment in public transportation creates hundreds of thousands of private-sector jobs. In addition, commuters who use public transportation save an average of nearly $9,800 a year.[25]

The economic benefits of urban rail networks have been known for a long time. Marcia Lowe of the Worldwatch Institute reported in the mid-1990s on a study regarding economic growth in Montgomery County, Maryland, in suburban Washington, DC:

A long-range planning study for the county found that if urban growth continued in the usual auto- and highway-oriented pattern—even at a slower pace—the resulting traffic congestion would stifle further economic development. In contrast, focusing most new urban growth in pedestrian- and bicycle-friendly clusters along an expanded rail and bus system—and revising commuter subsidies to discourage the use of cars—would enable the county to double its current number of jobs and households without exacerbating traffic congestion.[26]

A 1991 study reached the same conclusion for Philadelphia. The study

compared the economic effects of investing in rehabilitation and continued operation of SEPTA (the light rail, subway, and commuter rail system in the Philadelphia metropolitan area) with cutting or eliminating its services. The study found that for every dollar of public spending on rebuilding and operating SEPTA, $3 would accrue to the state and the region as a direct result of improved transport. The total economic impact . . . would be nine dollars for every dollar invested.[27]

The government promotes greater equality when it invests in economically justified public transportation with money raised by progressive taxation. Rich people pay most of the tax and middle-income people reap great benefits when they save $8,000 a year by selling one of the family's cars. Poor people are helped most because the cost of a car is a greater burden on them.

The poorest fifth of Americans spend 42 percent of their annual household budget on the purchase, operation, and maintenance of their cars. That's more than twice the national average. Low-income people typically have older cars and more unexpected repair costs. More than 90 percent of former welfare recipients do not have access to a car, and yet three in every five jobs suitable for welfare-to-work program participants are not accessible by public transportation.[28]

Intercity rail is also a good public investment. A report of the General Accounting Office titled "Excessive Truck Weight: An Expensive Burden We Can No Longer Support" maintains that an eighteen-wheel semi truck (with five axles and weighing the federal limit of 80,000 pounds) causes 9,600 times as much damage to a road surface when it rolls over that surface than a typical 2,000-pound car with two axles.[29] What is more, the average truck travels many more miles per year than the 10,000 to 15,000 miles for the typical car. Although the semi is not fully loaded all the time, it is likely to travel more miles per year fully loaded than the average car travels per year. So it's safe to say that the average eighteen-wheel semi damages our highways each year at least 10,000 times, and probably more than 20,000 times as much as a passenger car.

I pay in Illinois a fee of $106 dollars to register my car and this money is used largely, although not exclusively, for road maintenance. If a semi truck were to pay its proportional share for road maintenance through vehicle registration fees, its fee would have to be $1 to $2 million per year. Because such trucks pay only $8,545 in Illinois ($550 of which is the Federal Heavy Vehicle Use Tax),[30] taxpayers are subsidizing the trucking industry. In other words, the current method of hauling freight in the United States is so fundamentally inefficient that the industry could not exist in anything like its present state without massive government subsidies. Your tax dollars are paying for the trucks that clog the highways, create delays, pollute the atmosphere, contribute to global warming, and aggravate the balance of payment problems that imperil our economy. It makes sense for the government to invest instead in rail networks for freight. Railroads use less land (one track can replace several lanes of highway) and can run on electricity, which can be generated from fuels and renewable sources that our country has in abundant supply.

$ $ $

Health care is another important area where the United States can be more efficient. Like efficient sources of energy, efficient uses of energy, efficient transportation, and efficient public education, an efficient health-care system is a public good. Before the health care reform of 2010, American health care was the most inefficient among industrialized nations. We spent more on health care than any other country as a percentage of GDP. In 2006 Americans spent 15.2 percent of GDP on health care, whereas in Canada it was only 10 percent, in Australia 8.7 percent, in Britain 8.2 percent, and in New Zealand 8.0 percent.[31] Yet, we didn't get comparably better results. Overall life expectancy in the United States is worse than in these other four countries,[32] and our treatments for grave diseases are not always more successful. Although we lead these other countries in five-year survival rates for breast cancer, we're in last place in five-year survival rates for kidney transplants and only in the middle of the pack in five-year survival rates for childhood leukemia, non-Hodgkin's lymphoma, and colorectal cancer.[33] The life expectancy of people who are sixty years old is worse in the United States than in any other of the twenty-three wealthiest countries in the world.

How could we have spent 50 to 90 percent more of our GDP than other countries without getting better results? Part of the explanation is that before health-care legislation was passed in 2010, about 46 million Americans lacked health insurance at any given time. A much larger number, about 87 million, lacked insurance for at least part of any typical year.[34] Sociologist Susan Sered and health system analyst and activist Rushika Fernandopulle found that this situation harms the individuals involved and increases overall health-care costs. The uninsured and underinsured often delay going to the doctor when they have medical problems because they don't think they can afford to pay the out-of-pocket expense. As a result,

small tumors may be left untreated until they become big and metastasize. Diabetes is not managed properly, leading to amputations, end-stage renal failure, and expensive dialysis treatments. Asthma goes untreated until the individual ends up unable to breathe, turning blue in the emergency room. Hypertension progresses until it becomes a completely disabling disease, preventing the individual from working. . . . Sore throats become systemic infections, bladder infections become kidney infections, and earaches become the source of hearing loss.[35]

It really is true in medicine that an ounce of prevention is worth a pound of cure, and people who lack health insurance often can't afford preventive measures.

When the uninsured finally do go to the doctor their treatment is much more expensive than it would have been had they availed themselves of regular check-ups, preventive care, and timely interventions. When their pains become unbearable, they typically go to an emergency room where the cost of treatment is about four times the cost of treating the same ailment in a doctor's office.[36] Sered and Fernandopulle point out further that "in a bizarre economic and ethical twist, the chronically ill, if they are uninsured, are allowed to deteriorate to the point at which hospitals are legally required to take them in. They are covered if they have terminal cancer or renal failure, but not before."[37] At that point, when it's too late for a good quality of life, they're treated in expensive emergency rooms and end-stage treatment wards.

Insured Americans are often underinsured, but many don't know it. For example, Lawrence Yurdin, a sixty-four-year-old computer security specialist thought that his Aetna policy covered him up to $150,000 a year in the hospital, but found out too late that the fine print in the policy excluded almost all treatments for his heart disease. When his unpaid medical bills reached $200,000, he and his wife, Claire, filed for bankruptcy.[38] Medical bills are a common cause of bankruptcy, accounting for between one-third and one-half of the more than one-and-a-half million personal bankruptcies in the United States in 2002.[39] Three-quarters of those driven to bankruptcy by medical bills had health insurance.[40] These personal financial failures are a public problem because bankruptcy harms all of a family's creditors.

The increasing cost of insurance harms the economy as well. Most heath-care insurance is provided by employers in the United States. On average, when employer insurance rates go up by 10 percent, employers compensate by lowering worker pay by 2.3 percent.[41] Employers suffer as well, because increased health-care costs make it difficult for American manufacturers to compete globally. Testifying before a congressional committee in December 2008, then CEO of General Motors Rick Wagoner said, "Indeed, the United States' broken health care system puts enormous burdens on all employers—and has both helped create the Big Three's current financial troubles as well as fueled the overall economic downturn. Health care costs add $1,525 to the price tag of every GM car; the company spent $4.6 billion on health care in 2007, more than it paid for steel."[42]

Clearly, something had to be done and the 2010 health-care legislation is certainly part of a new progressive agenda. But it is insufficient because millions of people will still be uninsured when the plan is fully implemented in 2014. So, more work is needed. The sane center must evaluate new ideas as it gathers information generated through implementation of the 2010 legislation.

$ $ $

In sum, whether it's health care, education, energy production, energy use, or transportation, there's great potential for extraordinary financial returns from public investment. The fact that these returns are typically greater than those for private investments in the stock market explains why increasing rates of taxation generally correspond, contrary to George Will's expectation, to improved overall economic performance. Increasing taxation drains money from private investments that earn modest returns and makes that money available for public investments that get better returns. The economy flourishes when public investments create and maintain public goods.

The economic considerations highlighted in this chapter reinforce many of the conclusions of the previous three chapters. High tax rates on the wealthy are justified by the commonsense principle of people paying or working for the benefits they receive (chapter 7). Some of the revenue from those high taxes should be spent on education and health care to create a level playing field for competition (chapter 8). Such redistribution is what people would want if they were viewing the situation from behind a veil of ignorance (chapter 8). The resulting increase in equality of all Americans will promote democracy (chapter 9). Finally, public investments in energy, education, public transportation, and many other public goods provide high-quality jobs that can't be outsourced overseas. This helps average Americans regain their foothold in the middle class, stems the tide of economic polarization, and stimulates economic growth (this chapter).

In sum, a new progressive agenda that includes more steeply progressive taxation, support for unionization efforts, and public expenditures to create and maintain public goods in such areas as energy production, energy use, transportation, education, and health care is good public policy. It is recommended on grounds of economic performance, job growth, democratic revitalization, and social justice. Its implementation, guided by a sane center pledged to respect evidence more than ideology, will no longer be marginalized when its virtues become apparent to more Americans. Spread the word and take back the center.

Notes

Chapter 1

1. See Ezra Klein, "If You Build It . . . ," *Newsweek* (October 2, 2010): 21; Henry Fountain, "Danger Pent Up behind Aging Dams," *New York Times* (February 22, 2011): D1–D2.

2. Tamar Lewin, "Students, Not States, Are Now Paying More to Cover Costs for Public Universities," *New York Times* (January 24, 2011): A18; Jennifer Medina, "California Cuts Weigh Heavily on Its Colleges," *New York Times* (July 9, 2011): A1, A12; Tamar Lewin, "Average College Debt Rose to $24,000 in 2009, Report Finds," *New York Times* (October 22, 2010): A15.

3. See for example James C. McKinley "Aid Cuts Have Texas Schools Scrambling," *New York Times* (February 15, 2011): A16–A17.

4. Kevin Sack, "For Governors of Both Parties, Medicaid Looks Ripe to Slash," *New York Times* (January 29, 2011): A1, A3.

5. "Everett McKinley Dirksen's Finest Hour: June 10, 1964," *Peoria Journal Star* (June 10, 1964), http://www.congresslink.org/print _basics_histmats_civilrights64_cloturespeech.htm.

6. "Q: Voting Record for the Civil Rights Act," Google Answers, http://answers.google.com/answers/threadview/id/183344.html.

7. Ronald Reagan, "First Inaugural Address," http://www.reagan foundation.org/pdf/Inaugural_Address_012081.pdf, 1.

8. Ibid., 2.

9. Ibid., 3.

10. Ibid., 2.

11. Philip Gourevitch, "Fight on the Right," *The New Yorker* 80, no. 8 (April 12, 2004), 34–39, at 38.

12. Ibid., 39.

13. Ibid., 37.

14. Ibid.

15. Paul Krugman, "Ludicrous and Cruel," *New York Times* (April 8, 2011): A25.

16. For this estimate by Steven Rattner, former "car czar" for the Obama administration, and for the same estimate by commentator Fareed Zakaria, see http://super-economy.blogspot.com/2011_08_01 _archive.html. Some other estimates are closer to $3 trillion. For a more extended discussion see Michael Tomasky, "The Budget Battles on Which His Reelection Depends," *New York Review of Books* (May 26, 2011): 12–14.

17. Natalie Gewargis, "Spread the Wealth?" *ABC News: Political Punch* (October 14, 2008), http://abcnews.go.com/blogs/politics /2008/10/spread-the-weal, 2 of 75.

18. Ibid.

19. Michelle Malkin, "What Happened When They 'Spread the Wealth' in Zimbabwe" (October 20, 2008), http://michellemalkin .com/2008/10/20/what-happened-when-they-spread-the-wealth-in -zimbabwe.

20. Greg Mills and Jeffrey Herbst, "Bring Zimbabwe in from the Cold," *New York Times* (May 28, 2009): A27.

21. "Sarah Palin: Statement on the Current Health Care Debate," Facebook (August 7, 2009), http://www.facebook.com/note. php?note_id=113851103434.

22. Andy Barr, "Palin Doubles Down on 'Death Panels,'" Politico (August 13, 2009), http://dyn.politico.com/printstory.cfm? uuid=136EBBDB-18FE-70B2-A8CB12CB08EE4B9A, 2 of 2.

23. See Brad Sylvester, "The Health Care Reform Bill: Pundits Are Duping You," Associated Content from Yahoo!, http://www.associat edcontent.com/article/2050947/the_health_care_refrm_bill_pundits .html?cat=75.

24. See, for example, The Kent Reporter, http://www.kentreporter .com/opinion/letters/43391367.html.

25. Elyse Siegel, "Lindsey Graham Faces Tea Party Fury: 'Traitor,' 'Democrat in Drag,' 'Half-A-Sissy,'" *The Huffington Post* (October

13, 2009, updated March 18, 2010), http://www.huffingtonpost.com/2009/10/13/lindsey-graham-faces-tea-n-319225.html.

26. Michael Hirsh, "The Illustrated Man," *Newsweek* (September 6, 2010): 22–25, at 23.

27. Pew Center for Research for the People & the Press, "Fewer Want Spending to Grow, but Most Cuts Remain Unpopular" (February 10, 2011), http://www.people-press.org/2011/02/10/fewer-want-spending-to-grow-but-most-cuts-remain-unpopular.

28. For an account of poll results see Kate Zernike and Megan Thee-Brenan, "Poll Finds Tea Party Backers Wealthier and More Educated," *New York Times* (April 14, 2010), http://www.nytimes.com/2010/04/15/us/politics/15poll.html?pagewanted=print.

29. Pew Center for Research for the People & the Press, "Fewer Want Spending to Grow," Section 4, 2 (February 10, 2011).

Chapter 2

1. Geraldine Fabricant, "Old Nantucket Warily Meets the New," in *Class Matters*, written by correspondents of the *New York Times* (New York: Henry Holt and Company, 2005), 169–170.

2. Ibid., 177.

3. Ibid., 171.

4. Ibid., 179.

5. Joe Sharkey, "For the Super-Rich, It's Time to Upgrade the Old Jumbo Jet," *New York Times* (October 17, 2006): C10.

6. Jennifer Steinhauer, "When the Joneses Wear Jeans," in *Class Matters*, 136.

7. Nadav Kander, "At Their Service," *New York Times Magazine* (October 14, 2007): 76–81, at 79–80.

8. Robert Pear, "Median Incomes Shrank Further after Recession," *New York Times* (October 10, 2011): A1, A15. The years 2006 and to some extent 2007 are the last ones for statistics that were not affected by the Great Recession of 2008–2009. I want generally to stick with statistics that show the general trend of the last nearly forty years, not make matters look either better or worse than the general trend by cherry-picking years that may not be representative of that trend. However, I do occasionally cite more recent statistics.

9. Susan Starr Sered and Rushika Fernandopulle, *Uninsured in America* (Berkeley: University of California Press, 2007), 24. All information about Dave and Judy is from this work, 21–39.

10. Ibid., 25.

11. Ibid., 29.

12. Ibid., 31–32.

13. Ibid., 29–30.

14. Ibid., 30.

15. Barbara Ehrenreich, *Nickel and Dimed: On (Not) Getting By in America* (New York: Henry Holt and Company, 2001), 25.

16. Ibid., 27.

17. Randal C. Archibold, "Las Vegas Makes Feeding Homeless Illegal," *New York Times* (July 28, 2006): A23.

18. Kevin Sack, "Slump Pushing Cost of Drugs Out of Reach," *New York Times* (June 4, 2009): A3.

19. Dean Olsen, "Central Illinois Incomes Slip," *State Journal-Register* (Springfield, Illinois) (September 5, 2006): 1–2.

20. Grace Budrys, *Unequal Health* (Lanham, MD: Rowman and Littlefield, 2003), 164.

21. Kevin Phillips, *Wealth and Democracy: A Political History of the American Rich* (New York: Broadway Books, 2002), 128.

22. Ibid., 132.

23. David Cay Johnston, "Richest Are Leaving Even the Rich Far Behind," in *Class Matters*, 182–191, at 182.

24. Ibid., 184.

25. Steven Allen, personal communication, analyzing data in Thomas Piketty and Emmanuel Saez, "Income Inequality in the United States, 1913–1998," in *Top Incomes over the Twentieth Century: A Contrast between European and English-Speaking Countries*, A. B. Atkinson and Thomas Piketty, eds. (New York: Oxford University Press, 2007); "Tables and Figures Updated to 2007," http://elsa.berkeley.edu/~saez. Allen trained in mathematics and worked primarily in banking before retiring.

26. Phillips, *Wealth and Democracy*, 153.

27. Robert Reich, *Supercapitalism: The Transformation of Business, Democracy, and Everyday Life* (New York: Vintage Books, 2008), 108.

28. Jeff Kolnick and Doug Anderson, "Examining 'Redistribution of Wealth,'" *National Voter* (February 2009): 5.

29. Ibid., 4.

30. Phillips, *Wealth and Democracy*, 142.

31. Michael Tomasky, "The Budget Battles on Which His Reelection Depends," *New York Review of Books* (May 26, 2011): 12–14, at 13.

32. Phillips, *Wealth and Democracy*, 142.

33. T. R. Reid, *The Healing of America: A Global Quest for Better, Cheaper, and Fairer Health Care* (New York: Penguin, 2009), 208.

34. Lawrence R. Jacobs and Theda Skocpol, *Health Care Reform and American Politics: What Everyone Needs to Know* (New York: Oxford University Press, 2010), 149.

Chapter 3

1. See his website at http://johnboehner.house.gov/Issues/Issue/?IssueID=3944.

2. Natalie McPherson, *Machines and Economic Growth: The Implications for Growth Theory of the History of the Industrial Revolution* (Westport, CN: Greenwood Press, 1994), 1.

3. Christopher C. DeMuth, "The New Wealth of Nations," in *Taking Sides: Clashing Views on Political Issues* (15th ed.), George McKenna and Stanley Feingold, eds. (Dubuque, IA: McGraw-Hill, 2008), 242.

4. Ibid. Emphasis in original.

5. Jennifer Steinhauer, "When the Joneses Wear Jeans," in *Class Matters,* by correspondents of the *New York Times* (New York: Henry Holt, 2005), 139.

6. Ibid., 140.

7. DeMuth, "The New Wealth of Nations," 244.

8. Ibid., 246.

9. John Hospers, *Libertarianism: A Political Philosophy for Tomorrow* (New York: Authors Choice Press, 2007), 102.

10. Ibid., 103. Emphasis in original.

11. Ibid., 103–104.

12. Paul Krugman, "The Tax-Cut Con," in *Annual Editions: American Government 06/07* (36th ed.), Bruce Stinebrickner, ed. (Dubuque, IA; McGraw-Hill, 2007), 185–192, at 186.

13. Paul Krugman, *The Conscience of a Liberal* (New York: W. W. Norton, 2007), 254.

14. Kevin Phillips, *Wealth and Democracy: A Political History of the American Rich* (New York: Broadway Books, 2002), 113.

15. Krugman, *Conscience*, 254.

16. Susan Starr Sered and Rushika Fernandopulle, *Uninsured in America* (Berkeley: University of California Press, 2007), 13.

17. Krugman, *Conscience*, 246–247.

18. Ibid., 249.

19. Ibid., 188.

20. Ibid., 188–189.

21. Ibid., 189.

22. Robert B. Reich, *Supercapitalism: The Transformation of Business, Democracy, and Everyday Life* (New York: Vintage Books, 2007), 36.

23. Quotation 20487 in *Michael Moncur's (Cynical) Quotations*, http://www.quotationspage.com/quote/20487.html.

24. Sam Walton with John Huey, *Sam Walton: Made in America* (New York: Doubleday, 1992), 1.

25. Ibid., 173.

26. Ibid., 22.

27. Ibid., 24.

28. Ibid., 25.

29. Ibid., 27.

30. Ibid., 34.

31. Ibid., 109–110.

32. Ibid., 185.

33. Ibid., 185.

34. Ibid., 187.

35. Ibid., 128. Emphasis in original.

36. Ibid., 120.

37. Ibid.

38. Reich, *Supercapitalism*, 91–92.

39. With some fiddling and helpful assumptions, the $15,000 figure might be reduced to about $12,000, but the point would remain.

40. Allan Sloan, "There's Still No Free Lunch," *Newsweek* 127, no. 5(January 29, 1996): 24, http://web.ebscohost.com.ezproxy.uis .edu:2048/ehost/detail?vid=1&hid=4&sid=f6e4a641-a1e5-4b2d -8a7f-2faa03d38efa%40SRCSM2&bdata=JnNpdGU9ZWhvc3QtbG l2ZQ%3d%3d#db=mth&AN=9601257730, 2 of 5.

41. David Cay Johnston, "Richest Are Leaving Even the Rich Far Behind," in *Class Matters*, 185.

Chapter 4

1. Eric Dash, "Off to the Races Again, Leaving Many Behind," *New York Times*, Section 3 (April 9, 2006): 5.

2. Ibid.

3. Ibid.

4. Ibid.

5. Ibid.

6. Ibid., 1, 5.

7. Ibid., 5

8. Gretchen Morgenson, "For Consultants, It Can Pay to Back the Boss's Big Raise," *New York Times* (April 10, 2006): A1, A16, A17, at A1.

9. Ibid., A16.

10. Kevin Phillips, *Wealth and Democracy: A Political History of the American Rich* (New York: Broadway Books, 2002), 153.

11. See James Surowiecki, "The Financial Page: Board Stiff," *New Yorker* (June 1, 2009): 34.

12. Morgenson, "For Consultants," A1.

13. Ibid., A16.

14. Ibid.

15. Ibid., A17.

16. Gretchen Morgenson, "Peer Pressure: Inflating Executive Pay," *New York Times*, Section 3 (November 26, 2006): 1, 8–9, at 8.

17. Ibid.

18. Ibid.

19. Morgenson, "For Consultants," A16.

20. Paul Krugman, *The Conscience of a Liberal* (New York: W. W. Norton, 2007), 148.

21. Joseph E. Stiglitz, *The Roaring Nineties* (New York: W.W. Norton, 2003), 123–124.

22. Morgenson, "For Consultants," A16.

23. Daniel Costello, "The Drought Is Over (At Least for C.E.O.'s)," *New York Times*, Section 3 (April 10, 2011): 1, 6–9, at 1.

24. Ibid., 6.

25. Pradnya Joshi, "We Knew They Got Raises. But This?" *New York Times,* Section 3 (July 3, 2011): 1.

26. See http://www.westegg.com/inflation.

27. Costello, "The Drought Is Over," 1.

28. Ibid., 6.

29. S. Mills with Peter Wilenski, "There's No Smoke, but Lots of Fire," *The Age* (September 6, 1986), http://www.tobaccoinaustralia.org.au/fandi/fandi/c14s21.htm.

30. Helen Epstein, "Getting Away with Murder," *New York Review of Books* (July 19, 2007): 38–40, at 39.

31. Andrew C. Revkin, "On Climate Issue, Industry Ignored Its Scientists," *New York Times* (April 24, 2009): A1.

32. Andrew Revkin, "Skeptics Gather to Discuss Why Global Warming Isn't Such a Big Worry," *New York Times* (March 9, 2009): A12.

33. Revkin, "On Climate Issue," A14.

34. Ibid.

35. Robert B. Reich, *Supercapitalism: The Transformation of Business, Democracy, and Everyday Life* (New York: Vintage Books, 2007), 159–160.

36. Marcia Angell, "The Truth about the Drug Companies," *New York Review of Books*, LI, no. 12 (July 15, 2004): 55.

37. Marcia Angell, "Drug Companies and Doctors: A Story of Corruption," *New York Review of Books*, LVI, no. 1 (January 15, 2009): 8–12, at 8.

38. Ibid., 10.

39. Ibid.

40. Ibid.

41. Ibid., 12.

42. Ibid.

43. Donald M. Berwick, "Less Is More . . . and Better," *Newsweek* (October 16, 2006): 52.

44. Stiglitz, *Roaring Nineties*, 135–136.

45. Benjamin M. Friedman, "The Failure of the Economy & the Economists," *New York Review of Books* (May 28, 2009): 42–45, at 42.

46. Paul Krugman, *The Return of Depression Economics and the Crisis of 2008* (New York: W. W. Norton, 2009), 168.

47. Michael Lewis, "The End" (November 11, 2008), http://www .portfolio.com/news-markets/national-news/portfolio/2008/11/11/ The-End-of-Wall-Streets-Boom.

48. Robert M. Solow, "How to Understand the Disaster," *New York Review of Books* (May 14, 2009): 4–5. Emphasis in original.

49. Ben White, "What Red Ink? Wall St. Paid Hefty Bonuses," *New York Times* (January 29, 2009): A1.

50. Ibid., A17.

Chapter 5

1. Steven Greenhouse, *The Big Squeeze: Tough Times for the American Worker* (New York: Anchor Books, 2009), 136.

2. Ibid., 146.

3. Ibid., 146–147.

4. Ibid., 147.

5. Ibid., 148.

6. Ibid., 100.

7. Ibid., 149.

8. Ibid., 100.

9. Ibid., 100–101.

10. Greg Palast, *The Best Democracy Money Can Buy: The Truth about Corporate Cons, Globalization, and High-Finance Fraudsters* (New York: Plume, 2003), 211.

11. Barbara Ehrenreich, *Nickel and Dimed: On (Not) Getting By in America* (New York: Henry Holt and Company, 2001), 143.

12. Barbara Ehrenreich, "Earth to Wal-Mars," in *Inequality Matters: The Growing Economic Divide in America and Its Poisonous Consequences*, James Lardner and David A. Smith, eds. (New York: The New Press, 2005), 41–53, at 48.

13. Ibid., 49.

14. Ibid.

15. Ibid., 50.

16. Ehrenreich, *Nickel*, 145.

17. Greenhouse, *Big Squeeze*, 146.

18. Palast, *Best Democracy*, 211.

19. Ibid., 212.

20. Greenhouse, *Big Squeeze*, 140.

21. Greenhouse, *Big Squeeze*, 139–140.

22. Robert Reich, *Supercapitalism: The Transformation of Business, Democracy, and Everyday Life* (New York: Vintage, 2007), 90–92.

23. Greenhouse, *Big Squeeze*, 64.

24. Greenhouse, *Big Squeeze*, 67–68.

25. Greenhouse, *Big Squeeze*, 69–70.

26. Greenhouse, *Big Squeeze*, 11.

27. Ehrenreich, *Nickel*, 109.

28. Greenhouse, *Big Squeeze*, 11.

29. Steven Greenhouse, "Low-Wage Workers Are Often Cheated, Study Says," *New York Times* (September 2, 2009): 11. All references to this study are on this page.

30. Greenhouse, *Big Squeeze*, 10.

31. Greenhouse, "Low-Wage Workers," 11.

32. Thomas Frank, *What's the Matter with Kansas? How Conservatives Won the Heartland of America* (New York: Henry Holt and Company, 2005), 54.

33. Juliet B. Schor, *The Overworked American: The Unexpected Decline of Leisure* (New York: Basic Books, 1992), 20.

34. Ibid., 21.

35. Ibid., 22.

36. Kevin Phillips, *Wealth and Democracy: A Political History of the American Rich* (New York: Broadway Books, 2002), 163.

37. Paul Krugman, *The Conscience of a Liberal* (New York: W. W. Norton, 2007), 124. Emphasis in original.

38. Ibid., 125.

39. Ibid., 127.

40. Ibid. Emphasis in original.

41. Reich, *Supercapitalism*, 71.

42. Ibid., 72.

43. Ibid., 75.

44. Ibid., 171.

45. Greenhouse, *Big Squeeze*, 85.

46. Ibid., 87.

47. Ibid., 88.

48. Steven Greenhouse and David Leonhardt, "Real Wages Fail to Match a Rise in Productivity," *New York Times* (August 28, 2006): A1.

49. Ibid., A13.

50. Eric Dash, "Off to the Races Again, Leaving Many Behind," *New York Times*, Section 3 (April 9, 2006): 1, 5.

51. Robert Pear, "Median Incomes Shrank Further after Recession," *New York Times* (October 10, 2011), A1, A15.

Chapter 6

1. Jason Lee Steorts, "Sugar Daddies: How Sugar Interests Rip Off America and Harm the National Interest," in *Annual Editions: American Government 06/07* (36th ed.), Bruce Stinebrickner, ed. (Dubuque, IA: McGraw-Hill, 2007), 152. (Originally in *National Review* [July 18, 2005]: 35–36.)

2. Ibid., 153.

3. Ibid., 154.

4. Adam Smith, *The Wealth of Nations*, ed. Edwin Cannan (New York: Modern Library, 1994), 484–485.

5. Ibid., 109.

6. Ibid., 288.

7. Ibid., 527.

8. Gardiner Harris, "Pfizer Moves to Stem Canadian Drug Imports," *New York Times* (August 7, 2003), http://www.nytimes

.com/2003/08/07/business/pfizer-moves-to-stem-canadian-drug
-imports.html?scp=7&sq=drug+importation+Canada&st=nyt&page
wanted=print, 1 of 2.

9. Smith, *Wealth*, 715.

10. Marcia Angell, "The Truth about the Drug Companies," *New York Review of Books*, 51, no. 12 (July 15, 2004): 54.

11. *New York Times*, "Company News; Court Upholds Ruling that Extends Pfizer Patent" (April 29, 2004), http://www.nytimes
.com/2004/04/29/business/company-news-court-upholds-ruling-that
-extends-a-pfizer-patent.html?scp=2&sq=patent+extension&st=nyt
&pagewanted=print.

12. David Bollier, *Silent Theft: The Private Plunder of Our Common Wealth* (New York: Routledge, 2002), 85.

13. Ibid., 86–87.

14. Ibid., 88.

15. Ibid.

16. Ibid., 89–90.

17. Ibid., 94.

18. Angell, "The Truth": 52.

19. Ibid., 56.

20. Kevin Phillips, *American Theocracy: The Peril and Politics of Radical Religion, Oil, and Borrowed Money in the 21st Century* (New York: Viking, 2006), 284.

21. Ibid., 287.

22. Gretchen Morgenson, "The Cost of Saving These Whales," *New York Times*, Section 3 (October 4, 2009): 4.

23. Joseph E. Stiglitz, *The Roaring Nineties* (New York: W. W. Norton, 2003), 15–16.

24. Jeff Madrick, "They Didn't Regulate Enough and Still Don't," *New York Review of Books* (November 5, 2009): 54–57, at 56.

25. Ibid., 54.

26. Frank Sharry, "Comprehensive Immigration Reform II," in *Taking Sides: Controversial Political Issues* (15th ed.), George McKenna and Stanley Feingold, eds. (New York: McGraw-Hill, 2007), 287.

27. Mark Krikorian, "Comprehensive Immigration Reform II," in McKenna and Feingold, 280.

28. Nicholas Kristof, "Compassion That Hurts," *New York Times* (April 9, 2006): 13.

29. Ibid.

30. Eduardo Porter, "Here Illegally, Working Hard and Paying Taxes," *New York Times* (June 19, 2006): A14.

31. James K. Galbraith, "'Who Should Get In?' An Exchange," *New York Review of Books*, 49, no. 9 (May 23, 2002), www.nybooks.com/articles/15423. Emphasis in original, 2 of 6.

32. Ibid., 3 of 6.

33. Julia Preston, "Mexico Data Say Migration to U.S. Has Plummeted: Recession Stems a Tide," *New York Times* (May 15, 2009): A1.

34. Porter, "Here Illegally," A14.

35. Krikorian, "Comprehensive Immigration Reform II," 278–279.

36. Ibid., 284.

37. The Obama administration may be cracking down more than previous administrations on employers who employ illegal immigrants. See Julia Preston, "A Crackdown On Employing Illegal Workers," *New York Times* (May 30, 2011): A1, B2.

Chapter 7

1. Elizabeth Knowles, ed., *The Oxford Dictionary of Quotations* (5th ed.) (New York: Oxford University Press), 769.

2. "Margaret Thatcher on Socialism" (last updated July 7, 2009), http://www.snopes.com/politics/quotes/thatcher.asp.

3. Gar Alperovitz and Lew Daly, *Unjust Deserts: How the Rich Are Taking Our Common Heritage* (New York: The New Press, 2008), 96. Emphasis in original.

4. James Burke, *Connections* (Boston: Little, Brown and Company, 1978), 268–270.

5. Ibid., 271.

6. Ibid., 273.

7. Ibid., 274–275.

8. Ibid., 276.

9. Ibid., 282.

10. Ibid., 282–283.

11. Idea Finder, "Light Bulb History: Invention of the Light Bulb," http://www.ideafinder.com/history/inventions/lightbulb.htm, 3 of 8.

12. Ibid.

13. Alperovitz and Daly, *Unjust Deserts*, 71–72.

14. Ibid., 66–67.

15. Ibid., 67.

16. Ibid., 70–71.

17. Ibid., 40.

18. Isaac Newton, in *The Oxford Dictionary of Quotations*, 543.

19. Alperovitz and Daly, *Unjust Deserts*, 1.

20. Warren E. Buffett, "Stop Coddling the Super-Rich," *New York Times* (August 15, 2011): A19.

21. Alperovitz and Daly, *Unjust Deserts*, 79–80.

22. Ibid., 81.

23. Ibid., 82–83.

24. Ibid., 84.

25. David Bollier, *Silent Theft: The Private Plunder of Our Common Wealth* (New York: Routledge, 2002), 103.

26. Ibid., 104.

27. Alperovitz and Daly, *Unjust Deserts*, 78.

28. Ibid., 77.

29. Ibid., 76.

30. Ibid., 59.

31. Ibid., 60–61.

32. "Lighting a Revolution: Lamp Inventors 1880–1940: Carbon Filament Incandescent," http://americanhistory.si.edu/lighting/bios/swan.htm.

33. Alperovitz and Daly, *Unjust Deserts*, 61–62.

34. Ibid., 62.

35. Ibid., 61.

36. Ibid., 211, note 9. Emphasis in original.

37. Robert Frank, "More Billionaires Sign the Gates-Buffett Giving Pledge," *Wall Street Journal* (August 4, 2010), http://blogs.wsj.com/wealth/2010/08/04/40-billionaires-sign-the-gates-buffett-giving-pledge/.

38. Alperovitz and Daly, *Unjust Deserts*, 25.

39. Ibid., 26–27.

40. I use households rather than individuals here because households are the units subject to income and some other taxes that can be progressive.

41. Robert Pear, "Median Incomes Shrank Further after Recession," *New York Times* (October 10, 2011): A1, A15.

42. See the proposal made by Robert Reich, "Recover Our Spending Power," Sunday Opinion, *New York Times* (January 23, 2011): 12. He suggests a 30 percent marginal rate for households with incomes between $150,000 and $250,000 and a top rate of 60 percent on income in excess of $5 million in any given year.

43. William G. Gale, "Five Myths about the Bush Tax Cuts," *Washington Post* (August 1, 2010), http://www.washingtonpost.com/wp-dyn/content/article/2010/07/30/AR2010073002671.html. For the same estimate, see Roger Lowenstein, "Stop the Panic. It's Not 2008," *Newsweek* (August 22 and 29, 2011): 24–25.

44. The organization National Priorities estimates that in 2012 the federal government will take in about $1.14 trillion in personal income taxes. "People's Guide to the Federal Budget," http://nationalpriorities.org/resources/federal-budget-101/budget-briefs/federal-revenues/. The National Taxpayers Union estimates that nearly 40 percent of federal personal income taxes are paid by the richest 1 percent of households. "Who Pays Income Taxes and How Much?" http://ntu.org/tax-basics/who-pays-income-taxes.html. Put these together and the richest 1 percent of households contributes over $400 billion in federal personal income taxes each year. Increase this by one-half and the US Treasury has an additional $2 trillion over ten years.

45. David Kocieneiwski, "Where Pay for Chiefs Outstrips U.S. Taxes," *New York Times* (August 31, 2011): B1, B5.

46. David Kocieniewski, "G.E. Turns the Tax Man Away Empty-Handed," *New York Times* (March 25, 2011): A1, A17.

47. Buffett, "Stop Coddling the Super-Rich," A19.

48. Peter Orszag, "Safer Social Security," *New York Times* (November 15, 2010): A25.

49. See the Social Security website: "Updated 2011," http://ssa.gov/pubs/10003.html.

50. Jack Newfield, "How the Other Half Still Lives: In the Shadow of Wealth, New York's Poor Increase," *The Nation* (March 17, 2003): 13.

51. Ibid.

52. Jeff Madrick, "In the Shadow of Prosperity," *New York Review of Books* (August 14, 1997): 44.

53. Ibid., 41.

54. "US Inflation Calculator," http://www.usinflationcalculator.com.

55. See IRS Publication 596, "Earned Income Credit (EIC)," http://www.irs.gov/pub/irs-pdf/p596.pdf.

56. I am assuming here that the minimum wage is not allowed to decrease in relation to the cost of living. A significant decline in the minimum wage relative to the cost of living could cause government EIC payments to increase so much that they prop up inefficient businesses that should be allowed to fail.

57. In essence, this amounts to taxing poor families at a 50 percent rate, which is very high at the low end of the income spectrum, so some people might want a more gradual removal of EIC support from poor families. Recall that the Boss, whose memo was discussed in chapter 3, believed that neither he nor his employees would continue to work if 50 percent of their pay was taken by the government.

Chapter 8

1. Walter Lord, *A Night to Remember* (New York: Holt, Rinehart and Winston, 1955), 13.

2. Ibid., 14.

3. Geoffrey Marcus, *The Maiden Voyage* (New York: Viking Press, 1969), 31.

4. Lord, *A Night to Remember*, 110.

5. Ibid., 16.

6. Ibid., 34–35.

7. Ibid., 109.

8. Ibid., 107.

9. Ibid., 109.

10. Ibid., 109.

11. Ibid., 108–109.

12. Ibid., 108–109.

13. John Rawls, *A Theory of Justice* (Cambridge, MA: Harvard University Press, 1971).

14. Lord, *A Night to Remember,* 71.

15. Ibid., 120–121.

16. Amy Westfeldt, "It's Not What the Kids Know, It's Who the Parents Know," *The State Journal-Register* (Springfield, Illinois) (November 17, 2002): 42.

17. Randall Robinson, *The Debt: What America Owes to Blacks* (New York: Plume, 2000), 63–65. Emphasis in original.

18. Ibid., 69–72. Emphasis in original.

19. Ibid., 78. Emphasis in original.

20. Malcolm Gladwell, *Outliers: The Story of Success* (New York: Little, Brown and Company, 2008), 55.

21. Richard D. Kahlenberg, "The Return of 'Separate but Equal,'" in *Inequality Matters: The Growing Economic Divide in America and Its Poisonous Consequences*, James Lardner and David A. Smith, eds. (New York: The New Press, 2005), 60.

22. Gladwell, *Outliers*, 257–259.

23. Ibid., 259–260.

24. Steven Greenhouse, *The Big Squeeze: Tough Times for the American Worker* (New York: Anchor Books, 2009), 301.

25. Tamar Lewin, "College Costs Keep Rising, Report Says," *New York Times* (October 21, 2009), A14. See also Greenhouse, *The Big Squeeze*, 269, and Andrew Delbanco, "Colleges: An Endangered Species?" *New York Review of Books* (March 10, 2005): 18–20.

26. David Leonhardt, "The College Dropout Boom," in *Class Matters* (New York: Henry Holt, 2005), 89.

27. Greenhouse, *The Big Squeeze*, 269.

28. Leonhardt, "The College Dropout Boom," 97.

29. Sam Dillon, "Saving Money Means Less Time for School," *New York Times* (July 6, 2011): A14.

30. Tamar Lewin, "Students, Not States, Are Now Paying More to Cover Costs for Public Universities," *New York Times* (January 24, 2011): A18.

31. Tamar Lewin, "Average College Debt Rose to $24,000 in 2009, Report Finds," *New York Times* (October 22, 2010): A15.

Chapter 9

1. Danny Hakim and Nicholas Confessore, "Billionaire's Frustration Fueled a State Senate Rebellion," *New York Times* (June 10, 2009): 23–24.

2. Jim Dwyer, "Albany Drama Is Tragedy and Farce," *New York Times* (June 10, 2009): 23.

3. Hakim and Confessore, "Billionare's Frustration," 24.

4. Dwyer, "Albany Drama," 23.

5. Ibid., 24.

6. Ibid., 23.

7. Joel Magnuson, *Mindful Economics: How the U.S. Economy Works, Why It Matters, and How It Could Be Different* (New York: Seven Stories Press, 2007, 2008), 289–290. However, in 2009 the Obama administration increased CAFE standards to 35.5 miles per gallon (mpg) by 2016 and in 2011 they increased the standard to 54.5 mpg by 2025.

8. Ibid., 290.

9. Ibid., 289.

10. Ibid.

11. Kevin Phillips, *American Theocracy: The Peril and Politics of Radical Religion, Oil, and Borrowed Money in the 21st Century* (New York: Viking, 2006), 283.

12. Kevin Phillips, *Wealth and Democracy: A Political History of the American Rich* (New York: Broadway Books, 2002), 326. Emphasis in original.

13. Robert B. Reich, *Supercapitalism: The Transformation of Business, Democracy, and Everyday Life* (New York: Vintage Books, 2007), 162.

14. Ibid., 166.

15. Robert Kuttner, "Don't Drink the Kool-Aid," in *Inequality Matters: The Growing Economic Divide in America and Its Poisonous Consequences*, James Lardner and David A. Smith, eds. (New York: The New Press, 2005), 234–235.

16. Phillips, *Wealth*, 323.

17. Magnuson, *Mindful Economics*, 288.

18. Michael Luo and Griff Palmer, "Democrats Retain Edge in Campaign Spending," *New York Times* (October 26, 2010), http://www.nytimes.com/2010/10/27/us/politics/27money.html.

19. Jennifer Schlesinger and Devin Dwyer, "Political Parties Cede Campaign Power to Outside Groups," ABC News (October 26, 2010), http://abcnews.go.com/Politics/vote-2010-elections-campaign-spending-political-parties-eclipsed/story?id=11965623.

20. *Citizens United* v. *Federal Election Commission*, 558 U.S. 8 (2010). See also Michael Luo, "Changes Have Money Talking Louder Than Ever in Midterms," *New York Times* (October 8, 2010): A13.

21. Jonathan D. Salant, "Spending Doubled as Obama Led First Billion Dollar Race in 2008," *Bloomberg News* (December 26, 2008), http://www.bloomberg.com/apps/news?pid=newsarchive&sid=aerix7 6GvmRM.

22. Magnuson, *Mindful Economics*, 288.

23. Phillips, *Wealth*, 325.

24. Charles Lewis, "Of the Few, by the Few, for the Few," in Lardner and Smith, *Inequality Matters,* 125.

25. Magnuson, *Mindful Economics*, 293.

26. Ibid., 294.

27. John Stauber and Sheldon Rampton, *Toxic Sludge Is Good for You! Lies, Damn Lies and the Public Relations Industry* (Monroe, ME: Common Courage Press, 1995), 183–184.

28. Magnuson, *Mindful Economics*, 293.

29. Stauber and Rampton, *Toxic Sludge*, 184.

30. Reich, *Supercapitalism*, 191.

31. Ibid.

32. Ibid., 191–192.

33. Ibid., 193.

34. Ibid., 194.

35. Susan Davis, "NBC Poll: Myths Endure on Health Care, Highlighting Doubts on Overhaul," *Wall Street Journal* (August 18, 2009), http://blogs.wsj.com/washwire/2009/08/18/nbc-poll-myths-endure -on-health-care-highlighting-doubts-on-overhaul/tab/print.

36. Magnuson, *Mindful Economics*, 271.

37. Ibid., 273–275.

38. In David Cay Johnston, "Richest Are Leaving Even the Rich Far Behind," *New York Times* (June 5, 2005): A17.

39. Paul Krugman, *The Conscience of a Liberal* (New York: W. W. Norton, 2007), 249.

40. Krugman, *Conscience*, 192–193.

41. Magnuson, *Mindful Economics*, 279.

42. "Prime Number 11.9," *New York Times*, News of the Week in Review, (January 23, 2011): 3.

43. Krugman, *Conscience*, 69.

44. Jeff Kolnick and Doug Anderson, "Examining 'Redistribution of Wealth,'" *The National Voter* (February 2009): 5.

45. Reich, *Supercapitalism*, 80–81.

46. Sabrina Tavernise and A. G. Sulzberger, "After Wisconsin, Ohio and Indiana Face Union Fight," *New York Times* (February 23, 2011): A1, A3.

47. Krugman, *Conscience*, 70.

48. Julie Garber, "Overview of 2011 and 2012 Estate Tax and Gift Tax Laws: Overview of Estate and Gift Tax Exemption, Rate and Portability in 2011 and 2012," About.com, http://wills.about.com/od/understandingestatetaxes/qt/Overview-Of-2011-And-2012-Estate-Tax-Laws.htm.

49. Krugman, *Conscience*, 48.

50. Liam Murphy and Thomas Nagel, *The Myth of Ownership: Taxes and Justice* (New York: Oxford University Press, 2002), 143.

51. Ibid.

52. Krugman, *Conscience*, 162.

53. "Gilding the Elite," *Economist* 379, no. 8481 (June 10, 2006): 25.

54. Ibid.

55. Quoted in Adrienne Koch, *The Philosophy of Thomas Jefferson* (Chicago: Quadrangle Paperback, 1964), 174–175.

56. David Cay Johnston, "Dozens of Rich Americans Join in Fight to Retain the Estate Tax," *New York Times* (February 14, 2001), http://www.nytimes.com/2001/02/14/us/dozens-of-rich-americans-join-in-fight-to-retain-the-estate-tax.html.

Chapter 10

1. George F. Will, *Statecraft as Soulcraft* (New York: Touchstone, 1984).

2. George F. Will, "The 'Tax the Rich!' Reflex: It Will Make the Investor Class Anemic," *Newsweek* (July 27, 2009): 30.

3. Ibid.

4. Ibid.

5. See chapters 3 and 9 of this book.

6. Will, "The 'Tax the Rich!' Reflex," 30.

7. Benjamin M. Friedman, *The Moral Consequences of Economic Growth* (New York: Vintage, 2005), 405.

8. Adam Smith, *The Wealth of Nations* (New York: Modern Library Edition, 1994), 745.

9. Milton and Rose Friedman, *Free to Choose: A Personal Statement* (New York: Harcourt Brace Jovanovich, 1979), 30–32.

10. Friedrich A. Hayek, *The Road to Serfdom* (Chicago: University of Chicago Press, 1944), 38–39.

11. Joseph E. Stiglitz, *The Roaring Nineties* (New York: W. W. Norton, 2003), 277.

12. Liam Murphy and Thomas Nagel, *The Myth of Ownership: Taxes and Justice* (New York: Oxford University Press, 2002), 86.

13. B. Friedman, *Moral Consequences*, 423.

14. Ibid.

15. Tamar Lewin, "Value of College Degree Is Growing, Report Says," *New York Times* (September 21, 2010): A18.

16. Pete Sherman, "How Much to Overhaul City's High Schools?" *State Journal-Register* (Springfield, IL): 1, 4.

17. Ibid., 4.

18. B. Friedman, *Moral Consequences*, 424.

19. Evan Mills, "Insurance in a Climate of Change," *Science* (August 12, 2005): 1041.

20. Christopher Klein, "Climate Change, Part III: Liabilities Heating Up" (May 27, 2009), http://www.gccapitalideas.com/2009/05/27/climate-change-part-iii-liabilities-heating-up/.

21. Van Jones, *The Green-Collar Economy: How One Solution Can Fix Our Two Big Problems* (New York: HarperCollins, 2008), 10.

22. David Shrank, Tim Lomax, and Bill Eisele, "TTI's 2011 Urban Mobility Report" (September 2011), http://tti.tamu.edu/documents/mobility-report-2011.pdf, 1.

23. Ibid., 20.

24. Ibid., 1.

25. See Pubic Transportation, "Transit Savings Report," http://www .publictransportation.org/tools/transitsavings/Pages/default.aspx.

26. Marcia Lowe, "Back on Track: The Global Rail Revival," *World-Watch Paper #118* (Washington, DC: Worldwatch Institute, April 1994), 15–16.

27. Ibid., 42.

28. Jones, *The Green-Collar Economy*, 142.

29. Comptroller General's Report to Congress, "Excessive Truck Weight: An Expensive Burden We Can No Longer Support," 23–24, http://archive.gao.gov/f0302/109884.pdf.

30. See Illinois License Services, "Truck & Auto Licensing," http:// www.illinoislicenseservices.com/Truck_Auto_Licensing_.html and US Government, "Heavy Highway Vehicle Use Tax Return," http://www .irs.gov/pub/irs-pdf/f2290.pdf.

31. David Leonhardt, "Limits in a System That's Sick," *New York Times* (June 17, 2009): B1, B9, at B9.

32. Grace Budrys, *Unequal Health: How Inequality Contributes to Health or Illness* (Lanham, MD: Rowman and Littlefield, 2003), 26.

33. Leonhardt, "Limits," B9.

34. Senator John Kerry on "This Week with George Stephanopoulos," ABC News (August 30, 2009). http://abcnews.go.com/ThisWeek/Politics/story?id=8443218&page=2.

35. Susan Starr Sered and Rushika Fernandopulle, *Uninsured in America: Life & Death in the Land of Opportunity* (Berkeley: University of California Press, 2007), 11.

36. Ibid., 12.

37. Ibid., 18.

38. Reed Abelson, "Insured but Unprotected, and Driven Bankrupt by Health Crises," *New York Times* (July 1, 2009): A1, A4.

39. Sered and Fernandopulle, *Uninsured*, 13.

40. Abelson, "Insured but Unprotected," 1.

41. Leonhardt, "Limits," A1.

42. "GM CEO: Serious Health Care Reform 'Undoubtedly Would Help Level the Playing Field,'" Think Progress (December 5, 2008), http://thinkprogress.org/2008/12/05/gm-health-care-reform.

Index